THE ELEMENTARY APPLE

by William B. Sanders

Illustrations by
Martin Cannon

DISCLAIMER

DATAMOST, INC. shall have no liability or responsibility to the purchaser or any other person or entity with respect to any liability, loss or damage caused or alleged to be caused by this manual or its use, including but not limited to any interruption in service, loss of business and anticipatory profits or consequential damages resulting from the use of this product.

Published by Datamost, Inc.
9748 Cozycroft Avenue
Chatsworth, California 91311

Reston Publishing Company, Inc.
A Prentice-Hall Company
Reston, Virginia

ISBN 0-8359-1659-6

TABLE OF CONTENTS

Preface

My first formal introduction to the workings of a computer was in 1966. At that time our wise mentor told us that if we learned the lowest level operations of a computer, we would be set for life. As a result of this philosophy, we were taught how to do everything from counting in binary and conversion to octal to the essentials of FORTRAN. The problem was that we never really sat down and programmed at a terminal, and so while we had a terrific theoretical understanding of the workings of computers, we never really learned very much about actual programming.

Since that time, both computers and the people who use them have changed. To learn how to use a computer, it is unnecessary to learn everything about how they work or the theory behind their operation. It is true that by having a detailed understanding of the theory and operation of computers one can do more with them, but it is something that does not have to be done at the outset. One can learn how to program, and at a later date learn the more technical details of a computer's operation. After all, most people learn to drive without knowing the intricacies of the internal combustion engine of their automobile.

Another major change in computers has been in the transition from "main-frames" and "terminals" to small individual computers. Your Apple is not merely a terminal. It is a whole computer. Therefore, you are not dependent on using a piece of a larger computer, but you get the whole thing all to yourself. As a result, you are not subject to a set of policies and regulations for getting "on line" or paying for the time you use. You make your own policies and are the captain of your own computer ship. Therefore, it is unnecessary to spend a lot of time discussing the organizational aspects of accessing the CPU (Central Processing Unit) time-sharing, and so forth. We will go right to the heart of the matter, programming YOUR computer.

The purpose of this book is primarily to teach you how to work your computer and program in the language called BASIC. It is ELEMENTARY, and so while you will learn a good deal, don't expect to learn everything about working with your Apple. Once you are finished with this book, you will realize how much more you can do with your computer, and the more you learn, the more you will find to learn. However, by following the instructions and keying in the examples, you will learn how to write programs with most of the instructions in the version of BASIC on your Apple.

As a final note, don't expect to learn everything right away. Be patient with yourself and your computer, and you will be amazed at how much you will learn. If you do not understand a command or a procedure, you can always come back to it later. Try different things and play with your programs. Think up different projects you would like your computer to do and then try writing a program to do what you want. By all means, though, do not be afraid to make an attempt. With each step or attempt you will make some progress, and while it may be slow at times, the accumulated knowledge will eventually lead to understanding.

Acknowledgements

Several people helped directly or indirectly in the creation of *Elementary Apple*. First and foremost, I owe a great deal to Eric Goez of the Apple Corps of San Diego who taught me and several others how to program the Apple computer. Not only did Eric patiently show how to make the computer do all sorts of wonderful things, but he also sparked the imagination of the group of novices of which I was a member. Likewise, other members of the Apple Corps of San Diego were extremely helpful in furthering my knowledge of the Apple. The club's beginner's group that I was instructing taught me a good deal about what beginners need to know, and I hope I have done them justice. In particular, one newcomer, Bob Preston, went through the entire manuscript and discovered more bugs and mistakes than I thought possible in a work of this size. Bob's efforts saved the bugs from driving the book's users daffy since even the smallest mistake in a program can ruin it.

Dave Gordon of DATAMOST INC. provided a world of support for the book's production. Larry Bouyer edited the manuscript for style and consistency, making the work a good deal clearer. Martin Cannon did the art work in a way that communicated ideas creatively and visually. He gave life to the notion that a picture is worth a thousand words. The rest of the staff at DATAMOST were equally helpful and friendly.

Finally, my wife Eli and sons Billy and David, and even our dog Cassiopeia, put up with the inconvenience of a writer in the house. To every one of these people I owe a debt of gratitude, but as in all such efforts, if anything goes wrong, it is only the author who is to blame. Therefore, while I happily give those who assisted credit, any of the book's shortcomings are the sole responsibility of the author.

CHAPTER 1

Introduction

This book is intended to help you operate your new Apple II+ computer, get started programming and make life easier with your computer. It is not for professional programmers or more advanced applications. It is only the first step, and it is for BEGINNERS on the Apple II+ computer. Everything will be kept on an introductory level, but by the time you are finished, you should be able to write and use programs.

To best use *Elementary Apple* it is suggested that you start at the beginning and work your way through step-by-step. I have tried to arrange the book so that each part and section logically follows the one preceding it. Skipping around might result in your not understanding some important aspect of the computer's operation. The only exception to this rule is the last chapter where I have put a number of suggestions for programs you might want to buy in order to help you write programs (called UTILITY PROGRAMS). Also, there are descriptions of programs for doing other things such as business, word processing and so forth. When you're finished with this chapter, it would be a good idea to take a quick peek at some of the programs described in the last chapter to see if any of them fit your needs while you're learing about your Apple. You don't have to purchase any of them, but depending on your interests and needs, you will find some of them very useful.

The first thing to learn about your computer is that it will not "bite" you. It requires a certain amount of care. There are ways you can destroy diskettes, tapes, and information, but by following a few simple rules you should be all right. All of us have used sophisticated electronic equipment, such as our stereos, televisions, and video-tape recorders; and there is a certain amount of care they require. Otherwise, there is no need to fear them. Likewise, your computer is electronic; if you pour water or other liquids on the computer while the power is on you're likely to damage it. Using reasonable care, go ahead and put it to use. Remember, it is virtually impossible to write a program that will harm the hardware (or electronic circuits) in your machine; the worst thing any program you write can do is erase the information on a diskette. Throughout this book there will be tips about how to do things the right and wrong way, but for the most part, treat your computer as you would your microwave oven, garage door opener or radio—with care but without fear.

At this stage of the game it is unnecessary to learn a lot of computer jargon. Some of this jargon is necessary to help you understand how your

computer operates, however. As we go on more new terms will be introduced, but for the most part the text will be in plain English. Nevertheless, you should know the following just to get started.

Hardware

Hardware refers to the machine and all of its electronic parts. Basically, everything from the keyboard to the wires and little black chips in your computer are considered "hardware." You will also hear the terms "firmware." This is another type of hardware that is placed on boards that go in the slots in the back of your Apple. The flat card that connects your disk drive to the computer is what "firmware" looks like—but just consider it as a type of hardware. A biological analogy of hardware is the physical body, most importantly the brain.

Software

Software consists of the programs that tell the computer to do different things. Whatever goes into the computer's memory is software. It is analogous to the mind or ideas. Treating the hardware as the brain, any ideas that go into the hardware is the software. Software is to computers as records are to stereos. Software operates either in Random Access Memory (RAM) or Read Only Memory (ROM) memory.

RAM — You may hear people talk about expanding their RAM. This is the part of the computer's memory into which you can enter information in the form of data and programs. The more memory you have, the larger the program and more data you can enter. Think of RAM as a warehouse. When you first turn on your computer, the warehouse is just about empty, but as you run programs and enter information, the warehouse begins filling up. The larger the warehouse the more information you can store there, and when it is full, you have to stop. Most Apples come with 48K of RAM. The "K" for computerists refers to "kilobytes" or "thousands-of-bytes." (The new disk storage systems are measured in "megabytes" or "millions-of-bytes." The next time you're at a cocktail party, mention megabytes and you'll really impress everyone.) For now, all you need to know about "bytes" is that they are a measure of storage in computers. The more bytes, the more room you have. Think of them in the same way you would "gallons," "inches" or "meters"—simply a unit of measure.

DON'T WORRY - IT WON'T BITE YOU!

ROM — A second type of computer memory is ROM meaning "Read Only Memory." This type of memory is "locked" into your computer's chips. Your Apple's programming language, called BASIC, is stored in ROM. The difference between ROM and RAM is that whenever you turn off your computer, all information in RAM evaporates, but ROM keeps all of its information. Don't worry, though, you can save whatever is in RAM on diskettes and tape and get it back. We'll see how that is done later.

GO AHEAD -- LOOK INSIDE!

Now that you know a few terms and enough not to fear your computer, let's get it cranked up and running. If you already have your computer all hooked up and working properly, you can skip the next section and go directly to the POWER ON! section of this chapter.

Hooking Up Your Apple And Peripheral Equipment

The LAST thing you should do after reading this section is plug your Apple in and turn it on. Everything else should be done first. In this book, we will assume that most users will have a Disk Operating System (DOS)—that is a disk drive—and so most of the discussion will focus on setting up and operating your Apple with at least a single disk drive. Tape systems will be discussed as well, however.

Disk Drive

Take the top off your Apple and, sitting at the keyboard, look into the back of the computer. On your left there should be a big copper or silver colored box (your power supply). Moving to your right is a plug (in a white outlined box) labeled "POWER." Now right next to that are eight (8) slots numbered from zero to seven. Go ahead and look at them and make sure they are all there! Computerists begin counting at zero instead of one; so count them from zero to seven just to get used to it. (These slots should be numbered in the very back.)

Hard Disks: Some of you may have "hard disk" systems that have megabyte capacity. If you do, the hook-up process is essentially the same as for the standard Apple DISK II system described below. However, there may be special considerations, and I would strongly suggest you consult the store where you bought your hard disk and the manual that comes with it before installation.

NEVER PLACE AN INTERFACE CARD INTO A SLOT WHILE THE POWER IS ON!

Disk Drive Connection —

1. Find Slot #6, counting #0, #1, #2, #3, #4, #5, #6, #7. It is the second from the last slot counting from left to right. With your disk drive you should have also bought a "CONTROLLER CARD" to which you attach the cable from your disk drive. This card goes into Slot #6.Now, gently but firmly place the CONTROLLER CARD in Slot #6. It will only fit one way with all of the black chips and electronic gizmos on the right side. Make sure that the card is all the way in the slot and level.
2. On the back of the card you will find two sets of pins sticking up. One set is labeled DRIVE 1 and the other DRIVE 2. CAREFULLY place the connector on the end of the cable from your drive onto the pins labeled DRIVE 1. Make sure that the pins and the holes in the connector line up and gently but firmly press the connector into place. That's it! You now have your disk oper-

ating system hooked up! If you have more than 1 disk drive, connect the second drive in the same manner to the pins marked DRIVE 2. If you have more than 2 drives, you will need a second controller card. Put it in Slot #5 and hook up the drives as you did the ones in Slot #6.

Tape Recorder

If you are using a tape recorder, either with or without a disk operating system, hooking it up is quite simple. Supplied with your Apple are a set of cables to connect it to a tape recorder. Not all tape recorders work with the Apple and some work better than others; so if you do not have a tape recorder, check with your computer store to make sure you buy the correct type. (Luckily, you do not have to buy a fancy expensive recorder, and you can use your computer cassette recorder for regular recording as well!) Here's how to do it.

Tape Recorder Connection —

1. In the very back of your computer on the right hand side are 3 holes. Two holes are under a box labeled CASSETTE—one labeled IN and the other OUT. (The third hole is labeled OUT also, but don't use it for connecting your tape recorder.) Connect one end of the black cable into the hole marked CASSETTE OUT and the other end of the black cable into the hole marked MIC or MICROPHONE on your recorder. (What comes OUT of the computer goes into the MICROPHONE of the tape recorder—just as sound coming from a person speaking goes into the microphone.)
2. Take the plugs on the gray cable and put them into the CASSETTE IN hole in the computer and the MON, MONITOR, EAR or EARPHONE of the tape recorder. (The computer "listens" IN on the tape recorder with the "earphone.') That's all there is to it, except when you are ready to get started, you will want to plug in your tape recorder—using batteries is NOT recommended.

TV Or Monitor

In order to see what's going on in your computer, you need either a TV set or a monitor. We all know what a TV set does; a monitor is essentially a TV set for your computer. Monitors are preferable over TV sets since they are easier to hook up and have a higher resolution (they're clearer.) However, since one of the outstanding features of the Apple is the color graphics, (especially on some of the games!) a lot of people use color televisions (sometimes the family TV) with their Apples since they cost less than color monitors.

Types Of TV Sets

TV's come in a "jillion" different shapes, sizes, etc.; either a color or black and white will work fine. BE CAREFUL in the selection of the TV set you buy! Not all televisions work well with your Apple; so ask first before you buy. When I bought my TV set, a color one for the graphics, I simply looked at the color TV's being used on the computers in the stores and bought the same make and model at an "el cheapo" discount house. Whatever the case, check to make sure that the TV set you purchase will work with your Apple.

IF YOU USE A T.V., MAKE SURE IT'S COMPATIBLE!

TV Connection — Hooking up a black and white or color television is somewhat tricky. You will need an RF modulator to do so, and rather than pretending I know exactly what, why and how about an RF modulator, I suggest you simply ask your computer store for an "adaptor for a television." One popular such adaptor is called "SUP 'R' MOD. II" made by M & R Enterprises, and you can name it as an example of what you're looking for. Also, you should ask someone to show you how to hook up whatever RF modulator you buy. Finally, since most adaptors will only use certain channels for displaying computer output, be sure to test your output on the appropriate channel!

Types of Monitors

Green Screen — This type of monitor gives a green on black display and can be bought for between $100 and $200. The green and black display is quite good for people doing a lot of word processing and non-graphic programming since they are easy on the eyes. However, since these displays only present green and black, they are not too good for color graphics.

Black and White — These monitors are essentially the same as the green screen, but are in black and white instead of black and green.

Color — This type of monitor is the most expensive, but for people who work a lot with grapics, they are probably worth the added cost. They provide the high resolution for seeing graphics in detail.

Monitor Connection — To hook up any kind of monitor simply plug the monitor connector cord into the MONITOR OUT hole (right next to the cassette holes) in the back right-hand corner of the computer. The other end of the connector cord goes into a similar socket in the back of the monitor. (When I purchased my monitor, a connector cord did not come with it. I simply went into Radio Shack (!) and asked for an RCA standard jack connector for a monitor. Remember, "RCA Standard" is the kind of plug and cord to ask for since it refers to the size of jack connector you'll need.)

Printer

This section simply tells you how to hook up your printer and a little about the different kinds of printers. If your printer is already hooked up and working, take a look at chapter 9 for tips on maximizing your printer's use.

Types of Printers

There are three basic kinds of printers.

Dot Matrix — First, the most popular kind of printer is the "dot matrix" printer. This printer has a number of little pins that are fired to form little dots that print out as text or graphics. The advantage of dot matrix printers is their relatively low cost and the fact that many of them can do both text and graphics. The improved quality of text printing of dot matrix printers gives an almost "letter quality" product, and usually can give you several different type faces. In chapter 9 there are several examples of different printing modes on dot matrix printers.

Letter Quality — Second, for people whose major use of their computer is to do word processing, there are "letter quality" printers. Most of these are "daisy wheel" printers and type characters in much the same way as a typewritter does. Each symbol has a molded image as on typewriter heads. These printers are not good for graphics, but for the user who wants top notch looking letters, manuscripts, reports and other written documents, this type of printer is the best. They tend to be relatively expensive, however, and for most written materials, dot matrix printers are fine. The thing to do before you buy is to compare.

Thermal — Third, for those people who are really on a budget, there are "thermal printers." These printers work with a special kind of paper, usually on a roll, and make a "picture" of what is on the computer screen. They can easily handle both text and graphics, but the quality of output is relatively low and the paper is very expensive. The best feature of these printers is their small size and light weight, and for people who travel with their computers and need print-outs, they can be handy.

FREE ADVICE

Before you buy a printer, decide what you will need it for, and then look at the features of the different kinds before buying!!! And by all means, ask to see a demonstration on an Apple.

When you buy your printer, you will need an interface card and cable to hook it up to your computer just as you did with your disk drives. When buying a printer, make certain to get the correct interface and cable that go with your printer. The interfaces and cables are sold separately, and so it is possible to get the wrong interface and cable if you're not careful. This is why it is important to see a demonstration of the printer hooked up to an Apple. To connect the printer proceed as follows:

Printer Connection —

1. Connect the cable to the printer. On one end of the cable there will be a connector to the interface card and on the other a connector to the printer. As a rule of thumb, the connector to the printer is the larger one.
2. Connect the other end of the cable to the interface card, much in the same way as you connected the disk drive cable to the diskette controller card.
3. Make sure there is some slack in the cable from the printer and put the interface card into Slot #1, the SECOND slot from your left. REMEMBER THE SLOTS BEGIN AT SLOT #0! That's it!

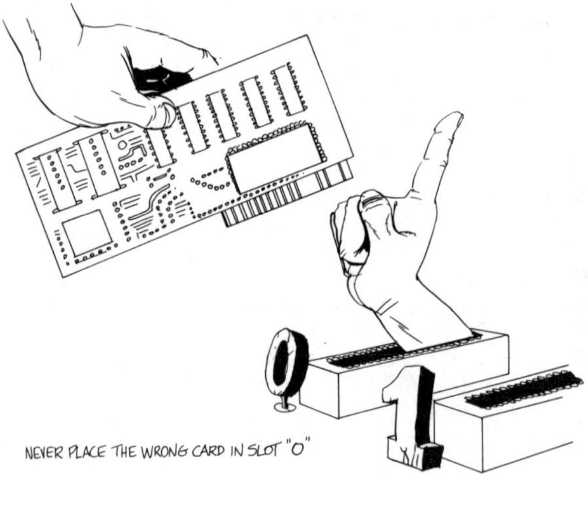

NEVER PLACE THE WRONG CARD IN SLOT "0"

CAUTION

NEVER insert or remove interface cards in your computer while the POWER IS ON! Even if you are rich and can afford to buy new chips every time you blow them by messing with the hardware in your Apple while the power is on, you might give yourself the SHOCK of a lifetime by doing so.

Other Gadgets

Besides the disk drive, TV/monitor, and printer, most new users do not have anything else to hook up at this point, and so you can skip on to the next section. However, if you plan on expanding your Apple or have other gadgets you bought with your system, you better read the following section.

Lots of Slots

The nicest feature of the Apple is its expandability and adaptability. The eight (8) slots in the back provide you with the ability to grow as your needs and interests do. So far, we've used three slots, and that leaves us with five more. So let's see what we can put in them.

INTEGER/APPLESOFT Card — There are two versions of BASIC in wide use on the Apple. Most people have the Apple II+ which means they have the APPLESOFT or floating point version of BASIC in ROM. However, there are programs, especially games, written in INTEGER BASIC. To run the Apple II+ on INTEGER programs, as well as APPLESOFT, many users buy the INTEGER firmware card. It goes in Slot #0 and will give you immediate access to either APPLESOFT (the one you already have) or INTEGER. Those who have the Apple II (without the "+") can get an APPLESOFT firmware card, also installed in Slot #0, to add APPLESOFT BASIC. However, before buying one or the other types of firmware cards, read on to save some money!

Language Or RAM Cards — The firmware known as *language cards* or *RAM cards* are 16K of additional memory. (Higher K cards are now available, but I will only be talking about the 16K ones here.) These cards go into Slot #0 and are used to add additional memory to the Apple for general use or to load in other languages. They can be used to load such languages as PASCAL, FORTRAN, COBOL, and either APPLESOFT or INTEGER BASIC. Therefore, if you buy a 16K RAM card, you won't need to get an INTEGER or APPLESOFT card, and you can load other languages as well or simply use the additional memory. Also, these cards have come way down in price (as little as $70 for a 16K RAM card).

However, unlike the INTEGER or APPLESOFT cards that give you immediate access to the language, it takes about 40 seconds to load the language into the 16K RAM card when it is first booted. However, if you don't mind waiting the extra 40 seconds, you're better off with the 16K card than with either the INTEGER or APPLESOFT cards. (If you can afford both, there are software programs available so that you can have immediate access to INTEGER or APPLESOFT as well as the extra 16K.)

Modem — A *modem* is a device that allows your computer to communicate with other computers over telephone lines. These devices usually require that you hook up your telephone to a part of the modem, or place the phone in an acoustic sender/receiver. The interface card is then placed in one of the empty slots, the number usually specified by the manufacturer.

80-column Card — These cards provide 80-column screen display on the Apple II and II+. They are useful for word processing. Look for a spare slot or where the directions suggest—we're running out of slots!

Clock Card — If you want your computer to time everything from the duration of a program, to telling you the hour and minute in Timbuktu, stick in a clock card. These cards also can be used to set up a home security system, timing the lighting, radio, and other devices that make it look like you're home when you're away. Another application of these cards is for "interrupts" for "spooling"—a form of time sharing where more than a single task is done on the computer. (Some spooling programs, such as Southwestern Data System's "DOUBLETIME PRINTER," come with an interrupt card, while others need a clock card.)

More Wonderful Gadgets — There are numerous other cards to make the Apple into many different computers. Special graphics printer drivers, Z-80 cards to give you CP/M, and cards to turn your Apple into just about anything you want! There are even multi-function cards that combine a number of the above cards into a single card using a single slot!

POWER ON!

System Check-out

Now that you have your Apple all set to go, you simply plug it in, along with your TV or monitor and printer, turn on the power and let her rip! In the back, on the left-hand side you will find a switch. Turn it to the ON position, and if everything is working correctly your disk drive will start whirling and the red "IN USE" light on the disk drive will be lighted. To stop the disk drive, depress the button marked CTRL (CONTROL) and the RESET button simultaneously. (On some, all that is necessary is to press RESET). You should hear a "beep," the disk drive should stop and a CURSOR should appear on your screen. Now press some keys and different characters will appear on the screen. If that happens, you know your disk drive system is hooked up correctly and your TV/monitor is working properly. Now press the RETURN key, and there will be a "beep" along with a "**SYNTAX ERROR" message on the screen.

To see if your printer is working correctly, first write in the word NEW and press RETURN; then put in the following program EXACTLY as it appears below (<RETURN> means press the button marked "RETURN"):

```
10 D$=CHR$(4) <RETURN>
20 PRINT D$; "PR#1" <RETURN>
30 PRINT "MY PRINTER IS WORKING!" <RETURN>
40 PRINT D$; "PR#0" <RETURN>
```

Make certain you have written the program as it appears above. If there are even minor differences, change it so that it is precisely the same. Put the ribbon and some paper in your printer. Now, turn on your printer and make certain that its switches and lights indicate it is ON-LINE. Now write in the word RUN on your computer and <RETURN>. If your printer is attached properly, it will print out the message, "MY PRINTER IS WORKING!" If a "SYNTAX ERROR" or some other error message jumps on the screen, it means that you wrote the little test program improperly; so go back and do it again. If the system "hangs up"—the screen goes blank and nothing happens, check to make sure the printer is turned on and is ON-LINE. If it still doesn't work, turn off the power on the printer and computer, and review the steps for hooking up your printer.

Booting Disks

Assuming your system is working correctly, let's *boot* a diskette. This will get your Disk Operating System (DOS—pronounced "DAS") operating.

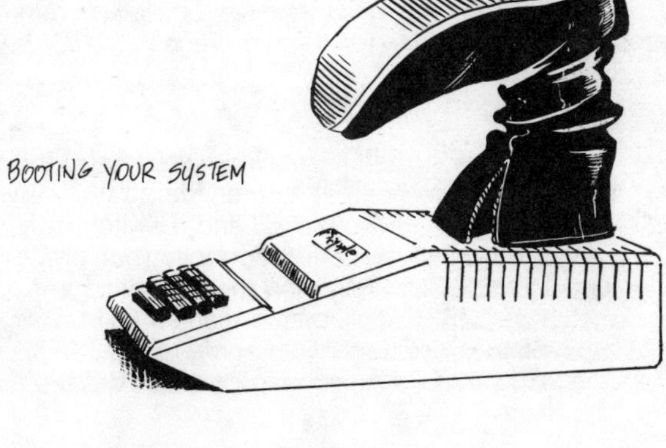

Here's how. Take the diskette marked "SYSTEM MASTER" that comes with your computer and place it in the disk drive. Insert it gently and evenly until it is all the way in. Now turn on your computer and the drive will start spinning. At this time, SLOWLY close the "door" on the disk drive. (Some manuals suggest you close your disk drive before you turn on the power, but with floppy diskettes, sometimes the diskette ring is not properly centered. By inserting the diskette before turning on the power, the spinning heads will center it for you, increasing the life of your diskettes and ensuring proper centering.) The disk drive will spin for a while and then there will appear a message on your screen with the title of the diskette. A cursor will appear indicating your system is all set to go.

CATALOG—Reading the Diskette's Contents

To find out what is on a diskette, simply write in the word "CATALOG." If your system is properly booted you will be presented with a listing on your screen showing you the various "files" on your diskette. If you get a "**SYNTAX ERROR", it means your system did not boot; so instead of shutting off the power, write in PR#6 <RETURN>. This is another way of "booting" your system except you do not have to turn off the power.

> **HOW TO IMPRESS YOUR FRIENDS**
>
> Remember we put the diskette controller card in Slot #6? By typing in PR#6, we accessed that slot. (If you had put the drive in Slot #5, PR#5 would have booted the diskette system.) To impress people, type in IN#6, and it will do the same thing as PR#6 ! If you really want to knock 'em dead, type in CALL −1401. It's simply a way to show off and another way to boot your system.

The System Master—RUNning Your FIRST Program

Assuming you now have your DOS (come on now, you remember that DOS means "Disk Operating System" and is pronounced "DAS") "booted," let's run a program. Write in:

```
RUN BRIAN'S THEME
```

Your disk drive will whirl and shortly a program showing you graphic displays will appear. You have successfuly run a program! That's just about all there is to it. . . . However, there are a few more things you should know before we continue. Let's look at a few files:

```
*A 006 APPLESOFT PROGRAM
 I 012 INTEGER PROGRAM
*B 003 BINARY PROGRAM
 T 119 TEXT FILE
```

The above four files represent the main types you will see on a diskette. The A, I, B, or T to the left of the program name is a code indicating the type of file saved on the diskette. Files coded with an "A" refer to APPLE-SOFT, those with an "I", INTEGER, "B" for "binary" or "machine" programs and "T" is for "text" files. Using the RUN command, you can operate either "A" or "I" files as long as you have the correct language installed when you make the "RUN." (If you try to run an INTEGER program on an APPLE-SOFT machine, you will get a "LANGUAGE NOT AVAILABLE" message unless you have an INTEGER card or INTEGER loaded into a language card.) For "B" files, you use the command "BRUN" instead of "RUN." Finally, for the time being, don't try to RUN or BRUN files marked with a "T". Some can be operated with the command EXEC, but for now, don't do anything to them. We'll cover them in detail in chapter 8.

UNLOCKING FILES

There are a couple of other commands we'd better cover now dealing with DOS. Notice the little asterisk (*) next to the files on the diskette. This means the file is LOCKed. (Ok, so what does LOCK do?) If a file is locked, it cannot be removed from the diskette with the DELETE command. (You mean it's there permanently?) If you wish to DELETE a locked file, first you must UNLOCK it. (I'm confused.) Let's sort all of this out:

DOS COMMAND	WHAT IT DOES
RUN	Operates either "A" or "I" files.
BRUN	Operates "B" files.
LOCK	Prevents a file from being overwritten or removed with a DELETE command.
DELETE	Removes a file from the diskette.
UNLOCK	Removes the LOCKed status of a file and enables the user to remove it with a DELETE command.

Initializing Blank Diskettes

We will discuss how to SAVE files to diskette in chapter 2. Now, we will take a look at a new diskette with nothing on it (a blank diskette). First, if you do not have a blank diskette, go get one. DO NOT use your SYSTEM MASTER for this next procedure except to boot your DOS. Now, let's look at the diskette.

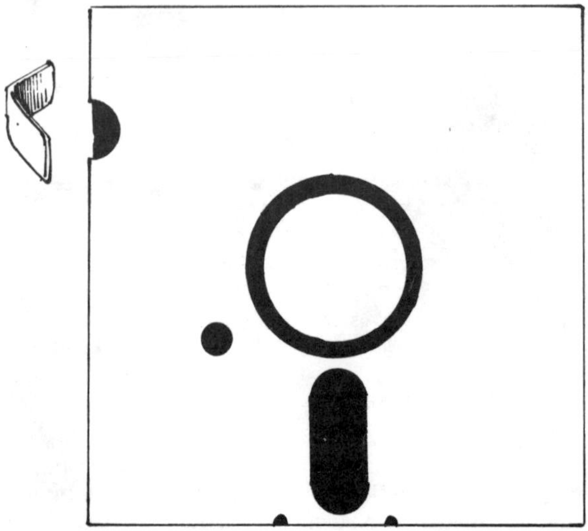

The item to notice on your blank diskette is the square notch in the upper right corner. This is the "write protect" notch. If there is no such notch on a diskette or if the notch is covered by a little tab, called a "write protect tab," you cannot add or delete files from that diskette—even if all of the files are unlocked. This is an important feature since it protects you against accidental erasure or overwriting. Now lets "initialize" a diskette so that it can be used to SAVE the programs we will begin writing in chapter 2. Here's how:

1. Boot your system with your SYSTEM MASTER diskette and remove the SYSTEM MASTER from the drive. Insert your blank diskette with the write protect tab removed.
2. Write in the word "NEW" (this clears the current program from memory).
3. Write the following little program EXACTLY as it is listed (at the end of each line press RETURN):

```
10 TEXT:HOME
20 PRINT "THIS DISKETTE WAS INITIALIZED ON <DATE>"
30 PRINT "BY <YOUR NAME>"
40 PRINT CHR$(4);"CATALOG"
50 END
```

4. Write in INIT HELLO and press RETURN.

Your disk drive will whirl for some time and make funny noises. When it stops and the cursor comes up, your disk is initialized. Now, to test it, write in PR#6 <RETURN> and your system will "re-boot." Your message, "THIS DISKETTE WAS INITIALIZED ON <DATE> BY <YOUR NAME>" will appear at the top of the screen, and your diskette will be automatically CATALOGed. The only file on the catalog will be HELLO. Now write in LOCK HELLO <RETURN> and then CATALOG your disk again. Now the HELLO file has a little asterisk (*) next to it indicating it is locked. DO NOT attempt to save another program to the disk using the INIT command—it will remove everything on the disk! Diskettes only need to be INITialized once; NEVER initialize a diskette with programs on it unless you want to erase all the programs on the disk. If you buy diskettes with programs on them they are already initialized. We'll get to saving regular programs on your diskette later. For now, just leave your initialized diskette alone, and go on and read about the Apple keyboard. The next section is about how to use a tape recorder with your computer. (You can read it even if you have a disk system, of course.)

LOADing And RUNning Programs From Tape

The procedure for loading and running programs from tape is quite simple, but there can be problems in troubleshooting if things do not work out. We'll go through the steps in loading and running a program from tape first, then we'll go through the troubleshooting procedures.

1. Make sure your tape recorder is plugged in; rewind it to the beginning. Use one of the demonstration tapes that is supplied with your computer.
2. Turn on your computer and when you get the bracket shaped cursor, write in the word LOAD. Do NOT press RETURN at this time.
3. Press the PLAY button on your tape recorder and press RETURN on your computer. At this point the cursor will disappear and soon you will hear a "beep" indicating the program has begun loading.
4. After a while, you will hear another "beep". This means the program has loaded, and you should press the STOP button on your recorder. Rewind the tape. (Actually, you don't have to rewind the tape now, but it's a good habit.)
5. Write in the word RUN on your keyboard, and your program will be executed. That's it.

Troubleshooting With Tape

Tapes seem to run into far more problems than diskettes, but there are usually some relatively simple solutions to the problem. Let's look at possible problems and some solutions.

Wrong Type Of Tape Recorder — One of the first things you should check out with your computer store is the correct type of tape recorder to purchase. Not all cassette recorders work with your system. It is is good idea to get a tape recorder with the following features:

1. Tone Control
2. Manual Volume Level Control (not automatic volume)
3. Tape counter—so you know where a program begins and ends.

Wrong Volume And/or Tone Level — Depending on the type of tape recorder you have, the volume and tone will affect loading and running tapes. Try a tone of 9 or 10 and a volume of 4 to 5 and make adjustments until your program loads and runs properly.

Incorrect Cable Connections — Check your cables to make sure the jack OUT of the computer goes to the MIC, and the IN socket on the computer is connected to the EAR or LISTEN on the tape recorder.

Computer Problem — Sometimes there will be something in the computer's memory that causes problems in loading. Just turn it off, and then on again and give it another try.

Tape Not Rewound — Make sure you have rewound your tape all the way.

If you still have trouble with loading your program from tape, take your tape recorder to the store where you got your computer and have them give it a try on one in the store. If they cannot get it to work, it is either the wrong kind of recorder or the tape is bad.

> **TAPE TO DISK TRANSFER**
>
> If you have both a tape and disk system, and you don't want to wait for a program to load from tape everytime your run it, why not transfer your tape files to disk? All you have to do is to boot your DOS, put in an initialized disk in the drive and then load your tape. Once your tape program is loaded, simply write in SAVE <name of file> and now your tape program is on disk! Makes life simpler.

The Apple Keyboard

Almost Like A Typewriter:The Familiar Keys

If your are familiar with a typewriter keyboard, you will see most of the same keys on your Apple II. For the most part, they do almost the same thing as your typewriter keys. If you type in the word COMPUTER, hitting the same keys you would on a typewriter, the word "COMPUTER" appears on the screen just as it would on paper in a typewriter. However, the upper-case (capital letters) and lower-case letters do not work exactly the same as a typewriter. On the standard Apple II, there are no lower case letters to the screen. You have to buy a "lower case adapter" to put in your computer for that, and I would recommend you get one. They are inexpensive and your computer store should have them. Also, the screen has only 40 columns instead of 80 like most typewriters. Of course, you cannot type just anything on the screen. If you start typing away, you'll get a SYNTAX ERROR unless you put in the proper commands. Otherwise, though, think of your keyboard as you would a typewriter keyboard.

Keys You Won't See On A Typewriter

While most of the keys on your Apple look like those on a typewriter, many do not, and they are important to know about. The following keys are peculiar to computers; you will soon get used to them even though they will be a bit mysterious at first:

ESCape — The ESC key in the upper left-hand corner of your computer stands for "escape" and depending on the program in memory or the particular task you're working on it will do different things. It is used in editing programs, and we will cover that in the next chapter. For now, you should know that when pressing ESC, the next keyboard entry will be affected by it. Also, you do not have to hold the ESC key down while simultaneously holding another key to operate it.

CTRL (Control) — Right below the ESC key is the CTRL or *control* key. To use this key, you must hold it down while pressing another key. Try holding it down and pressing the "G" key. Ring a bell? Later, we will be getting into the use of "control characters" that are initiated by pressing CTRL and another key simultaneously.

Reset — The RESET key is often a "panic button." When things freeze up on your computer, often the only way to unjam them is to hit RESET, or CTRL-RESET. Again, depending on the program in memory, hitting the

RESET key will do different things. If you accidentally hit RESET instead of the "-" or RETURN key, for example, usually by typing in RUN you will get your program back. With certain programs in memory, though, strange things can happen if you hit RESET. Don't be afraid of it, but for now only use it when instructed or when a program freezes up on you. (As a rule of thumb, NEVER press RESET when your disk drive light is on and the door is closed!)

REPT (Repeat) — This key allows you to automatically repeat a key by simultaneously holding down the desired key you want repeated and the REPT key. Try it by holding down the "P" key and REPT key. You should get a line of "P's" across you screen.

Left and Right Arrows and Space Bar — The left and right arrows move the cursor without affecting the characters on the screen. If you advance the cursor with the "space bar" (the long key at the bottom of your keyboard) it will wipe out any characters you see on the screen. This is because it puts a "space" in as the "character." The arrows are used extensively in editing. If you retrace a line with the right arrow, it "verifies" the line. Later when we discuss editing, we will see the many uses of the arrow keys.

Return — The RETURN key is something like the carriage return on a typewriter. In fact, you may see it referred to as a "Carriage Return" or "CR" in computer articles. It works in an analogous manner to a typewriter's carriage return, in that after you press it, the cursor bounces back to the left-hand side of the display screen. However, there are other uses for the RETURN key.

Some New Meanings For Old Keys

Some of the familiar keys have different meanings for the computer than we usually associate with the key symbols. Many are math symbols you may or may not recognize. In the next chapter, we will illustrate how these keys can be operated and discuss them in detail. For now let's just take a quick look at the math symbols

SYMBOL	MEANING
+	Add
–	Subtract
*	Multiply (different from conventional)
/	Divide (different from conventional)
∧	Exponentiation (symbol called "caret")

In addition to some of the new representations for math symbols, other keys will be used in ways that you are not used to. As we go on, we will explain the meanings of these keys, but just to get used to the idea that your Apple has some special meanings for keys. We'll show you some more here that will have special meanings later.

SYMBOL	MEANING
$	Used to indicate a string variable and hexadecimal value.
:	Used to indicate "end of line" in program.
%	Indicates an integer variable.
?	Can be used as PRINT command.

Don't worry about understanding what all these symbols do for the time being. Simply be prepared to think in "computer talk" about symbols. As you become familiar with the keyboard and the uses and meanings of these symbols, you will be able to handle them easily, but the first step is to be aware that the different meanings exist.

Your Apple On The Screen

We have mentioned the CURSOR, but we really have not told you too much about it. If you haven't already noticed, the prompt for APPLESOFT is a bracket "]". Perhaps the easiest way to understand the cursor is to

UNDERSTAND WHAT PROMPTS YOU.

think of it as a "marker" telling you where you are and what your computer is doing. When the cursor disappears, it means that your computer is: (1) running a program or (2) hung up and not operating. If you think it is hung up, you can hit RESET or re-boot your system by turning it off and then on again. However, there are different cursors representing different states.

Different Prompts

As we have seen, the APPLESOFT prompt is the bracket-shaped cursor meaning that the language APPLESOFT is ready to go. If you have INTEGER BASIC loaded in memory or have an Apple II (without the "+," your cursor looks like an arrowhead, like this ">." Whenever you see the ">" prompt, you know that INTEGER BASIC and not APPLESOFT is in operation. Finally, if your prompt is an asterisk "*," you are in the monitor (not the TV set!). For the most part, you DO NOT want to be in the monitor, for that's where machine level programming is done. If you see the "*," press CTRL-C or CTRL-B to get back into BASIC—either APPLESOFT or INTEGER. (Just for fun, if you find yourself in the monitor, press "L" and you will get an "assembly listing." This is useful, for if you're showing off your Apple

DON'T WORRY IF YOU BOMB AT FIRST

to a friend and you accidentally bomb, ending up in the monitor, by pressing "L" and listing the assembly/machine code, they'll think you know what you're doing.)

Summary

This first chapter has been an overview of your new machine. You should now know how to hook up the different parts of your Apple and get it running. Also, you should be able to boot and initialize a disk, CATALOG the contents of a disk, and run a program from disk or tape. You should know some of the basic DOS commands for manipulating files on your diskette. Finally, you should be familiar with the keyboard and know what the cursor means. At this point, there is still much to learn, and don't feel badly if you don't understand everything. As we go along, you will pick up more and more, and what may be confusing now, later will become clear. Have faith in yourself, and in no time, you will be able to do things you never thought possible.

The next chapter will get you started in learning how to program your Apple. It is vitally important that you key in and run the sample programs. Also, it is recommended you make changes in them after you have first tried them out to see if you can make them do slightly different things. Both practical and fun (and crazy!) programs are included so that you can see the purpose behind what you will be doing and enjoy it at the same time.

CHAPTER 2
Getting Started

This chapter will introduce you to writing programs in the language known as APPLESOFT BASIC, also called "Floating Point" BASIC. The rest of the book will reference programs in this version of BASIC. If you have an Apple II+, or an Apple II with an APPLESOFT firmware card or a 16K Language Card, you can easily follow the instructions writing commands in APPLESOFT. All you have to remember is to look for the bracket prompt "]," and you are all set. If you have the arrowhead prompt ">" of INTEGER BASIC and yet believe you have APPLESOFT available to you, put your SYSTEM MASTER in your disk drive and type in the letters "FP" (for Floating Point). This should either immediately give you the APPLESOFT bracket prompt or load APPLESOFT in your language card from your SYSTEM MASTER. If you cannot get APPLESOFT "up" and must use INTEGER BASIC; then you will find a number of differences between the commands written for APPLESOFT BASIC and your version of BASIC. Despair not! Throughout, I will attempt to note where differences exist between the two languages. However, the main orientation will be to working in APPLESOFT.

Your Very First Command!

PRINT

Probably the most often used command in APPLESOFT is PRINT. Words enclosed in quotation marks following the PRINT command will be printed to your screen, and numbers and variables will be printed if they are preceded by a print command. It is used to command your computer to print output to the screen or printer from within a program or in the Immediate mode. You may well ask what the difference is between the Immediate and Program mode. Let's take a look, but first turn on your computer and make sure the bracket cursor is on your screen and prompt is blinking. Also, to clear memory and make sure nothing is there to get mixed up with your commands enter in the NEW command. (You can also clear memory by keying in FP.)

Immediate Mode — The *immediate mode* executes a command as soon as you press RETURN. For example, try the following:

PRINT "THIS IS THE IMMEDIATE MODE" <RETURN>

If everything is working correctly, your screen should look like this:

```
PRINT "THIS IS THE IMMEDIATE MODE"
THIS IS THE IMMEDIATE MODE
```

See how easy that was? Now try PRINTing some numbers, but don't put in the quote marks. Try the following:

```
PRINT 6 <RETURN>
PRINT 54321 <RETURN>
```

As you can see, numbers can be entered without having to use quote marks, but as we will see later, the actual value of the number is placed in memory rather than a "picture" of it.

Program Mode — This mode "delays" the execution of the commands until your program is "RUN." All commands that begin with numbers on the left side will be treated as part of a program. Try the following.

```
10 PRINT "THIS IS THE PROGRAM MODE" <RETURN>
```

Nothing happens, right? Enter the RUN command and your screen should look like this:

```
10 PRINT "THIS IS THE PROGRAM MODE"
THIS IS THE PROGRAM MODE
```

Your Very First Program!

Clearing The Screen And Writing Your Name

Let's write a program and learn three new commands. First, the new commands are TEXT, HOME and END. The TEXT command clears any graphics from the screen and puts you in the text screen placing the cursor in the lower left hand corner, and the HOME command clears the screen and places the cursor in the upper left hand corner. The END command tells the computer to stop executing commands. From the Immediate mode write in the TEXT and HOME commands to see what happens. Now, let's write a program using TEXT, HOME, END and PRINT. From now on, press the RETURN key at the end of each line. Throughout the rest of the book, I will no longer be putting in <RETURN> except in reference to entries in the Immediate mode. (In INTEGER BASIC, there is no HOME command. Use the command CALL −936 instead.)

```
10 TEXT
20 HOME
30 PRINT "<YOUR NAME>"
40 END
RUN <RETURN>
```

All you should see on the screen is your name and the blinking cursor. Now, we're going to introduce two shortcuts that will save you time in programming and in memory. First, instead of entering new line numbers, it is possible to put multiple commands on the same line by using a colon ":" between commands. Also, instead of typing in PRINT, you can key in a question mark "?". (The question mark substitution does not work in INTEGER BASIC.) Try the following program to see how this works.

```
10 TEXT : HOME
20 ? "<YOUR NAME>" : END
```

THE COMMANDS CAN BE PUT ON THE SAME LINE BY USING A COLON!

It did exactly the same thing, but you did not have to put in as many lines or write out the word PRINT. Neat, huh? Now, as a rule of thumb, ALWAYS begin your programs with TEXT : HOME. This will help you get into a habit that will pay off later when you're running all kinds of different programs with text and graphics all over the place. There will be exceptions to the rule, but for the most part, by beginning your programs with TEXT : HOME, you will start off with a nice clear screen in the proper mode for most of your applications.

While we're just getting started, it will probably be a good idea to use the colon sparingly. This is because it is easier to understand a program with a minimum number of commands in a single line. Later, when you become more adept at writing programs, and want to figure out ways to save memory and speed up program execution, you will probably want to use the colon a good deal more. Also, we want to make liberal use of the REM command (or non-command). After the computer sees a REM command in a line, it goes on to the next line number, executing nothing until it comes to an executable command. The REM command works as a REMark in your program lines so that others will know what you are doing and as a reminder to yourself what you have done. Just to see how it works, let's put it in our little program.

```
10 TEXT : HOME : REM THIS SETS THE FULL TEXT WINDOW
AND CLEARS THE SCREEN
20 PRINT "<YOUR NAME>" : END
30 REM THIS MAGNIFICENT PROGRAM WAS CREATED BY
<YOUR NAME>
```

Now RUN the program and you will see that the REM statements did not affect it at all! However, it is much clearer as to what your program is doing since you can read what the commands do in the program listing.

Setting Up A Program

Using Line Numbers

Now that we've written a little program let's take a look at using line numbers. In your first program, we used the line numbers 10, 20 and 30. We could have used line numbers 1, 2 and 3 or 0, 1 and 2 or even 1000, 2000 and 3000. In fact, there is no need at all to have regular intervals between numbers, and line numbers 1, 32 and 1543 would have worked just fine.

However, we usually want to number our programs by 10's, starting at 10. You may well ask, "Wouldn't it be easier to number them 1, 2, 3, 4, 5, etc.?" In some ways maybe it would, but overall, it definitely would not! Here's why. Type in the word LIST <RETURN>, and if your program is still in memory it will appear on the screen. Suppose you want to inset a line between lines 20 and 30 that prints your home address. Rather than rewriting the entire program, all you have to do is to enter a line number with a value between 20 and 30 (such as 25) and enter the line. Let's try it, but first remove the END command in line 20.

```
25 PRINT "<YOUR ADDRESS>"
RUN <RETURN>
```

Aha! You now have your name and address printed on the screen, and all you had to do was to write in one line instead of retyping the whole program. Now if we had numbered the program by 1's instead of 10's you would not have been able to to that since there would be no room between lines numbered 2 and 3 as there was between 20 and 30. You would have to rewrite the whole program. Now with a small program, this would not be much of a problem, but when you start getting into 100 and 1000 line programs, you'll be glad you have space between line numbers!

Listing Your Program

As we just saw, using the word LIST gives us a listing of our program. To make it neat, type in HOME : LIST <RETURN>, and you'll get a listing on a clear screen. However, once you start writing longer programs, you won't want to list everything, but only portions. Let's examine the options available with the LIST command

WHAT YOU WRITE	WHAT YOU GET
LIST	Lists entire program.
LIST 20	Only line 20 is listed (or any line number you choose).
LIST 20,30	All lines from 20 to 30 inclusive are listed (or any other range of lines you choose).
LIST −40	Lists from the beginning of the program to line 40 (or any other line number chosen).
LIST 40− (or 40,)	Lists from line 40 (or any other line number chosen) to the end of the program.

Try listing different portions of your program with the options available to see what you get. The following commands will give you some examples of the different options:

```
LIST 25
LIST 20-
LIST -20
LIST 25,30
```

WANNA HAVE SOME FUN?

Usually you will want to use the LIST command from the Immediate mode as you write your program. However, you can use it from within a program. Just for fun, add the following line to your program.

```
40 LIST
```

RUN your program and see what happens. Believe it or not, there are some very practical applications we will see in some programs much later in the book. For the time being, though, it's just for fun. Now, back to some serious stuff.

Saving Your Program

Suppose you write a program, get it working perfectly and then turn off your computer. Since the program is stored in the RAM memory, it will go to Never-Never Land, and you will have to write it in again if you want to use it. Fortunately, it is a simple matter to SAVE a program to your diskette. Let's use our program for an example of SAVEing a program to disk. Make sure your program is still in memory by LISTing it, and if it is not, re-write it. Make sure an initialized disk is in the drive and write in the following:

SAVE MY PROGRAM

The disk will start whirling and the red light will glow on the disk drive. This means the disk drive is writing your program to disk. When the red light goes out, write in the word CATALOG <RETURN> and you should see:

HELLO
MY PROGRAM

That means your program has been successfully saved to disk.

Saving Programs On Tape

To save a program to tape, put a blank cassette in your tape recorder and rewind it. Write in the word SAVE and press the RECORD button(s) on your tape recorder. Now press RETURN on your computer. The cursor will disappear and soon there will be a "beep" followed shortly by another "beep." After the second "beep," turn off your recorder and rewind it. Your program is now SAVEed to tape. Unlike SAVEing to disk, you do not enter a name after the SAVE command.

Retrieving Your Programs

The best way to make sure you have SAVEed a program to disk or tape is to completely turn off your Apple, and then turn it on again. Go ahead and do it, and then CATALOG your disk. You should be able to see your program, (MY PROGRAM) in the catalog. Now, enter the word RUN and the name of your program.

RUN MY PROGRAM

The disk drive will whirl for a while, and then your program will be executed. In this case the screen should go blank, and your name and address should appear at the top of the screen and a listing of your program. This means that you have successfully SAVEed a program to disk.

Now, let's try something else. Enter the following:

NEW (this will clear memory)

LIST (this will show you that nothing is in memory)

LOAD MY PROGRAM

LIST

RUN

Now you could have just RUN the program directly from disk, but you can also LOAD a program and then RUN it. There will be several occasions when you will want to only LOAD and list a program but not RUN it. When you begin working on larger programs, you may spend several days working on the same one. Since you do not want to leave your computer ON the entire time, you will save parts of the program as you go along.

A SAFETY NET

As you begin writing longer programs, every so many lines, you should SAVE your program to disk. In this way, if your dog accidently trips over your cord and turns off your computer, you won't lose your program and have to shoot the offending pooch. Saves both programs and dogs.

Now that you have SAVEed and LOADed programs, let's look at another neat trick. Remembering you SAVEed your file under the name MY PROGRAM, let's change the contents of that file. First, add the following line and then LIST your program:

27 PRINT "<YOUR CITY, STATE & ZIP>"

Your program is now different than the program you SAVEed in the file MY PROGRAM since you have added line 27. Now write in

SAVE MY PROGRAM <RETURN>

Clear memory with NEW, LOAD the file MY PROGRAM and LIST it. As you can see, line 27 is now part of MY PROGRAM. All you have to do to update a program is to LOAD it, make any changes you want, and then SAVE it under the same file name. However, BE CAREFUL. No matter what program is in memory, that program will be SAVEed when you enter the SAVE command; therefore, if your disk has PROGRAM A and you write PROGRAM B, and then SAVE it under the title PROGRAM A, it will destroy PROGRAM A and the SAVEed program will actually be PROGRAM B. The best way to avoid "overwriting" a cherished program is to LOCK it. Then if you try to SAVE a program to that file name, your computer will tell you "FILE LOCKED" and not to "overwrite" it with any other program until you UNLOCK it. Also, if you have a really important program, it is a good idea to make a "back-up" file. For example, if you saved your current program under the file names, MY PROGRAM and MY PROGRAM B, it would have two files with exactly the same program. To really play it safe, save the program on two different diskettes.

IT'S NICE TO KEEP COPIES, IN CASE SOMETHING HAPPENS TO THE ORIGINAL

I TOLD YOU SO DEPT.

Sooner or later the following will happen to you: You will have several disks, one of which you want to initialize. You will pick up the wrong diskette, one with valuable programs on it—possibly one you bought for $157.23. There will be no write protect tab on the diskette, and after you initialize it and blow away everything on it, you will realize your mistake and say, "!&$#!%&," and kick your dog. You cannot avoid that from happening at least once, believe me. Therefore, to insure that such a mistake is not irreversible, do the following: MAKE BACK-UP's. The COPYA program on your SYSTEM MASTER is very handy. Simply RUN it, and copy valuable programs from one diskette to another. Take your ORIGINAL and put it somewhere out of reach, and when you accidentally erase a disk, you can make another copy. Remember, if you fail to follow this advice, your dog will have sore ribs. Be kind to your dog.

Using Your Editor: Fixing Mistakes On The RUN

The Error Message And Repairing Them

By now you probably entered something and got a **SYNTAX ERROR or ?SYNTAX ERROR IN 30 (referring to line 30 or any other line where an error is detected). This occurs in the Immediate mode as soon as you hit RETURN and in the program mode as soon as you RUN your program. (In INTEGER BASIC you get error messages for program lines as soon as you press RETURN after a mistake.) Depending on the error, you will get a different type of message. As we go along, we will see different messages depending on the operation. For now, we will concentrate on how to fix errors in program lines rather than the nature of the errors themselves. This process is referred to as "editing" programs. (See Appendix A for a complete list of error messages.)

Deleting Lines

The most simple type of editing involves inserting and deleting lines. Let's write a program with an error in it and fix it up.

```
NEW <RETURN>
10 TEXT : HOME
20 PRINT " AS LONG AS SOMETHING CAN"
30 PRINT : "GO WRONG" : REM LINE WITH ERROR
40 PRINT "IT WILL"
50 END
RUN <RETURN>
```

If the program is written exactly as depicted above you will get a ?SYNTAX error. Now, write in,

```
30 <RETURN>
LIST <RETURN>
```

What happened to line 30?! You just learned about deleting a line. Whenever you enter a line number and nothing else, you delete the line. We already learned how to insert a line; so all you have to do to fix the program is enter the following:

```
30 PRINT "GO WRONG"
```

Now run the program. It should work fine. The error was inserting the colon between the PRINT statement and the words to be printed. Another way you could have fixed the program is simply to re-enter line 30 correctly without first deleting it, but I wanted to show you how to delete a line by entering the line number.

Now suppose you have several lines you want deleted. Instead of having to write all of the line numbers, you can use the DEL statement. Try the following:

```
DEL 20,50
LIST <RETURN>
```

Only line 10 is left. To DELete a range of lines, enter the first line you want deleted, a comma "," and the last line you want deleted.

Using The Apple Editor

Within your Apple is a trusty little editor; however, before describing it to you, I strongly suggest you take a look at the discussion of UTILITIES in Chapter 10. The editor in your Apple works just fine; however, there are some really powerful editors available. The Applesoft Command Editor (A. C. E.) and Program Line Editor (PLE) are two among several excellent editors commercially available. Using them instead of the one that is in your Apple will save you a considerable amount of time and speed with your progress in learning how to use programming commands. For the time being, though, let's concentrate on the editor in your computer—it has one huge advantage—it's right in front of you!

To begin, we'll write another bad program and fix it. Also, just for fun we'll learn something new. In line 40, after you put in the first quote marks, press the CTRL key and while holding it down, press the "G" key. You will hear a bell, but you will not see the "G". Ok, write the following program and RUN it.

```
NEW
10 TEXT : HOME
20 PRINT "IF I CAN GOOF UP A PROGRAM "
```

```
30 PRINT "I CAN" : FIX IT : REM BAD LINE
40 PRINT " ": REM CTRL-G IN BETWEEN QUOTES
50 END
RUN <RETURN>
```

All right, you got a ?SYNTAX ERROR IN 30. To repair it, instead of rewriting line 30 do the following:

1. LIST your program.
2. Press the ESC key.
3. Press the I key repeatedly until cursor is on line 30.
4. Press the B key so that the cursor is directly over the "3" in line 30.
5. Press the right arrow key until you get to the second quote mark in line 30 and then press the space bar twice. This will erase the quote mark.
6. Continue pressing the right arrow key until the cursor is to the right of the word "IT" and enter a quote mark (") and then press RETURN.

Now LIST the program again. Line 30 should now be correct and the REM statement gone. Now RUN the program. You should have seen the statement, IF I CAN GOOF UP A PROGRAM I CAN FIX IT and heard a bell ring. When you LISTed your program you should have heard a bell ring, also. That bell is the invisible CTRL-G ringing whenever you RUN or LIST a program. In longer programs, it is sometimes helpful to put in CTRL-G's as part of REM statements to flag various parts of the program. This makes locating parts of long programs easier.

However, we have a mystery! What happened to our REM statement in line 30? Well, it just so happens that when using the editor in your Apple that the entire line must be retraced with the cursor for it to be maintained in the line. Essentially, it is like re-writing the line and as soon as you hit RETURN the line is terminated. Since you did not re-trace over the REM statement, it was erased. Let's learn more about the editor. Put in the following program: (Remember, in APPLESOFT we can use the question marks to replace PRINT statements. If you LIST the program before you run it, you will see that all of the question marks have magically been transformed to PRINT statements.)

```
10 TEXT : HOME
20 ? "SOMETIMES I LIKE TO WRITE LONG, LONG LINES
AND REALLY EXPRESS MYSELF AND TELL THE COMPUTER
THE WAY THE WORLD WAS CREATED " : WHEW!
30 ?"AND SOMETIMES I LIKE SHORT LINES"
40 ?"DING, DING" : PRINT "   ": REM ENTER CTRL-G TWICE
```

INSIDE THE QUOTE MARKS
50 END
LIST <RETURN> See what happened to the question marks.
RUN <RETURN>

Ok, after you ran the program it went El Bombo. The problem was that we stuck in that WHEW! without a PRINT statement or quote marks after the colon had terminated the line. To repair it, LIST the program, hit ESC and "walk" the cursor up to line 20 using the "I" key and starting at line 20 retrace the line up to where the mistake was made. To make it simple, remove the second quote mark, and leaving the colon in place, add a quote mark after the word WHEW!. Since the colon is now inside the quote marks, it will be printed as part of the PRINT statement and be ignored as a line termination statement. After running the cursor over the rest of line 20, press RETURN. Now RUN the program.

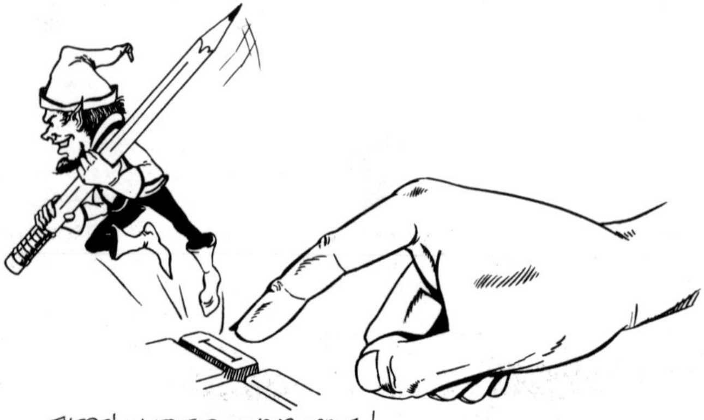

THERE' AN EDITOR IN YOUR APPLE !

Something strange happened to the statement in line 20. It has a big space in it, but you did not put it there. Here's what happened, when you retraced the line. The cursor went out into "space" as you traced past the end of the line first line and the computer thought you were entering spaces. To avoid this problem in the future, before entering the editor write in:

POKE 33,33

This statement resets the text window so that as soon as the cursor hits the end of a line, instead of going into "space" it immediately wraps around to pick the next entry. Ok, to test it, do the following:

1. Re-enter line 20 in the original wrong way. (Just write in 20 and the line.)
2. Enter HOME <RETURN> and then POKE 33,33 <RETURN>.
3. LIST the program and hit ESC and "walk" the cursor to line 20 and press B.
4. Now retrace the line, and make the same repairs you did the first time.

RUN the program and notice how the line is now correctly formatted. The TEXT statement in line 10 reset the text "window" to its full size; were there no TEXT statement in line 10, the lines would have extended only out part of the way. As a rule of thumb, whenever you perform editing, especially with longer lines to repair, use the POKE 33,33 first.

More Editing

There is a lot more you can do with your editor. Besides using the I key to move up, you can also use the J, K and M keys. Think of the I, J, K and M keys as a "cross" with the I key moving up, the J key moving left, the K key moving right and the M key moving down.

As long as you are in the "Edit mode" (i.e., after you hit ESC and before you press any other key than I,J,K, or M) the cursor can be moved without affecting anything on the screen. To get used to it, LIST a program, press

ESC and "walk" around the screen using the I, J, K, and M keys. None of the characters on the screen are affected.

Now, let's try the editor out on something a little trickier, but as you will see, very useful. Suppose you have typed in a program and after you have RUN it, you realize that you left out a word in the middle of a line. Even using the tricks we know so far, it will take a long time to insert a single word since you'd have to re-type the entire line. So, let's see how we can use the editor to do "insertions." Try the following little program:

```
10 TEXT : HOME
20 PRINT "NOW IS THE TIME FOR ALL GOOD MEN TO
COME TO THE AID OF THEIR COUNTRY"
30 END
```

So far so good, but you meant to include women as well as men in line 20. You could retype the entire line, but all you really need to add is AND WOMEN after MEN. Do the following to make the change with the editor:

1. Write in HOME : POKE 33,33 : LIST 20 <RETURN>
2. Enter ESC and "walk" the cursor up to the beginning of the line using the I key, and then back it over the "2" in 20 with the J key.
3. Trace over the line to the point where you want to insert AND WOMEN (right after the word MEN).
4. At the point of insertion, press ESC and then the "I" key. This will take the cursor right above the line you're fixing.
5. Once you are above the line, press the space bar to release you from the editor and type in (SPACE) AND WOMEN.
6. Now, press ESC again to get back into editor and press "M" to take you back down into the line and the "J" key to take you back to the point where you want the insertion. Once at the insertion point press the space bar to get out of the editor; then retrace the remainder of line 20 with the right arrow key.

The following diagram illustrates the above steps:

. . . GOOD MEN ˆ TO COME . . . (ˆ indicates point of insertion—when cursor is here, press ESC and "I")

```
              AND WOMEN
... GOOD MEN TO COME ...

           AND WOMEN
... GOOD MEN ˆ TO COME ...
```

(ˆ point to exit the editor and begin retracing line with right arrow key)

Now enter TEXT : HOME : LIST 20 <RETURN> and you will find line 20 now reads,

```
20 PRINT "NOW IS THE TIME FOR ALL GOOD MEN AND
WOMEN TO COME TO THE AID OF THEIR COUNTRY"
```

You will save yourself a great deal of time if you use the editor rather than retyping every mistake you make. (You will save yourself even more time using a commercial editor.) Therefore, to practice with it, there are several pairs of lines below to repair. The first line shows the wrong way and the second line in the pair shows the correct way. Since "little" things can make a big difference, there are a number of little changes to be made. However, as you will soon see, those little gliches are the ones we are most likely to get snagged on. Practice on these examples until you feel comfortable with the editor—time spent now will save you a great deal later. (Note: Once you have entered POKE 33,33, you will have strange things happen on your screen when you LIST a program sometimes. To set everything back to normal, enter the command TEXT.)

Editor Practice

```
50 PRINT NOBODY EVER WENT BROKE UNDERESTIMATING
THE TASTE OF THE AMERICAN PUBLIC."
50 PRINT "NOBODY EVER WENT BROKE
UNDERESTIMATING THE TASTE OF THE AMERICAN
PUBLIC."
10 TEXT HOME
10 TEXT : HOME
80 PRINT "A GOOD MAN IS HARD TO FIND"
80 PRINT "A GOOD PERSON IS HARD TO FIND"
40 HOME : TEXT PRINT "WE'RE OFF!
40 TEXT : HOME : PRINT "WE'RE OFF!"
```

If you fixed all of those lines, you can repair just about anything. Once you get the hang of it, it's quite simple.

ELEMENTARY MATH OPERATIONS

So far all we've done is to PRINT out a lot of text, but that isn't too different than having a fancy typewriter. Now, let's do some simple math operations to show you your computer can compute! Enter the following:

```
HOME
PRINT 2 + 2
```

This is what your screen should look like now:

```
PRINT 2 + 2
4
```

Big deal, so the computer can add—so can my $5 calculator and my 7 year old kid. Who said computers are smart? The programmer (you) is who is smart. Ok, so let's give it a little tougher problem.

```
HOME
PRINT 7.87 * 123.65
```

Still nothing your calculator can't do, but it'd be a little rough on the 7 year old.

As we progress, we can include more and more aspects of mathmatical problems, and in the next chapter, we will see how we can store values in variables and a lot of things that would choke your calculator. For now, though, all we'll do is to introduce the format of mathematical manipulations. The "+" and "−" signs work just as they do in regular math, and the "x" is replaced by "*" (asterisk) for multiplication and "÷" is replaced by the "/" (slash) for division.

As we begin dealing with more and more complex math, we will need to observe a certain order in which problems are executed. This is called "precedence." Depending on the operations we use, and the results we are attempting to obtain, we will use one order or another. For example, let's suppose we want to multiply the sum of two numbers by a third number—say the sum of 15 and 20 multiplied by 3. If you entered

```
3 * 15 + 20
```

you would get 3 multiplied by 15 with 20 added on. That's not what you wanted. The reason for that is precedence—multiplication precedes addition. To help you remember the precedence, let's write a little program you can run and then play with some math problems in the Immediate mode to see the results and refer to your "Precedence Chart" on the screen. (This little program is quite handy; so save it to disk or tape to be used later.)

```
10 TEXT : HOME
20 PRINT "1. − (MINUS SIGNS FOR NEGATIVE NUMBERS −
NOT SUBTRACTION)"
30 PRINT "2. ^ (EXPONENTIATIONS)"
40 PRINT "3. */(MULTIPLCATION AND DIVISION)"
50 PRINT "4. + − (ADDITIONS AND SUBTRACTIONS)"
60 PRINT "NOTE: ALL PRECEDENCE IS FROM LEFT TO
RIGHT"
70 PRINT "YOUR COMPUTER FIRST EXECUTES THE
NUMBERS IN PARENTHESES, WORKING ITS WAY FROM THE
INSIDE OUT IN MULTIPLE PARENTHESES."
80 POKE 34,10 : END : REM THE POKE STATEMENT RESETS
YOUR TEXT WINDOW SO YOU CAN DO MATH OPERATIONS
AND KEEP YOUR PRECEDENCE CHART ON THE SCREEN
```

Try some different problems and see if you can get what you want.

Re-ordering Precedence

Once you get the knack of the order in which math operations work, there is a way to simplify organizing math problems. By placing two or more numbers in PARENTHESES, it is possible to move them up in priority. Let's go back to our example of adding 15 and 20 and then multiplying by 3, but this time we will use parentheses.

```
PRINT 3 * (15 + 20)
```

Now since the multiplication sign has precedence over the addition sign, without the parentheses we would have gotten 3 times 15 plus 20. However, since all operations inside parentheses are executed first, your computer FIRST added 15 and 20 and then multiplied the sum by 3. If more than a single set of parentheses is used in an equation, then the innermost is executed first, working its way out.

THE PARENTHESES DUNGEON

To help you remember the order in which math operations are executed within parentheses, think of the operations as being locked up in multi-layer dungeon. Each cell represents the innermost operation, and the cells are lined up from left to right. Each "prisoner" is an operation surrounded by walls of parentheses. To escape the dungeon, the prisoner must first get out of the innermost cell, then the prisoner goes to his right and releases any other prisoners in their cells. Then they break out of the "cell-block" and finally out in the open. Unfortunately, since operations are "executed," this is a lethal analogy for our poor escaping "prisoners." Do some of the examples and see if you can come up with a better analogy.

The following examples show you some operations with parentheses.

```
PRINT 20 + (10 * (8 - 4))
PRINT (12.43 + 92)/(3 ^ (11 - 3))
PRINT (22 * 3.1415) * (22 * 3.1415)
PRINT ((16/4) * (3 + 5))/18
PRINT 19 + 2 * (51/3) - (100/14)
```

Now, try some of these problems in the proper format expected by your computer:

Multiply the sum of 4 , 9 and 20 by 15.

Multiply 3.14159265 by 35 and then multiply the result by itself.

Add up the charges on your long distance calls and divide the sum by the number of calls you made. This will give you the average expense of your calls. Remember, though, you have to do this in one set of statements in a single line. Do the same thing with your check book for a month to see the average (mean) amount for your checks.

Summary

This chapter has covered the most basic aspects of programming, and at this point you should be able to use the editor in your Apple, write commands in the immediate and deferred (program) mode. Also, you should be able to manipulate basic math operations. However, we have only just begun to uncover the power of your computer, and at this stage, we are treating it more as a glorified calculator than a computer. Nevertheless, what we have covered in this chapter is extremely important to understand, for it is the foundation upon which your understanding of programming is to be built. If there are parts you do not understand, review them before continuing. If you still do not understand certain operations after a review; don't worry, you will be able to pick them up later, but it is still important that you try and get everything to do what it is supposed to do and what you want it to do.

The next chapter will take us into the realm of computer programming and increase your understanding of your Apple considerably. If you take it one step at a time, you will be amazed at the power you have at your fingertips and how easy it is to program. Also, we will be leaving the realm of calculator-like commands and getting down to some honest-to-goodness computer work. This is where the fun really begins.

CHAPTER 3
Moving Along

In the last chapter, we saw how to get started in executing commands in both the Immediate and Program mode. From now on we will concentrate our efforts on building from the foundation set in chapter 2 in the Program mode, tying various commands together in a program. We will, however, use the Immediate mode to provide simple examples and to give you an idea of how a certain command works. Also, as we learn more and more commands, it would be a good idea if you started saving the example programs on your disk (or tape) so that they can be used for review and a quick "look-up" of examples. Use file names that you can recognize, such as VARIABLE EXAMPLE or HOW TO SUBROUTINES, and REMEMBER each file has to have a different name; so be sure to number example file names (e.g., ARRAYS 1, ARRAYS 2, etc.)

Variables

Perhaps the single most important computer function is in variable commands. Basically, a variable is a symbol that can have more than a single value. If we say, for example, X = 10, we assign the value of 10 to the variable we call "X". Try the following:

```
X = 10 <RETURN>
PRINT X <RETURN>
```

Your computer responded,

```
10
```

Now type in,

```
X=55.7 <RETURN>
PRINT X <RETURN>
```

This time you got,

```
55.7
```

Each time you assign a value to a variable, it will respond with the last assigned value when your PRINT that variable. Now try the following:

```
X = 10 <RETURN>
Y = 15 <RETURN>
PRINT X + Y <RETURN>
```

And your Apple responsed with,

```
25
```

As you can see, variables can be treated in the same way as math problems using numbers. However, instead of using the numbers, you use the variables. Now let's try a little program using variables to calculate the area of a circle.

```
10 TEXT : HOME
20 PI = 3.14159265 : REM YOU REMEMBER THE VALUE OF
PI FROM YOUR GEOMETRY CLASS
30 R = 15 : REM R IS THE RADIUS OF OUR CIRCLE
40 PRINT PI * (R * R) : REM THIS GIVES US PI TIMES THE
RADIUS SQUARED
50 END
```

When you RUN the program, you will get the area of a circle with a radius of 15. If you change the value of "R" in line 30, it is a simple matter to quickly calculate the area of any circle you want! Since our example "squares" a number, why don't we use our exponential sign "^". Change line 40 to read:

```
40 PRINT PI * R ^ 2
```

That saves typing, doesn't it. RUN the program again and see if you get the same results. You should. Also, change the value of R to see the different areas of circles.

Variable Names

When you name a variable, the computer only looks at the first two characters. For example, if you name a variable NUMBER, all your computer is interested in is NU. Try the following:

```
NUMBER = 63
PRINT NU
```

You got 63 even though you only entered the first two characters of the variable you called NUMBER. Now try this next one:

```
NUMBER = 123
PRINT NUDE
```

The value 123 is printed because the only characters of interest to the computer are still the first two; so even if you undress NUMBER you still get 123!

Now it may seem the best thing to do is to use variable names with only two characters, and while you're getting used to variables, that's probably not a bad idea. However, as you get into more and more sophisticated programs, it helps to use variable names that are descriptive. For example, the following program uses MEAN as a descriptive variable name:

```
10 TEXT : HOME
```

```
20 A = 15 : B = 23 : C = 38
30 MEAN = (A + B + C )/3
40 PRINT MEAN
50 END
```

If the above program were a hundred or more lines long, you would know what the variable MEAN does—it calculates a "mean." Now you'd have to be careful not to have another variable named MEATBALL or some other name beginning with "ME," but it would certainly make it easier to understand what it does.

Other considerations in naming variables include not using "reserved words" (i.e., programming commands) and beginning variable names with a capital letter. Let's look at some examples of what is and what is not a valid variable name:

TEXTURE = 987 (Invalid name since TEXT, a reserved word, is part of the variable name.)

R1 = 321 (Valid name since first character is a capital letter.)

1R = 55 (Invalid since first character is not a capital letter.)

HOMEWORK = 222 (Invalid since variable name contains reserved word HOME.)

TE = 99 (Valid name, for even though reserved word TEXT begins with TE, only part of the reserved word is used in variable name.)

TO = 983 (Invalid name since TO is a reserved 2 character word.)

ADFETDCVRRWRDAAF = 10 (Valid name, but really dumb.)

It is also possible to give values to variables with other variables or a combination of variables and numbers. In our example with the variable MEAN we defined it with other variables. Here are some more examples:

```
T = A * (B + C)
N = N + 1
SUM = X + Y + Z
```

Types Of Variables

Real Variables

So far we've only used "real" or "floating point" variables in our examples. Any variable that begins with a capital letter and does not end with a dollar sign ($) or percentage sign (%) is a real variable. The value for a real variable can be from zero to + or −9.99999999E+37. The "E" is the scientific notation for very big numbers. For the time being, don't worry about it, but if you get a result with such a letter in a numeric result, get in touch with a math instructor. (If your checkbook debit or income tax payments have a scientific notations in them, leave the country.) Think of real variables as being able to hold just about any number you would need along with the decimal fractions.

Integer Variables

Integer variables contain only "integer" or "whole" numbers—ones without fractions. The following are some examples:

```
AB% = 345
K% = R% + N%
ADD% = ADD% + NUM%
WXY% = 88 + LR%
```

The values of integer variables can range from −32767 to +32767, and, like real variables, only the first two characters are read. However, the "%" is always read, no matter how many characters are used. So, a variable named WA% is the same as WAX%. Also, a variable named ABC is different from one named ABC%; therefore, both variables could be used in the same program and each be considered unique. As they have a lower range than real variables, integer variables have limited applications; however, integer variables take up less memory and execute faster than real variables and so they have many useful applications. They can be used in mathematical operations in the same way as are real variables, but since they do not store fractions, operations using division and similar fraction operations must be done with care. Try some of the following operations from the Immediate mode to see how they work:

```
A% = 15 : B% = 21 : C% = B% + A% : PRINT C%
<RETURN>
36
LL% = 17 :JJ% = LL%/5 : PRINT JJ% <RETURN>
3
Z% = -11 :XY% = Z% + 51 : PRINT XY% <RETURN>
40
```

String Variables

String variables are extremely useful in formatting what you will see on the screen, and like real and integer variables, they are sent to the screen by the PRINT statement. However, rather than printing only numbers, string variables send all kinds of characters, called "strings,"to the screen. String variables are indicated by a dollar sign ($) on the end of a variable. For example, A$, BAD$, G$, and PULL$ are all legitimate string variables. (In computer parlance, we use the term "string" for the dollar sign. Thus, our examples would be called "A string," "BAD string," etc.) String variables are defined by placing the "string" in quotation marks, just as we did with other messages we printed out.

Let's try out a few examples from the immediate mode:

```
ABC$ = "ABC" : PRINT ABC$ <RETURN>
G$ = "BURLESQUE" : PRINT G$ <RETURN>
KAT$ = "CAT" : PRINT KAT$ <RETURN>
NUMBER$ = "123456789" : PRINT NUMBER$ <RETURN>
B1$ = "5 + 10 + 20" : PRINT B1$ <RETURN>
```

In the same way that real and integer variables only use the first two characters, a string variable, must begin with a capital letters and use non-reserved words. More importantly, you probably noticed in our examples that numbers in string variables are not treated as numbers, but rather as "words" or "messages." For example, you may have noticed that when you PRINTed B1$, instead of printing out "35" (the sum of 5, 10 and 20), B1$ printed out exactly what you put in quotes, 5 + 10 + 20. Do not attempt to do math with string variables. (In later chapters, we'll see some tricks to convert string variables to numeric real or integer variables, but for now, just treat them as messages.)

Now, let's put all of our accumulated knowledge together and write a program that uses variables. We will start a little program that will allow you subtract a check from your check book and print the amount. This program will be the beginning of something we will develop to give you a handy little program to do check book balancing with later.

```
10 TEXT : HOME
20 BALANCE = 571.88 : REM ANY FIGURE WILL DO.
BALANCE (BA) IS A REAL VARIABLE
30 CHECK = 29.95 : REM WHAT YOU LAST SPENT IN THE
COMPUTER STORE. CHECK (CH) IS A REAL VARIABLE
40 B$ = "YOUR BEGINNING BALANCE IS $"
50 C$ = "YOUR CHECK IS FOR $"
60 NB$ = "YOUR NEW BALANCE IS $": REM B$, C$ AND
NB$ ARE STRING VARIABLES
70 PRINT B$;BALANCE
80 PRINT C$;CHECK
90 N = BALANCE - CHECK
100 PRINT NB$; N
110 END
```

Since this is a fairly long program for this stage of the game, make sure you put in everything correctly. For the computer, it is critical that you distinguish between commas, semi-colons, periods, etc. Also, save it to disk. To play with it, change the values in lines 20 and 30.

Let's quickly review what we have done.

1. First we defined the real variables "BALANCE" and "CHECK" (which your Apple read as BA and CH since it only cares about the first two characters).
2. Then we defined string variables B$, C$, and NB$ to use as labels in screen formatting.
3. Finally, we printed out all of our information using our variables, with one new variable, "N" defined as the difference between BALANCE and CHECK.

Note how we formatted the "OUTPUT" (what you see on your screen) of our PRINT statements. The semi-colon ";" between the variables accomplished two things: (1) it told the computer where one variable ended and the next began, and (2) it told the computer to PRINT the second variable right after the first one. Thus, it took the string variable NB$

YOUR NEW BALANCE IS $^

and stuck the value of the real variable N right after the dollar sign (exactly where we placed the carat ^). Later we will go more into the formatting of OUTPUT, but for now, let's take a quick look at using punctuation in formatting text. We will use the comma "," and semi-colon ";" and "new line" to illustrate basic formatting. Put in the following little program:

```
FP <RETURN>
10 TEXT : HOME
20 A$ = "HERE" : B$ = "THERE" : C$ = "WHERE"
30 PRINT A$; : PRINT B$; : PRINT C$; : REM SEMI-COLONS
35 PRINT
40 PRINT A$, : PRINT B$, : PRINT C$,: REM COMMAS
45 PRINT : REM A 'PRINT' BY ITSELF GIVES A VERTICAL
'SPACE' IN FORMATTING
50 PRINT A$ : PRINT B$ : PRINT C$ : REM 'NEW LINES'
60 END
```

Now RUN the program. As you should see, the little differences in lines 30, 40, and 50 made big differences on the screen. The first set is all crammed together, the second set is spaced evenly across the screen, and the third set is stacked one on top of the other. As we saw in the previous program, semi-colons put numbers and strings right next to one another. However, using commas after a PRINTed variable will space output in groups of three across the screen, and using "new lines" in the form of colons or new line numbers will make the output start on a new line. A PRINT statement all by itself will put a vertical "linefeed" between statements. Try the following little program to see how PRINT statements all by themselves can be used.

```
NEW <RETURN>
10 TEXT : HOME
20 PRINT "WHENEVER YOU PUT IN A PRINT STATEMENT"; :
REM NOTE PLACEMENT OF SEMI-COLON
30 PRINT "ALL BY ITSELF, IT GIVES A 'LINEFEED.'"
40 PRINT
50 PRINT "SEE WHAT I MEAN?"
60 END
```

Play with commas, semi-colons, and "new lines" with variables and string variables until you get the hang of it. They are very important and are the source of program "bugs."

BUGS and BOMBS

We've mentioned "bugs" and "bombs" in programs but never really explained what they meant. "Bugs" are simply errors in programs that either create ?SYNTAX ERRORs or prevent your program from doing what you want it to do. "Debugging" is the process of removing "bugs." "Bombing" is what your program does when it encounters a "bug." This is all computer lingo, and if you use it in your conversations, people will think you really know a lot about computers or have a bug in your personality.

Input And Output (I/O)

Input and output, often referred to as I/O, are ways of putting things into your computer and getting it out. Usually we put IN information from the keyboard, save it to disk or tape, and then later put it in from the disk drive or cassette recorder. When we want information OUT of the computer, we want it to go to our screen or printer. This is what I/O means. So far, we have entered information IN the computer from the keyboard either in the Program or in the Immediate mode. Using the PRINT statement, we have sent information OUT to the screen. However, there are other ways we can INPUT information with a combination of programming and keyboard commands. Let's look at some of these ways and make our CHECKBOOK program a lot simpler to use.

INPUT

The INPUT command is placed in a program and expects some kind of response from the keyboard and then a RETURN. It must be part of a program and cannot be used from the Immediate mode. Let's look at a simple example:

```
NEW <RETURN>
10 TEXT : HOME
20 INPUT X : REM 'X' IS A NUMERIC VARIABLE SO ENTER A
NUMBER
30 PRINT X
40 END
```

RUN the program and your screen will go blank and a "?" along with a blinking cursor will sit there until you enter a number and then the computer will PRINT the number you just entered. Really interesting, huh?

Let's try INPUTing the same information but using a slightly different format. The nice thing about INPUT statements is that they have some of the same features as PRINT statements for getting messages on the screen. Look at the following program:

```
NEW <RETURN>
10 TEXT : HOME
20 INPUT "ENTER YOUR AGE "; X
30 HOME : PRINT : PRINT : PRINT
40 PRINT "YOUR AGE IS "; X
```

Now RUN the program; you will see that the presentation is a little more interesting. Also notice we did not put an END command at the end of the program. In APPLESOFT it is not necessary to enter an END command, but it is usually a good idea to do so. As we get into more advanced topics, we will see that our program can jump around, and the place we want it to END will be in the middle, and we will need an END statement so that it will not crash into an area we don't want it to go. So, while an END command really has not been necessary up to now, it is nevertheless a good habit to develop.

Let's soup up our program a little more with the INPUT statement.

```
NEW <RETURN>
10 TEXT : HOME
20 INPUT "ENTER YOUR NAME –> "; NA$
30 PRINT
40 INPUT "ENTER YOUR AGE –> "; AG%
50 PRINT
60 INPUT "PRESS <RETURN> TO CONTINUE "; RT$
70 HOME : ? : ? : ? : ? : ? : REM USING "?" AS SUBSTITUTES
FOR PRINT
80 PRINT NA$; " IS "; AG% ; " YEARS OLD. " : REM BE
CAREFUL WHERE YOU PUT YOUR QUOTE MARKS AND
SEMI-COLONS IN THIS LINE
90 END
```

Now we're getting somewhere. You can enter information as numeric or string variables and the OUTPUT is formatted so you know what's going on. As your programs become larger and more complicated, it is very important to connect your string variables and numeric variables in such a way that it is easy to see what the numbers on the screen mean. Let's face it, a computer wouldn't be very helpful if it filled the screen with numbers, but you did not know what they meant! Line 60 is the format for a pause in your program. RT$ doesn't hold any information, but since INPUT statements expect something from the keyboard a variable, RT$ (for RETURN), is as good as any.

GETing Information

The GET statement is something like the INPUT statement, except it is executed as soon as you hit a key. To see how it works try the following program.

```
NEW <RETURN>
10 TEXT : HOME
20 ? : ? : ? : ?
30 PRINT " ENTER A NUMBER FROM 0–9 "; : GET N
40 ? : ?
50 PRINT " HIT ANY KEY TO CONTINUE "; : GET K$
60 HOME : ? : ? : ? : ?
70 PRINT "YOUR NUMBER IS -->" ; N
80 END
```

Notice that as soon as you hit a key, the GET statement is executed. With an INPUT statement you first enter information and then press the RETURN key before the program executes. The good thing about the GET statement is that it is a faster way to enter and execute from the keyboard, but the problem is that you can only enter a single character before the program takes off again. If you press the wrong key there is no chance to correct the error before pressing the RETURN key as there is with the INPUT command.

READing In DATA

A third way to enter data into a program is with READ and DATA statements. However, instead of entering the data through the keyboard, DATA in one part of the program is READ in from another part. Each READ statement looks at elements in DATA statements sequentially. The READ command is associated with a variable which looks at the next DATA statement and places the numeric value or string in the variable. Let's look at the following example:

```
NEW <RETURN>
10 TEXT : HOME
20 READ NA$ : REM READS NAME
30 READ OC$ : REM READS OCCUPATION
40 READ SN : REM READS STREET NUMBER
50 READ ST$ : REM READS STREET NAME
60 READ CT$ : REM READS CITY
70 READ SA$ : REM READS STATE
80 READ ZIP : REM READS ZIP CODE
90 PRINT : PRINT : PRINT
100 REM BEGIN PRINTING OUT WHAT 'READ' READ IN. BE
CAREFUL TO PUT IN EVERYTHING EXACTLY AS IT IS LISTED.
110 PRINT NA$
120 PRINT OC$
130 PRINT SN; " "; ST$
140 PRINT CT$ ; ", " ; SA$ ;" "; ZIP
150 END
1000 DATA DAVID GORDON, SOFTWARE TYCOON, 9748,
COZYCROFT AVE
1010 DATA CHATSWORTH, CALIFORNIA, 91311
```

In the DATA statements there is a comma separating the various elements, unless the DATA statement is at the end of a line. If you have one of the elements out of place or omit a comma, strange things can happen. For example if the READ statement is expecting a numeric variable (such as the street address) and runs into a string (such as the street name) you will get an error message. Think of the DATA statements as a stack of strings and numbers. Each time a READ statement is encountered in the program the first element of the DATA is removed from the stack. The next READ statement looks at the element on top of the stack, moving from left to right. Go ahead and SAVE this program and let's put an error in it. (SAVE it first, though, so you will have a correct listing of how READ and DATA statements work.)

READ/DATA

LIST the program to make sure you have it in memory and enter the following line:

85 READ EX$

Now RUN the program and you should get an OUT OF DATA ERROR. This means that you have a READ statement without enough DATA statements (or elements); so, be sure that 1) there are enough elements in the DATA statements to take care of your READ statements, and 2) the variables in your READ statements are compatible with the elements of the DATA statements (i.e., your numeric variables read numbers and string variables read strings). To repair your program, simply type in:

1020 DATA WORD

This will give it something to READ. (Of course you could have DELETEd line 85.)

If an element is a DATA statement (and is enclosed in quotation marks), all the characters inside the quotes are considered to be a single string element. For example, make the following changes in your program and RUN it.

```
145 PRINT EX$
1020 DATA "10 DOWNING ST, LONDON, 45, ENGLAND"
```

Both numbers and commas were happily accepted by a READ statement with a string variable since they were all enclosed in quotation marks. Now remove the quote marks and RUN it again. This time it only printed up to the first comma, '10 DOWNING ST,' but the string variable EX$ had no problem accepting a numeric character! (However, since it read the '10' as a string, it cannot be used in a mathmatical operation.) Experiment with different elements in the DATA statements to see what happens. Also, just for fun, put the DATA statements at different places in the program. You will quickly find that they can go anywhere in the program.

Looping With FOR/NEXT

The FOR/NEXT loop is one of the most useful operations in BASIC programming. It allows the user to instruct the computer to go through a determined number of steps, at variable increments if desired, and execute them until the total number of steps is completed. Let's look at a simple example to get started.

```
NEW <RETURN>
10 TEXT : HOME
20 NA$ = "<YOUR NAME>"
30 FOR I = 1 TO 10 : REM BEGINNING OF LOOP
40      PRINT NA$
50 NEXT I : REM LOOP TERMINAL
60 END
```

Now RUN the program and you will see your name printed 10 times along the left side of the screen. That's nice, but so what? OK, not too impressive, but we will see how useful this can be in a bit, but first let's look at another simple illustration to show what's happening to "I" as the loop is being executed.

```
NEW <RETURN>
10 TEXT : HOME
20 FOR I = 1 TO 10
30      PRINT I
40 NEXT I
```

As we can see when the program is RUN, the value of "I" changes each time the program proceeds through the loop. Think of a loop as a child on a merry-go-round. Each time the merry-go-round completes a revolution, the child gets a gold ring, beginning with one and ending, in our example, with 10.

FLASH!

INVERSE

TRIVIA

As you begin looking at more and more programs, you will see that the variable "I" is used in FOR/NEXT loops a lot. Actually, you can use any variable you want, but the "I" keeps cropping up. Like yourself, I was most curious as to why programmers kept using the letter "I", and after several moments of exhaustive research I found out. The "I" stands for "increment." I told you it was trivia.

Having seen how loops function, let's do something practical with a loop. We'll fix up our CHECK-BOOK program we've been playing with. Before we do that, though, I want to introduce you to some fancy output statements. They are:

1. INVERSE
2. FLASH
3. NORMAL

So far, we've been doing all of our output in NORMAL, the default mode. However, we can also make our text INVERSE or FLASH if we want, resetting it with a NORMAL statement. Here's a quickie to see how they work:

```
NEW <RETURN>
10 TEXT : HOME
20 INVERSE : PRINT " INVERSE "
30 FLASH : PRINT : PRINT " FLASH "
40 NORMAL : PRINT : PRINT "NORMAL"
```

These commands help highlight output to make it easier to see what you're supposed to do. All right, now back to work.

In our souped up CHECK BOOK program, we are going to use variables in many ways. First, our FOR/NEXT loop will use a variable. We'll stick with tradition and use "I". Second, we will use a variable to indicate the number of loops to be executed. We will use N%, an integer variable. Third, we will use variables for the balance, the amount of the check, and the new balance. This program is going to be a little longer; so be sure to SAVE it to disk every 5 lines or so.

```
NEW <RETURN>
10 TEXT : HOME
20 CB$ = "CHECK BOOK"
30 PRINT : PRINT : FLASH : PRINT CB$ : NORMAL
40 INPUT "HOW MANY CHECKS? ->" ; N%
50 INPUT "WHAT IS YOUR CURRENT BALANCE? ->" ;BA
60 REM BEGIN LOOP
70 FOR I = 1 TO N%
80      PRINT "YOUR BALANCE IS NOW $";BA
90          INVERSE : PRINT " AMOUNT OF CHECK #";I; "->";
: NORMAL
100       INPUT CK : REM VARIABLE FOR CHECK
110       BA = BA - CK : REM KEEPS A RUNNING BALANCE
120      NEXT I : REM TOP OF LOOP
130         HOME : REM CLEAR SCREEN WHEN ALL CHECKS
ARE ENTERED
140      PRINT : PRINT : PRINT
150         PRINT "YOU NOW HAVE $"; BA ; " IN YOUR
ACCOUNT"
160         PRINT : FLASH : PRINT " THANK YOU AND COME
AGAIN " : NORMAL
170 END
```

Our check book program is coming along, making it easier to use, and that is the purpose of computers. Now, let's look at something else with loops.

Nested Loops

With certain applications, it is going to be necessary have one or more FOR/NEXT loops working inside one another. Let's look at a simple application. Suppose you had two teams with 10 members on each team. You want to make a team roster indicating the team number (#1 or #2) and member number (#1 through #10). Using a nested loop, we can do this in the following program:

```
NEW <RETURN>
10 TEXT : HOME
20 FOR T = 1 TO 2 : REM T FOR TEAM #
30    FOR M = 1 TO 10 : REM M FOR MEMBER #
40      PRINT "TEAM #" ; T ; "PLAYER #"; M
50    NEXT M
60 NEXT T
70 END
```

In using nested loops, it is important to keep the loops straight. The innermost loop (the "M loop" in our example) must not have any other FOR or NEXT statement inside of it. Think of nested loops as a series of fish eating one another, the largest fish's mouth encompasing the next largest and so forth on down to the smallest fish.

FOR/NEXT LOOPS

Look at the following structure of nested loops:

```
FOR A = 1 TO N
  FOR B = 1 TO N
    FOR C = 1 TO N
      FOR D = 1 TO N
      NEXT D
    NEXT C
  NEXT B
NEXT A
```

Note how each loop begins (a FOR statement is executed) and is terminated (encounters a NEXT statement) in a "nested" sequence. If you have ever stacked a set of different sized cooking bowls, each one fits inside the other; that is because the outer edge of one is larger than the next one. Likewise, in nested loops, the "edge" of each loop is "larger" than the one inside it and "smaller" than the one it is inside.

Stepping Forward And Backward

Loops can go one step at a time, as we have been using, or they can step at different increments. For example, the following program "steps" by 10.

```
NEW <RETURN>
10 TEXT : HOME
20  FOR I = 10 TO 100 STEP 10
30     PRINT I
40  NEXT I
```

This allows you to increment your count by whatever you want. You can even use variables or anything else that has a numeric value. For example

```
NEW <RETURN>
10  TEXT : HOME
20  K = 5 : N = 25
30  FOR I = K TO N STEP K
40     PRINT I
50  NEXT
```

Go ahead and RUN the program. But WAIT!!, you say. In line 50 you detect a BUG, a typo and big mistake. After the word NEXT, there should be an "I" but there is none, right? Well, actually, in APPLESOFT BASIC you really do not need it, and you can save a little memory if you use NEXT statements without the variable name. Even in nested loops, as long as you put in enough NEXT statements, it is possible to run your program without variable names after NEXT statements. However, it is good programming practice to use variable names after NEXT statements, especially in nested loops so that you can keep everything thing straight.

It is also possible to go backward. Try this program:

```
NEW <RETURN>
10 FOR I = 4 TO 1 STEP -1
20     PRINT "FINISHING POSITION IN RACE = ";I
30 NEXT I
```

As we get into more and more sophisticated (and useful) programs, we will begin to see how all of these different features of APPLESOFT BASIC are very useful. Oftentimes, you may not see the practicality of a command initially, but when you need it later on, you will wonder how you could program without it!

> **IN CASE YOU WONDERED**
>
> You may have noticed that the lines inside the loops were indented. If you tried that on your Apple you probably found that as soon as you LISTed your program, all the indentations were gone. Unfortunately, that will happen, and without special utilities, there's nothing you can do about it. However, don't worry about it. It is a programming convention for clarity to indent or "tab" loops to make it easier to understand what the program is doing, but they do not affect your program at all.

Counters

Oftentimes, you will want to count the number of times a loop is executed and keep a record of it in your program for later use. For example, if you run a program that loops with a STEP of 3, you may not know exactly how many times the loop will execute. To find out, programmers use "counters," variables that are incremented, usually by +1, each time a loop is executed. The following program illustrates the use of a counter:

```
NEW <RETURN>
10 TEXT : HOME
20 FOR I = 3 TO 99 STEP 3
30     PRINT I
40     N = N + 1 : REM THIS IS THE COUNTER
50 NEXT I
60 PRINT : PRINT "YOUR LOOP EXECUTED "; N ; " TIMES."
```

The first time the loop was entered, the value of "N" was 0, but when the program got to line 40, the value of 1 was added to N to make it 1 (i.e., 0 + 1 = 1). The second time through the loop, the value of N began at 1, then 1 was added, and at the top of the loop, line 50, the value of N was

2. This went on until the program exited the loop. Then, after all the looping was finished, presto!, your N told you how many times the loop was executed. Of course, counters are not restricted to counting loops, and they can be incremented by any value, including other variables, you need. For example, change line 40 to read:

```
40 N = N + (I * 2)
```

RUN your program again and your "counter total" will be a good deal higher.

Summary

This chapter has begun to show you the power of your computer, and we have really began programming. One of the most important concepts we have covered is that of the "variable." The significant feature of variables is that they "vary" (change depending on what your program does). This is true not only with numeric variables, but also with string variables. The various input commands show how we enter values or strings into variables depending on what we want the computer to compute for us. Finally, we have learned how to loop. This allows us, with a minimal amount of effort, to tell the computer to go through a process several times with a single set of instructions. With loops, we can set the parameters of an operation at any increment we want, and then sit back and let our Apples go to work for us.

However, we have only just begun programming! In the next chapter we will begin getting into more commands and operations that allow us to delve deeper into the Apple's capabilities and make our programming jobs easier. The more commands we know, the less work it is to write a program.

CHAPTER 4
Branching Out

Introduction

In this chapter we will begin exploring new programming constructs that will geometrically increase your programming ability. We will be getting into some more sophisticated techniques, but by taking each a step at a time, you will begin using them with ease. Later, when you are developing your own programs, be bold and try out new commands. One problem new programmers have is a tendency to stick with the simple commands they have learned to get a job done. After all, why use "complicated" commands to do what simpler ones can do. Well, the answer to that has to do with simplicity. If one "complicated" command can do the work of 10 "simple" commands, which one is actually simpler? As you get into more and more sophisticated programming applications, your programs can become longer and subject to more bugs. The more commands you have to sift through, the more difficult it is to find the bugs; therefore, while it is perfectly OK to write a long program using a lot of simple commands while you're learning, begin thinking about short-cuts through the use of the more advanced commands.

Related to this issue of maximizing your knowledge of different commands is that of letting the computer perform the computing. This may sound strange at first, but oftentimes novices will figure everything out for the computer and use it as a glorified calculator. In the last chapter you may remember we set up a counter to count the times a loop was executed when we used a STEP 3 loop. We could have figured out how many loops were executed instead of letting the computer do it with the counter, but that would have defeated the purpose of programming! So, as you learn new commands, see how they can be used to perform the calculations you had to work out yourself.

Branching

So far all of our programs have gone straight from the top to the bottom with the exception of loops. However, if our Apple is to do some real decision making, we must have some way of giving it options. When a program leaves a straight path, it is referred to as either "looping" or "branching." We already know the purpose of a loop, but what is a branch? Well, using the IF/THEN and GOTO commands, we will see. Consider the following program: (NOTE: By now you should know enough to clear memory with a NEW or FP command; so I won't keep on insulting your intelligence by putting them at the beginning of each program.)

```
10  TEXT : HOME
20  PRINT "CHOOSE ONE OF THE FOLLOWING BY NUMBER:
"
30  PRINT
40  PRINT "1. APPLES"
50  PRINT "2. ORANGES"
60  PRINT "3. PEACHES"
70  PRINT "4. WATERMELONS"
80  PRINT
90  INPUT "WHICH? "; X
100  HOME
110  IF X = 1 THEN GOTO 200
120  IF X = 2 THEN GOTO 300
130  IF X = 3 THEN GOTO 400
140  IF X = 4 THEN GOTO 500
150  GOTO 10 : REM THIS IS A 'TRAP' TO MAKE SURE THE
USER CHOOSES 1, 2, 3, OR 4
200  PRINT "APPLES" : END
300  PRINT "ORANGES" : END
400  PRINT "PEACHES" : END
500  PRINT "WATERMELONS" : END
```

GOTO COMMAND

As you can see, your computer "branched" to the appropriate place, did what it was told and ENDed. Not very inspiring I admit, but it is a clear example. Now, let's try something a little more practical for your kids to play with in their math homework.

```
10 TEXT : HOME
20 TI$=" ADDITION GAME ": INVERSE : PRINT TI$ :
NORMAL
30 PRINT : PRINT
40 INPUT "ENTER FIRST NUMBER -->" ; A
50 PRINT
60 INPUT "ENTER SECOND NUMBER -->" ; B
70 PRINT
80 PRINT "WHAT IS "; A ; "+" ; B ; : INPUT C
90 IF C = A + B THEN GOTO 200
100 PRINT : INVERSE : PRINT "THAT'S NOT QUITE IT. TRY
AGAIN." : NORMAL : PRINT
110 GOTO 80
200 FLASH : PRINT " THAT'S RIGHT! VERY GOOD " :
NORMAL
210 PRINT
220 PRINT "WOULD YOU LIKE TO DO MORE? (Y/N): "; : GET
AN$
230 IF AN$ = "Y" THEN HOME : GOTO 30
240 HOME : PRINT : PRINT : PRINT
250 PRINT "HOPE TO SEE YOU AGAIN SOON" : END
```

As you can see, the more commands we learn, the more fun we can have. Just for fun, change the program so that it will handle multiplication, division, and subtraction.

WHAT'S IN A NAME?

Kids (of all ages) like to have their names displayed. See if you can change the above program so that it asks the child's name; then when the program responds with either a correction or affirmation command, it mentions the child's name. (e.g., THAT'S RIGHT! VERY GOOD, SAM). Use "NA$" as the name variable.

Let's look carefully at our program to learn something about IF/THEN statements. First, note in line 230, the branch is to clear the screen (HOME) if AN$ ="Y". If any other response is encountered it ends the program. You may ask why the program did not branch to line 30 regardless of the response since the "GOTO 30" command is after a colon, making it a new line. Good point. The reason for that is after an IF statement, when the response or condition is nul, the program immediately drops to the next LINE NUMBER. That is, any statements after a colon in a line beginning with an IF statement will only be executed if the condition of the IF statement is met. Secondly, the condition of AN$ is queried as being a "Y" and not simply a Y without quotes. Since the user INPUTs a Y and not a "Y", we assume that the program will accept a Y, but remember AN$ is a "string" and not a numeric variable. Therefore in setting of the conditional, we must remember what kind of variable we are using. On the other hand, if we used a numeric variable, such as AN or AN%, we could have entered a line such as,

```
IF AN = 1 THEN. . .
```

Relationals

So far we have only used " = " to determine whether or not our program should branch. However, there are other states, referred to as "relationals," that we can also query. The following is a complete list of the relationals we can employ:

SYMBOL	MEANING
=	Equal to
<	Less than
>	Greater than
<>	Not equal to
>=	Greater than or equal to
<=	Less than or equal to

Now let's play with some of these, and then we'll examine them for their full power. Here are some quickie programs:

```
10 TEXT : HOME
20 INPUT "NUMBER 1-->";A
30 INPUT "NUMBER 2-->";B
40 IF A > B THEN GOTO 100
50 IF A < B THEN GOTO 200
60 IF A = B THEN GOTO 300
100 PRINT "NUMBER 1 IS GREATER THAN NUMBER 2" :
END
200 PRINT "NUMBER 1 IS LESS THAN NUMBER 2" : END
300 PRINT "NUMBER 1 IS EQUAL TO NUMBER 2"

10 TEXT : HOME
```

```
20 INPUT "DO YOU WANT TO CONTINUE? (Y/N)"; AN$
30 IF AN$ <> "Y" THEN END
40 GOTO 10
```

```
10 TEXT : HOME
20 INPUT "HOW OLD ARE YOU? "; AG%
30 IF AG% >= 21 THEN GOTO 100
40 HOME : PRINT : PRINT "SORRY, YOU'VE GOT TO BE 21
OR OLDER TO COME IN HERE!" : END
100 HOME : PRINT : PRINT "WHAT WOULD YOU LIKE TO
DRINK?"
```

RELATIONALS

Ok, you have the idea how relationals can be used with IF/THEN commands; note they work with strings as well as numeric variables. However, there is another way to use relationals. Try the following from the Immediate mode:

```
A = 10 : B = 20 : PRINT A = B
```

Your computer responded with a Ø, right? This is a logical operation. If a condition is false, your Apple responds with a Ø, but if it is true, it responds with a 1. Now try the following little program.

```
10 TEXT : HOME
20 A = 10
```

```
30 B = 20
40 C = A > B
50 PRINT C
```

When you RUN the program, you again get a 0. This is because the variable C was defined as A being greater than B. Since A was less than B the variable C was 0, or "false." Now, let's take it a step further:

```
10 TEXT : HOME
20 A = 10
30 B = 20
40 C = A > B
50 IF C = 0 THEN PRINT "A IS LESS THAN B" : END
60 IF C = 1 THEN PRINT "A IS GREATER THAN B"
```

Later, we will see further applications of these logical operations of the Apple. For now, though, it is important to understand that a true condition is represented by a "1" and a false condition by a "0".

AND/OR/NOT

Sometimes we need to set up more than a single relational. Suppose, for example, that you are organizing your finances into 3 categories of expenses: (1) Under $10; (2) between $10 and $100 and (3) over $100. With our relationals it would be simple to compare input under $10 and over $100. But what if we wanted to do something in between. In this case we might have some difficulty without added commands. The AND, OR and NOT statements allow us to set ranges with our relationals.

AND	If all conditions are met then true
OR	If one condition is met then true
NOT	If condition is not met then true

For example:

```
10 TEXT : HOME
20 INPUT "ENTER AMOUNT --->$"; A
30 IF A < 10 THEN 100
40 IF A > 10 AND A <= 100 THEN 200
50 IF A > 100 THEN 300
100 PRINT " PETTY CASH " : GOTO 400
200 INVERSE : PRINT " GENERAL EXPENSES " : NORMAL :
GOTO 400
300 FLASH : PRINT " BIG BUCKS " : NORMAL
400 PRINT " DO YOU WISH TO CONTINUE? ";
410 GET AN$
420 IF AN$ < > "Y" AND AN$ < > "N" THEN PRINT
```

```
"ANSWER 'Y' OR 'N' PLEASE " : GOTO 400
430  IF AN$ = "Y" THEN 10
440  HOME : PRINT "GOODBYE"
```

In line 40 we set the conditional branch to be BOTH greater than 10 and equal to or less than 100. The variable "A" had to meet both conditions to branch. Similarly, in line 420, using the AND statement again, we made sure that the response had to be either "Y" or "N'.

If you are very perceptive, you may have asked yourself about some fishy format in the program. There are conditional IF/THEN lines that simply say THEN 100 and stuff like that. What's going on? Shouldn't there be a GOTO statement there? Again, we have slipped in another feature of APPLESOFT BASIC. When using IF/THEN statements, it is possible to drop the GOTO on a branch and simply put in the line number. However, note that we have used GOTO statements elsewhere in the program where no conditional is used within the same line or within a single set of colons. Until you become more familiar with programming you might want to keep your GOTO statements after IF/THEN statements, but they are not required.

Another question you may have had involves the AND statement in line 420. In normal English if we say, if something is not "Y" or "N" we mean that it must be one or the other. However, in programming, if we use OR, we are telling the program to branch if either condition is met. Thus, if we wrote line 420 as,

```
IF AN$ < > "Y" OR AN$ < > "N" THEN PRINT "ANSWER 'Y'
OR 'N' PLEASE " : GOTO 400
```

the program would have branched if AN$ was not equal to EITHER "Y" or "N'. Thus, for example, if we responded with a "Y', that "Y" would have NOT been equal to "N'; and so the program would have branched to "ANSWER 'Y' OR 'N' PLEASE"—not what we intended. To check this, change the AND to an OR in line 420 and RUN the program.

Now, let's use the OR and NOT statements in a program:

```
10  TEXT : HOME
20  READ A
30  READ B
40  READ C
50  DATA 10,20,30
60  IF A + B = C OR A < B OR A - B = C THEN 100
70  END
100  HOME : PRINT "ONE OF 'EM MUST BE TRUE"
```

Looking at line 60 we can see that A − B does not equal C; however, A + B does equal C and A is less than B. Using the OR statement, only one statement has to be true to branch. Now, let's try the following program:

```
10 TEXT : HOME
20 READ A : READ B : READ C
30 DATA 10,20,30
40 Z = A - B = C
50 IF NOT Z THEN 100
60 END
100 PRINT " THAT'S RIGHT! A - B = C IS NOT RIGHT! -
DID I SAY THAT RIGHT?"
```

As can be seen from the example, it is possible to use the "negation" of a formula to calculate a branch condition. In most cases, you will use < > (not equal) or the positive case, but at other times, it will be simpler to employ NOT.

Subroutines

Often in programming there is some operation you will want your computer to perform at several different places in the program. Now, you can repeat the instructions again and again or use GOTO's all over the place and return to your original spot after branching to the operation. On the other hand, you can set up "subroutines" and jump to them using GOSUB and get back to your starting point using the RETURN command. Up to a point

GOSUB COMMANDS

the GOSUB command works pretty much like the GOTO command since it sends your program bouncing off to a line out of sequence. Also, the RETURN command is something like GOTO since it also sends your program to an out-of-sequence line. However, the GOSUB/RETURN pair is unique in what it does. Let's take a look at a simple example to see how it works:

```
10 TEXT : HOME
20 A$ = "HELLO" : GOSUB 100
30 A$ = "HOW ARE YOUR TODAY?" : GOSUB 100
40 A$ = "I'M FINE" : GOSUB 100
50 END
100 PRINT A$
110 RETURN
```

Our example shows that a GOSUB statement works exactly like a command on the line itself except that it is executed elsewhere in the program. The RETURN statement brings it back to the next line after the GOSUB statement. Using the GOSUB/RETURN pair it is much easier to weave in and out of a program than using GOTO since the RETURN automatically takes you back to the jump-off point.

BLOCK YOUR PROGRAMS

To better illustrate the usefulness of GOSUB, let's change line 100 to something more elaborate. Try the following. (Note: We will be getting ahead of ourselves a bit with this example, but the following is meant to illustrate something very useful in GOSUB's.)

```
100 HTAB 20 - LEN (A$)/2 : PRINT A$
```

Now when you RUN the program, all of your strings are centered. As you can see, a single routine handled all of the centering, and instead of having to rewrite the routine every time you want a string centered all you had to do was to use a GOSUB to line 100.

NEATNESS COUNTS

We really have not discussed the structure of programs too much up to this point. In part, this is because we have not really had the need to do so. However, as our instruction set grows, so too does the possibility for errors, and by now if you haven't made an error, you haven't been keying in these programs! One way to minimize errors, especially using GOSUBs, is to organize them into coherent *blocks.* Basically, a *block* is a subroutine within a range of lines. For example, you might block your subroutines by 100s or 1000s, depending on how long the subroutines are. Thus, you might have subroutines beginning at lines 500, 600 and 700. It doesn't matter if the subroutine is 1 line or 10 lines, as long as it is confined to the block, it is easier to debug, easier for others and you to understand what is happening in the program, and in general a good programming practice.

Computed GOTO and GOSUB

Now we're going to get a little fancier, but in the long run, it will result in clearer and simpler programming. As we have seen, we can GOTO or GOSUB on a "conditional" (e.g., IF A = 1 THEN GOTO 200). The easier way to make a conditional jump is to use "computed" branches using the ON statement. For example,

```
10 TEXT : HOME
20 INPUT "ENTER A NUMBER FROM 1 TO 5 " ; A
30 IF A < 1 OR A > 5 THEN 20 : REM TRAP
40 ON A GOSUB 100,200,300,400,500 : REM COMPUTED
GOSUB
50 PRINT "DO YOU WISH TO CONTINUE? (Y/N)" ; : GET AN$
: IF AN$ < > "Y" THEN END
60 GOTO 10
100 PRINT "ONE" : PRINT : RETURN
200 PRINT "TWO" : PRINT : RETURN
300 PRINT "THREE" : PRINT : RETURN
400 PRINT "FOUR" : PRINT : RETURN
500 PRINT "FIVE" : PRINT : RETURN
```

The format for a computed GOSUB/GOTO is to enter a variable following the ON command. The program will then jump the number of "commas" to the appropriate line number. If a 1 is entered, it takes the first line number, a 2, the second, and so forth. It's a lot easier than entering " IF A = 1 THEN GOSUB 100 : IF A = 2 THEN GOSUB 200 : . . . etc." However, it is necessary to use relatively small numbers in the "ON" variable since there is a limited number of subroutines. If your program is computing larger numbers, all you have to do is to convert the larger numbers into smaller ones by changing the variables. For example:

```
10 TEXT : HOME
20 INPUT "ENTER ANY NUMBER-->"; A
30 IF A < 100 THEN B = 1
40 IF A >= 100 AND A < 200 THEN B = 2
50 IF A >= 200 THEN B = 3
60 ON B GOSUB 100, 200, 300 : REM COMPUTED GOSUB
ON 'B' VARIABLE
70 PRINT "DO YOU WISH TO CONTINUE?(Y/N)"; : GET AN$ :
IF AN$ <> "Y" THEN END
80 GOTO 10
100 PRINT "LESS THAN 100" : RETURN
200 PRINT "MORE THAN 100 BUT LESS THAN 200 " :
RETURN
300 PRINT "MORE THAN 200" : RETURN
```

RUN the program and enter any number you want. Since the program is branching on the variable B, and not on A (the INPUT variable), you will not get an error since the greatest value of B can only be 3.

Now let's get back to relationals and see how they can be used with computed GOSUBS. Remember, in using relationals, the only numbers we get are 0's and 1's for false and true respectively. However, we can use these 0's and 1's just like regular numbers. Try the following:

```
10 TEXT : HOME
20 X = 1 : Y = 2 : Z = 3
30 A = X < Z
40 B = Y > Z
50 C = Z > X
60 PRINT "A + A =" ; A + A
70 PRINT : PRINT "A + B =" ; A + B
80 PRINT : PRINT "A + B + C =" ; A + B + C
90 END
```

Now before you RUN the program, see if you can determine what will be printed by lines 60, 70 and 80. Once you have made a determination, RUN the program and see what happens. Go ahead and do it. How'd you do? Let's go over it step by step.

1. Since X is less than Z, A will be "true" with a value of one (1). Therefore A + A (1 + 1) will equal 2.

2. Since Y is not less than Z, (Y = 2 and Z = 3, remember) B will be "false" with a value of 0. Therefore, A + B (1 + 0) will total 1.

3. Since Z is greater than X, C will be "true" with a value of 1. Therefore A + B + C (1 + 0 + 1) will equal 2.

If you got it right, congratulations! If not, go over it again. Remember, very simple things are happening, so don't look for a complicated explanation! (For a more in-depth explanation of using logical operations, see "Our Logical Apples" by Ralph Swerdlow, M.D., *CALL A.P.P.L.E.* Vol. 5, No. 2 (Feb. 1982) pp. 17–21.)

Now that we see how we can get numbers by manipulating relationals, let's use them in computed GOSUB's. The following program shows how:

```
10 TEXT : HOME
20 INPUT "HOW BIG WAS THE HOME CROWD?"; HC
30 R = 1 + (HC => 500) + (HC >= 1000)
40 ON R GOSUB 100,200,300
50 PRINT : PRINT "DO YOU WISH TO CONTINUE? (Y/N) "; :
GET AN$
60 IF AN$ < > "Y" THEN END
70 GOTO 10
100 HOME : PRINT "THE HOME CROWD WAS NOT VERY BIG
– LESS THAN 500" : RETURN
200 HOME : PRINT "THE HOME CROWD WAS A PRETTY
GOOD SIZE – BETWEEN 500 AND 1000." : RETURN
300 HOME : PRINT "THE HOME CROWD WAS VERY BIG –
OVER 1000! " : RETURN
```

This program is hinged on line 30's formula or algorithm. Let's see how it works:

1. There are 3 conditions:
    a. HC is less than 500
    b. HC is between 500 and 1000
    c. HC is greater than 1000
2. If the first condition exists both HC >= 500 and HC >= 1000 would be false. Thus 1 + 0 + 0 = 1. Therefore R = 1.
3. If HC is >= 500 but less than 1000 then HC >= 500 would be true but HC >= 1000 would be false. Thus we would have 1 + 1 + 0 = 2. Therefore R = 2.
4. Finally, if HC is both >= 500 and >=1000 then our formula would result in 1 + 1 + 1 = 3. Therefore R = 3.

REST AREA

At this point let's take a little rest and reflection. In programming, there is no such thing as THE RIGHT WAY and THE WRONG WAY. Certain programs are more efficient, faster or take less code and memory than others, but the computer makes no moral judgements. If a program does what you want it to do, no matter how slowly it does it or how long it took you to write it, it is "right." In the above example we used an algorithm with relationals to do something we could have done with more code. Don't expect to use such formulas right off the bat unless you have a strong background in math. If you're not used to using algorithms, don't expect to understand their full potential right away. The one we used is relatively simple, and you will find far more elaborate ones as you begin looking at more programs. The main point is to keep plugging ahead. With practice, you will learn all kinds of little shortcuts and formulas, but if you get stuck along the way, just keep on going. Remember, as long as you can get your program running the way you want it to, you're doing the "right" thing.

HOW YOUR PROGRAMS "BRANCH OUT"

Strings And Relationals

Before we leave our discussion of computed GOTO's and GOSUB's with relationals, let's take a look at how relationals handle strings. Try the following:

```
A$ = "A" : B$ = "B" : PRINT B$ > A$ <RETURN>
```

Surprised? In addition to comparing numeric variables, relationals can compare string variables with "A" being the lowest and "Z" the highest. So if we ask is B$ greater than A$, we get a "1" (true) since B$ was a B and A$ was an A. Now you might be wondering what on earth you could possibly want to do with this knowledge. Well, in sorting strings (like putting names in alphabetical order) such an operation is crucial. Later on we will show you a routine for sorting strings, but for now, let's make a simple string sorter for sorting two strings.

```
10 TEXT : HOME
20 INPUT "WORD #1 - -> " ; A$
30 INPUT "WORD #2 - -> " ; B$
40 PRINT : PRINT : PRINT
50 IF A$ < B$ THEN PRINT A$ : PRINT B$
60 IF A$ > B$ THEN PRINT B$ : PRINT A$
```

Just what you needed! A program that will put two words in alphabetical order!

Arrays

The best way to think about arrays is as a kind of variable. As we have seen, we can name variables A, D$, KK%, X1 and so forth. An array uses a single name with a number to differentiate different variables. Consider the following two lists, one using regular string variables and the other using a string array:

STRING VARIABLE	STRING ARRAY
P$ = "PIG"	AM$(1) = "PIG"
C$ = "CHICKEN"	AM$(2) = "CHICKEN"
D$ = "DOG"	AM$(3) = "DOG"
H$ = "HORSE"	AM$(4) = "HORSE"

Now if we PRINT H$ we'd get HORSE and if we PRINT AM$(4) we'd also get HORSE. Likewise, we could use arrays for numeric variables such as:

```
A(1) = 1
A(2) = 2
A(3) = 3
A(4) = 4
. . . etc.
```

Again, you may well ask, "So what? Why not just use regular numeric or string variables instead of arrays?" Well, for one thing, it can be a lot easier to keep track of what you're doing in a program using arrays, and for another, it can save a lot of time. Consider the following program for INPUTing a list of 10 names using a string array.

```
10 TEXT : HOME
20 FOR I = 1 TO 10
30 PRINT "NAME #"; I ; : INPUT NA$(I)
40 NEXT I
50 FOR I = 1 TO 10 : PRINT NA$(I)
60 NEXT I
```

Now, write a program that does the same thing using non-array variables. It would take a lot more code to do so, but go ahead and try it. Use the variables N0$ through N9$ for the names just to see what it would take.

If you re-wrote the program, you saw how much time using arrays saved, but before going on, let's take a closer look at how the program worked with the FOR/NEXT loop and array variable:

1. The FOR/NEXT loop generated the numbers sequentially so that the array would be the following:

```
FOR I = 1 TO 10
   NA$(1)  ← First time through loop
   NA$(2)  ← Second time through loop
   NA$(3)  ← Third time through loop
   NA$(4)  . . . etc.
   NA$(5)
   NA$(6)
   NA$(7)
   NA$(8)
   NA$(9)
   NA$(10)
NEXT I
```

2. Each string INPUT by the user was stored in a sequentially numbered array variable.
3. Output, using the PRINT statement, was generated by the FOR/NEXT loop sequentially supplying numbers to be entered into array variables.

Now to get used to the idea that an array variable is a variable, enter the following:

```
A(10) = 432 : PRINT A(10) <RETURN>
XYZ(9) = 2.432 : PRINT XYZ(2) <RETURN>
R2D2$(1) = "BEEP!" + CHR$(7) : PRINT R2D2$(1)
```

<RETURN>
J%(5) = 321 : PRINT J%(5) <RETURN>

Ok, maybe it didn't take all that to convince you that an array is a variable with a number in parentheses after it, but it's easy to forget and think of arrays as something more exotic than they are.

THE DIMension Of An Array

If you've been very observant, you may have noticed we haven't gone over the number 10 in our array examples. The reason behind that is because, once our array is larger than 10 we have to use the DIM (dimension) statement to reserve space for our array. (We actually get 11 'free' arrays—0 through 10.) The following is an example of the format for DIMensioning an array.

```
10 TEXT : HOME
20 DIM AB(150) : REM DIMENSION OF ARRAY VARIABLE
'AB'
30 FOR I = 1 TO 150
40    AB(I) = I
50 NEXT I
60 FOR I = 1 TO 150
70    PRINT AB(I),
80 NEXT I
```

RUN the program as it is written. It should work fine. Now delete line 20 by simply entering 20. (Remember how we learned to delete single line numbers by entering that number?) Now RUN the program, and you will get an error for not DIMing the ARRAY. So, whenever your arrays are going to have more than 11 values from 0 to 10, be sure to DIM them.

> **BETTER SAFE THAN SORRY DEPT.**
>
> Many programmers always DIM arrays, regardless of the number in the array. It is perfectly all right to do so, and statements such as DIM X$(3) or DIM N% (5) are valid. Often when copying programs from books or magazines you may run across these lower level DIM statements, not because they are necessary, but rather because the programmer thinks its a good idea to DIM all arrays as part of programming style and clarity.

Multi-dimensional Arrays

So far, all we have examined are single dimension arrays. However, it is possible to have arrays with two or more dimensions. Let's begin with two-dimensional arrays, and examine how to use arrays with more than a single dimension.

The best way to think of a 2-dimensional array is as a matrix. For example, if our array ranged from 1 to 3 on two dimensions, the entire set would include: A(1,1) A(1,2) A(1,3) A(2,1) A(2,2) A(2,3) A(3,1) A(3,2) and A(3,3). By laying it out on a matrix, we can think of the first number as a row and the second as a column. This makes it much clearer:

	COLUMN #1	COLUMN #2	COLUMN #3
ROW #1	A(1,1)	A(1,2)	A(1,3)
ROW #2	A(2,1)	A(2,2)	A(2,3)
ROW #3	A(3,1)	A(3,2)	A(3,3)

Again, it is important to remember that each element in the array is simply a type of variable. To drum that into your head do the following:

```
XV$(3,1) = "I'M A VARIABLE" : PRINT XV$(3,1) <RETURN>
JK%(2,2) = 21 : PRINT JK% <RETURN>
MM (1,1) = 3.212 : PRINT MM(1,1) <RETURN>
```

Ok, so you were reminded a bit much, but in order to use arrays to their fullest advantage in programs, they must be envisioned as an orderly set of variables and not something else. Now, let's use a 2-dimension array in a program. Our program will be to line up people in a 9 member marching band.

```
10 TEXT : HOME
20 DIM BA$(3,3) : REM MAKE 3 'ROWS' AND 3 'COLUMNS'
30 FOR I = 1 TO 3 : REM ROWS
40    FOR J = 1 TO 3 : REM COLUMNS
50       READ BA$(I,J)
60    NEXT J
70 NEXT I
80 DATA MARY, TOM, SUE, PETE, JACK, NANCY, BETTY,
BILL, RALPH
100 REM OUTPUT BLOCK
110 FOR I = 1 TO 3 : REM ROWS
120    FOR J = 1 TO 3 : REM COLUMNS
130       PRINT BA$(I,J) , : REM COMMA WILL FORMAT
OUTPUT 3 ACROSS
140    NEXT J
150 NEXT I
```

When you RUN this program, all of your band members will be lined up. However, you could have done the same thing with a single dimension array since all that "lines them up" is the use of the comma to format the PRINT statement in line 130. So, what's the big deal about a 2-dimension array? Well, to see, let's add some lines to our program:

```
160 PRINT : PRINT "HIT ANY KEY TO CONTINUE "; : GET
AN$
170 HOME : PRINT "WHAT ROW & COLUMN WOULD YOU
LIKE TO SEE? " : INPUT "ROW #-> ";R :INPUT "COL #->
";C
180 PRINT : PRINT BA$(R,C); " IS IN ROW "; R; " COLUMN ";
C
190 PRINT : INVERSE : PRINT "MORE?(Y/N) "; : NORMAL :
GET M$
200 IF M$ = "Y" THEN 170
```

Now you can locate the value or contents on a specific array on two dimensions. In our example, if you know the row number and column number, you can find the band member in that position. The use of 2-dimensional arrays in problems dealing with matrixes is an important addition to your programming commands.

It is also possible to have several more dimensions in an array variable. As you add more and more dimensions, you have to be careful not to confuse the different aspects of a single array. Sometimes, when a multi-dimensional array becomes difficult to manage (or use), it is better to break it down into several 1- or 2-dimensional arrays. But just for fun, let's see what we might want to do with a 3 dimensional array with the following program : (By the way, this problem is based on an actual application!)

```
10 TEXT : HOME
20 INVERSE : PRINT "WINECELLAR ORGANIZER ": NORMAL
30 PRINT : PRINT "HOW MANY RACKS, ROWS, COLUMNS?":
INPUT "(ENTER EACH SEPARATED BY A COMMA)";RK,R,C
40 DIM WI$(RK,R,C)
50 INPUT "HOW MANY BOTTLES WOULD YOU LIKE TO
STORE? ";N%
60 PRINT : FOR I = 1 TO N%
70 INPUT "RACK #-> ";RA
80 INPUT "ROW #-> ";RO
90 INPUT "COL #-> ";CO
100 INVERSE : INPUT "NAME OF WINE : ";WN$: NORMAL
110 WI$(RA,RO,CO) = WN$
120 NEXT I
200 REM ROUTINE FOR CHECKING CONTENTS OF WINE
CELLAR
```

```
210  HOME : INPUT "WHICH RACK # WOULD YOU LIKE TO
CHECK? ";RR
220  FOR I = 1 TO R
230     FOR J = 1 TO C
240        IF WI$(RR,I,J) = "" THEN WI$(RR,I,J) = "EMPTY"
250           PRINT "RACK #";RR;" ROW #";I;" COLUMN #";J;"
CONTAINS ";WI$(RR,I,J)
260        NEXT J
270     NEXT I
280  END
```

Now that was a pretty long program, but go over it carefully to make sure you understand what it is doing. Again, let me remind you that the 3-dimensional array is a variable with a lot of numbers in parentheses. Also, note on line 30 how we INPUT several values with a single INPUT statement. We used the format,

```
INPUT A, B, C
```

and as long as the operator (program user) is told to enter the appropriate number of responses and separate each with a comma, every thing will work fine. Also, it would be a good idea to save this program on a disk as an example of a multi-dimensional array.

Summary

We covered a good deal in this chapter, and if you understood everything, excellent! If you did not, don't worry, for with practice, it will all become very clear. Whatever your understanding of the material, though, experiment with all the statements. Be BOLD and daring with your computer's commands, and as long as you have a disk with which you can practice your skills, the worst that can happen is that you will erase a few programs!

We learned that your Apple computer can compute! Using the IF/THEN commands and relationals we can give the computer the power of "decision making." Using subroutines it is possible to branch at decision points to anywhere we want in our program. Computed GOTOs and GOSUBs allow the execution to move appropriately with a minimal amount of programming.

Finally, we examined array variables. Arrays allow us to enter values into sequentially arranged variables (or elements). Using FOR/NEXT loops it is possible to quickly program multiple variables up to the limits of our DIMensions. Not only do arrays assist us in keeping variables orderly, they save a good deal of work as well.

In the next chapter, we will begin working with commands that help arrange everything for us. As our programs become more and more sophisticated, we will need to keep better track of what we're doing. By organizing our programs into small, manageable chunks, we can create clear useful programs.

CHAPTER 5

Organizing The Parts

Introduction

As we accumulate more and more information, work, or just about anything else, unless we organize, things get confusing. Good organization allows us to do more and to handle more complex and larger problems. These principles hold with programming. As we learn more commands, we can do more things, but the more we do, the more likely we are to get tangled up and lost.

One of the areas that is likely to be the first to suffer from "overflow" is that of formatting output. Variables get mixed up, arrays are misnumbered and the screen is a mess. In order to handle this kind of problem, we will deal extensively with text and string formatting. Not only will we be able to put things where we want them, but we will do it with style!

The second major area of disorganization is I/O (INPUT/OUTPUT). Some of the problem has to do with formatting, but even more elementary is the problem of organizing the input and output so that data is properly analyzed. Data has to be connected to the proper variables and be subject to the correct computations. Thus, in addition to examining string formatting, we will also look at organizing data manipulation.

Formatting Text

In Chapter 1 we said that the Apple keyboard works in many ways like a typewriter. One feature of a typewriter is its ability to set "tabs" so that the user can automatically place text a given number of spaces from the left margin. With your Apple, not only can you TAB, horizontally, you can HTAB, VTAB and SPC. Let's look at what each of these means:

COMMAND	MEANING
TAB (N)	Used within PRINT statement to place next character N spaces from left margin.
HTAB	Sets horizontal placement of next output character. (In INTEGER BASIC use TAB not in PRINT statement.)
VTAB	Sets vertical placement of next output character.

SPC (N)	Used within PRINT statement, creates specified number of spaces. (SPC starts printing non-space 1 space after N.)

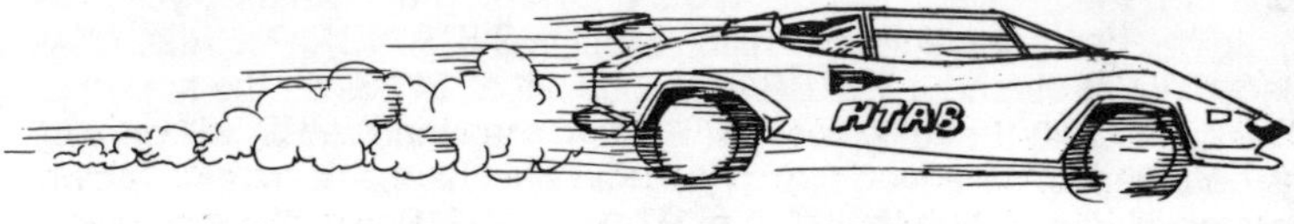

PLACING YOURSELF HORIZONTALLY

Now, to better see how these commands format text output, let's USE THEM!

```
10 TEXT : HOME
20 PRINT TAB (20);"TAB TO HERE"
30 HTAB 20 : PRINT "HTAB TO HERE" : REM NOTE
DIFFERENT FORMAT BETWEEN TAB & HTAB
40 VTAB 18 : PRINT "VTAB DOWN HERE"
50 PRINT SPC(20);"SPC TO HERE"
```

Now let's have a little fun with our commands. Here's a little program that will give you a strange affect on your cursor. (Note: the left bracket is made with a "SHIFT-M".)

```
10 TEXT : HOME : VTAB 20
20 FOR I = 38 TO 1 STEP -1
30    FOR J = 1 TO 100 : NEXT : REM DELAY LOOP
40       HTAB I : PRINT "]"; SPC(1); : REM USE 'SHIFT M' TO
MAKE BRACKET
50 NEXT I
60 HTAB 2 : PRINT "HIT ANY KEY TO CONTINUE OR 'Q' TO
QUIT--> ";: GET A$
70 IF A$ < > "Q" THEN 10
```

And here's another one to play with:

```
10 TEXT : HOME : VTAB 4
20 INPUT "ENTER MESSAGE--> "; MS$
30 PRINT : INPUT "HORIZONTAL PLACEMENT (1-40) -> ";
H
40 PRINT : INPUT "VERTICAL PLACEMENT (1-24) -> "; V
50 HOME
60 HTAB H : VTAB V : PRINT MS$
70 PRINT : PRINT "HIT ANY KEY TO CONTINUE OR 'Q' TO
QUIT "; : GET A$
```

```
80 IF A$ < > "Q" THEN 10
90 END
```

As you can see, variables can be used with formatting statements. Thus, HTAB H, is read in the same way as HTAB 10 or HTAB 15 or any other number between 1 and 40. Using the above program, what do you think would happen if you entered "THIS IS A LONG STRING," a HORIZONTAL placement of 39 and a VERTICAL placement of 24? Since the maximum HTAB is 40 and the maximum VTAB is 24, the string (MS$) will go over the boundaries. Go ahead and try it to see what happens. In fact, it would be a good idea to test the limits of HTAB and VTAB with this program to get a clear understanding of their parameters.

Paddle Formatting

(NOTE: If you do not have game paddles, skip this section.)

In some applications, you may wish to use your game paddles to output numbers or text. By turning the paddle wheel, you can change the value

of variables. Later, in our discussion of graphics, we will see how the paddles can be used to develop interesting graphic effects and even games, but for now, we will simply look at some commands that will show you how your paddles can be used with a program. Try the following little program to see:

```
10 TEXT : HOME
20 X = PDL(0)
30 HTAB 10 : VTAB 10
40 PRINT X
50     FOR I = 1 TO 15 : NEXT I : REM PADDLE 'REFRESH'
LOOP
60 GOTO 20 : REM ENDLESS LOOP
```

Note the FOR/NEXT loop in line 50. For some reason, the Apple paddle readings need to be "refreshed" with a little loop. Anyway, run the program and turn the dial on your paddle to see the effect.

Unraveling Strings

Our discussion of strings up to this point has involved "whole" strings. That is, whatever we define a string to be, no matter how long or short, can be considered a "whole" string. For example, if we define R$ as "WALK" then we can consider "WALK" to be the whole of R$. Likewise, if we defined R$ as "A VERY LONG AND WORDY MESSAGE" then, "A VERY LONG AND WORDY MESSAGE" would be the whole string of R$. There will be occasions, however, when we want to use only part of a string or tie several strings together. (When we get into data base programs, we will find this to be very important.) Also, there are applications where we will need to know the length of strings, find the numeric values of strings, and even change strings into numeric variables and back again.

TRUST ME!

I hate to admit it, but when I first learned about all of the commands we are about to discuss, I thought, "Boy, what a waste of time!" It was enough to get the simple material straight, but why in the world would anyone want to chop up strings and put them back together again? If you want only a certain segment of a string, why not simply define it in terms of that segment? And if you want a longer string, then just define it to be longer! Those were my thoughts on the matter of string formatting. However, I have now come to the point that I find it very difficult to even conceive of programming without these powerful commands. So, trust me! String formatting commands are teriffic little devices to have, and if you do not see their applicability right away, you will as you begin writing more programs.

String Formatting

We will divide our discussion of string formatting into four parts: 1) Calculating the length of a string; 2) Locating parts of strings; 3) Changing strings to numeric variables and back again; and 4) Tying strings together (concatenation).

Calculating The LENgth Of Strings

Sometimes it is necessary to calculate the length of a string for formatting output. Happily, your Apple is very good at telling you the length of a particular string. By the command, PRINT LEN (A$) you will be given the number of characters, including spaces, your string has. Try the following little program to see how this works:

```
10 TEXT : HOME
20 INPUT "NAME OF STRING–> "; A$
30 PRINT A$; " HAS "; LEN(A$); " CHARACTERS"
40 PRINT : INVERSE : PRINT " MORE?(Y/N) ";: NORMAL :GET
AN$
50 IF AN$ = "Y" THEN 20
```

Now to see a more practical application, we will look at a modified version of the centering routine we used in the last chapter.

```
10 TEXT : HOME
20 INPUT "40 OR 80 COLUMN SCREEN? "; CS
30 PRINT "ENTER A STRING OF LESS THAN "; CS ;"
CHARACTERS" : INPUT"–> "; S$
40 HTAB (CS/2) – LEN(S$)/2 : PRINT S$
50 VTAB 22 : PRINT "HIT ANY KEY TO CONTINUE OR 'Q' TO
QUIT ";: GET AN$
60 IF AN$ < > "Q" THEN HOME : GOTO 30
70 END
```

Now that we can see how to compute the LENgth of a string and then use that LENgth to compute our tabbing, let's see how we can control the input with the LEN command. Suppose you want to write a program that will print out mailing labels, but your labels will only hold 30 characters. You want to make sure all of your entries are 30 or fewer characters long, including spaces. To do this we will write a program that checks the LENgth of a string before it is accepted.

```
10 TEXT : HOME
20 PRINT "ENTER A NAME LESS THAN 30 CHARACTERS
INCLUDING SPACES" : INPUT "DO NOT USE COMMAS -> ";
NA$
30 IF LEN (NA$) > 30 THEN GOTO 100 : REM TRAP
40 PRINT : INVERSE : PRINT NA$ : NORMAL
50 PRINT : PRINT "ANOTHER NAME?(Y/N) "; : GET AN$
60 IF AN$ < > "Y" THEN END
70 GOTO 10
100 HOME : FLASH : PRINT "PLEASE USE 30 CHARACTERS
OR LESS " : NORMAL
110 PRINT : GOTO 20
```

Now the first thing you should do is to break the rule!!! Go ahead and enter a string of more than 30 characters to see what happens. (If your computer gets snotty with you, you can always re-program it. It helps to remind it of that fact periodically.) If the program was entered properly, it is impossible to enter a string over 30 characters.

From the above examples, you can begin to see how the LEN command can be useful in several ways. There are many other ways that such commands can be employed to reduce programming time, clarify output, and compute information. The key to understanding its usefulness is to experiment with it and see how other programmers use the same command.

Finding The MIDdle$, LEFT$, and RIGHT$ Parts Of A String

Suppose you want to use a single string variable to describe three different conditions, such as "POOR FAIR GOOD," but you want to use only part of that string to describe an outcome. Using MID$, LEFT$ and RIGHT$, it is possible to PRINT only that part of the string you want. For example, the following program let's you use a single string to describe three different conditions:

```
10 TEXT : HOME
20 X$ = "POOR FAIR GOOD"
30 PRINT "HOW DO YOU FEEL TODAY? (<P>OOR, <F>AIR
OR <G>OOD)"; : GET F$
40 IF F$ = "P" THEN PRINT LEFT$(X$,4)
50 IF F$ = "F" THEN PRINT MID$(X$,6,4)
60 IF F$ = "G" THEN PRINT RIGHT$(X$,4)
70 VTAB 22 : PRINT "ANOTHER GO?(Y/N) "; : GET AN$
80 IF AN$ = "Y" THEN 10
```

SUBSTRING COMMANDS

Let's face it, it would have been easier to simply branch to a PRINT 'GOOD' 'FAIR' or 'POOR' and no less efficient. But, no matter, let's see what the new commands do.

COMMAND	MEANING
MID$(A$,N,L)	Finds the portion of A$, beginning at Nth character L characters long.
LEFT$(A$,L)	Finds the portion A$, L characters long starting at the LEFT side of the string.
RIGHT$(A$,L)	Finds the portion of A$, L characters long starting at the RIGHT side of the string.

To give you some immediate experience with these commands, try the following:

```
W$ = “WHAT A MESS” : PRINT LEFT$(W$,4) <RETURN>
G$ = “BURLESQUE” : PRINT MID$(G$,4,3) <RETURN>
X$ = “A PLACE IN SPACE” : PRINT RIGHT$(X$,5) : PRINT
RIGHT$(X$,3) <RETURN>
```

Another trick with partial strings is to assign parts of one string to another string. For example:

```
10 TEXT : HOME
20 BIG$ = “LONG LONG AGO AND FAR FAR AWAY”
30 LITTLE$ = MID$(BIG$,11,3)
40 AWY$ = RIGHT$(BIG$,4)
50 LG$ = LEFT$(BIG$,4)
60 VTAB 10 : PRINT AWY$;“  ”;LG$;“  ”;LITTLE$
70 REM BEFORE YOU RUN IT, SEE IF YOU CAN GUESS THE
MESSAGE
```

For an interesting effect, try the following little program:

```
10 TEXT : HOME : VTAB 10
20 INPUT “YOUR NAME– – > ”; NA$
30 INVERSE : FOR I = LEN(NA$) TO 1 STEP -1 : PRINT
MID$(NA$,I,1); : NEXT I
40 NORMAL : FOR I = 1 TO 1000 : NEXT I : REM DELAY
LOOP
50 HTAB 1 : VTAB 11 : FOR I = 1 TO LEN(NA$) : PRINT
MID$(NA$, I,1); : FOR K = 1 TO 50 : NEXT K : NEXT I : REM
'K LOOP' SLOWS IT DOWN FOR SLOW MOTION EFFECT
60 HTAB 7 : VTAB 20 : PRINT “WANNA DO IT AGAIN?(Y/N) ”; :
GET AN$: IF AN$ = “Y” THEN 10
```

Now you have probably been wondering ever since you got your computer how to make it print your name backwards. Well, now you know! (If your name is BOB you probably didn't notice it was printed backwards—try ROBERT.) Actually, the above exercise did a couple of things besides goofing off. First, it is a demonstration of how loops and partial strings (or substrings) can be used together for formatting output. Second, we showed how output could be slowed down for either an interesting effect or simply to give the user time to see what's happening.

Since we're on the topic of speed, let's learn a SPEED command. The command is called SPEED and it can be from 0 to 255. SPEED defaults at 255; we have been operating at a speed of 255 from the outset. Let's do some SPEED tests:

```
10 TEXT : HOME : SPEED = 255 : REM RESETS SPEED
20 K$ = "ONCE UPON A TIME IN THE KINGDOM OF SNEW
. . ."
30 INPUT "WHAT SPEED WOULD YOU LIKE? (0-255) " ; S
40 SPEED = S
50 FOR I = 1 TO LEN(K$) : VTAB 10 : HTAB I : PRINT
MID$(K$,I,1) : NEXT I
60 VTAB 20 : FLASH : PRINT "AGAIN?(Y/N)"; : NORMAL : GET
AN$ : IF AN$ "Y" THEN 10
70 SPEED = 255 : END : REM WHEN YOU CHANGE THE
SPEED, IT IS ALWAYS A GOOD IDEA TO RESET IT TO 255 AT
THE END OF THE PROGRAM.
```

Now let's write a program that will do all kinds of things with our strings!

```
10 TEXT : HOME : GOTO 20
20 PRINT CHR$ (7): VTAB 10: INPUT "STRING > ";S$: IF S$
= " " THEN GOTO 90
30 L = LEN (S$): IF L > 10 THEN PRINT : PRINT "TEN OR
FEWER CHARACTERS PLEASE!": GOTO 20
40 HOME : PRINT S$;: INVERSE : HTAB 20 - LEN (S$)/2:
PRINT S$;: FLASH : HTAB 41 - LEN (S$): PRINT S$: NORMAL
: PRINT
50 FOR I = 1 TO LEN (S$): VTAB I + 2: PRINT MID$ (S$,I,1):
HTAB 19: VTAB I + 2: INVERSE : PRINT MID$ (S$,I,1): HTAB
40: VTAB I + 2: FLASH : PRINT MID$ (S$,I,1): NORMAL :
NEXT I
60 FOR I = 1 TO LEN (S$): HTAB I: PRINT MID$ (S$,I,1):
NEXT I
70 FLASH : FOR I = 1 TO LEN (S$): VTAB LEN (S$) + 3 + I:
HTAB 41 - I: PRINT MID$ (S$,I,1): NEXT : INVERSE
80 FOR I = 1 TO LEN (S$): HTAB 19: VTAB LEN (S$) + 3 +
I: PRINT MID$ (S$,1 + LEN (S$) - I,1): NEXT : NORMAL :
GET A$: PRINT A$: GOTO 10
90 HOME : END
```

Changing Strings To Numbers And Back Again

Now we're going to learn about changing strings to numbers and numbers to strings. If you're like me, when I first found out about these commands, I thought they were pretty useless. After all, if you want a string use a string variable, and if you want a number use a numeric variable. Simple enough, but again, once you understand their value, you wonder how you could do without them. To get started, let's RUN the following program:

```
10 TEXT : HOME
20 FOR I = 1 TO 5 : READ NA$(I) : NEXT I
30 FOR I = 1 TO 5
40 X(I) = VAL(RIGHT$(NA$(I),1))
50 NEXT I
60 FOR I = 1 TO 5 : PRINT "OVERTIME PAY= $"; X(I) * (1.5 *
7) : NEXT I
70 DATA SMITH 7, JONES 8, MCKNAP 6, JOHNSON 2,
KELLY 3
```

Using DATA that were originally in a string format, we were able to change a portion of that string array to a numeric array. By making such a conversion, we were able to use our mathematical operations on line 60 to figure out the overtime pay for someone receiving time and a half at seven dollars ($7) an hour. Well, that's pretty interesting, but we don't have a list of who got what and the total overtime paid! Why don't you try it yourself. Change the program so that everyone's name appears with the amount of overtime they received and a total overtime paid. (Hint: You are looking for the substring LEFT$ (NA$(I), LEN (NA$(I) – 2) since you want to drop the number and space after each name.) When you get it, drop me a letter to show me how you figured it out.

It always helps to do a few immediate exercises with a new command to get the right feel; so try these:

```
A$ = "123" : PRINT VAL(A$) + 11 <RETURN>
Q$ = "99.5" : PRINT VAL(Q$) * 7 <RETURN>
SALE$ = "44.95" : PRINT "ON SALE AT HALF PRICE ->$";
VAL(SALE$)/2 <RETURN>
DO$ = "$103.88" : DN$ = "$18.34" : PRINT VAL
(RIGHT$(DO$,6)) + VAL (RIGHT$(DN$,5)) <RETURN>
```

NOTE: Since you may want to SAVE the above examples on tape or disk, all you have to do is to add a line number and SAVE them as little programs.

From Numbers To Strings

All right, let's now go the other way. We saw why we might want to change strings to numbers, but we may also want to change numbers to strings.

To make the conversion we use the STR$ command. For example, look at the following program:

```
10 TEXT : HOME
20 INPUT "ENTER A NUMBER WITH 5 NUMBERS AFTER THE
DECIMAL POINT " ; A
30 A$ = STR$(A)
40 PRINT : PRINT LEFT$ (A$,4)
```

As you can see you have truncated the number to 4 characters. Now, let's do some in the immediate mode to get the idea firmly into your mind, and a little later we will do something very practical with these commands.

```
A = 5.00 : A$ = STR$(A) : PRINT A$ <RETURN>
V = 2345 : V$ = STR$(V) : PRINT V$ <RETURN>
BUCKS = 22.36 : BUCKS$ = STR$(BUCKS) : PRINT
LEFT$(BUCKS$,2) <RETURN>
```

Remember these commands, and when you are dealing with decimal points you will often find them handy.

Tying Strings Together: Concatenation

We have seen how we can take a portion of a string and PRINT it to the screen. Now, we will tie strings together. This is called *concatenation* and

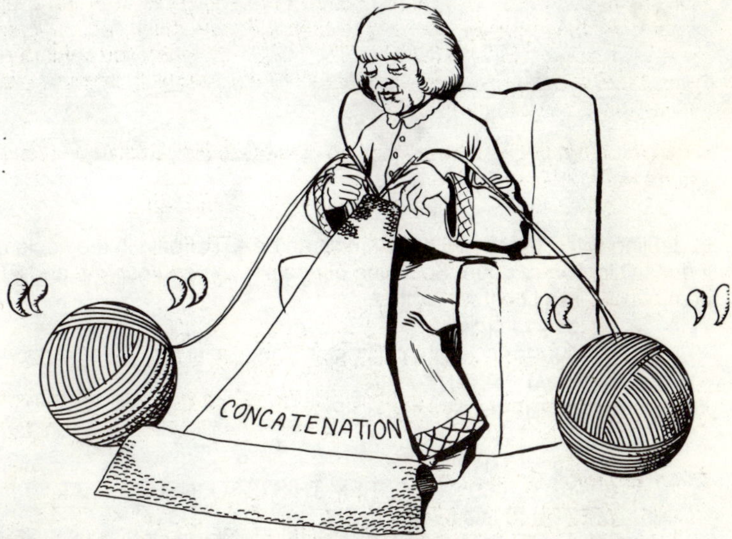

TYING STRINGS TOGETHER

is accomplished by using the "+" sign with strings. For example:

```
10 TEXT : HOME
20 INPUT "YOUR FIRST NAME -> "; NF$
30 INPUT "YOUR LAST NAME -> "; NL$
40 NA$ = NF$ + NL$
50 PRINT NA$
```

A little messy, huh? However, you can see how NF$ and NL$ were tied together into a single larger string. Now, change line 40 to read

```
40 NA$ = NF$ + " " + NL$
```

This time when you RUN the program, your name will turn out fine. Not only did we concatenate string variables, we also concatenated strings themselves. For example, it is perfectly all right to do the following:

```
PRINT "ONE" + "ONE" <RETURN>
```

Now there isn't much you can do with ONEONE, but we can see the principle of operation with concatenating strings.

One of the problems with the way your Apple formats numbers is that it drops 0's off the end. For example, try the following:

```
PRINT 19.80
PRINT 5.00
```

PADDING

In dealing with dollars and cents, this can be a real pain in the neck, and it doesn't look very good. So, using concatenation and our VAL and STR$ commands, let's see if we fix that.

```
10 TEXT : HOME
20 INVERSE : PRINT "BE SURE TO INCLUDE ALL CENTS!":
NORMAL : PRINT : PRINT
30 INPUT "HOW MUCH SPENT?-> $"; S
40 T = T + S
50 T$ = STR$(T)
60 T$ = "000" + T$ : REM THIS IS TO INSURE THAT
LEN(T$) IS LONG ENOUGH
70 IF MID$ (T$,(LEN(T$)-1),1) = "." THEN T$ = T$ + "0" :
```

```
GOTO 90
80 IF MID$ (T$,(LEN(T$)-2),1) < > "." THEN T$ = T$ +
".00"
90 PRINT : PRINT : PRINT "YOU NOW HAVE SPENT $";
RIGHT$(T$,LEN(T$)-3)
```

This may look pretty complicated, but let's break it down to see what has been done.

1. We entered numeric variables in line 30 and computed their sum in line 40.
2. The sum represented by T was then converted to a string variable T$ in line 50.
3. In line 60 we "padded" T$ with 3 0's to give it a minimum length we will need in lines 70 and 80.
4. Line 70 computes the second from the last character in T$. If that character is a decimal point (.) then we know it must be a figure that dropped off the last cent column (e.g., 5.4, 19.5, etc.). So we tack on a "0", and jump to line 90.
5. Line 80 computes the third from the last character, and if it is not a decimal point (.) then we know it must have dropped all the cents completely—an even dollar number. So we tack on the decimal point and two 0's (.00).
6. Finally, we print out our results but first dropping the "padding" we added in line 60 using RIGHT$.

All of this may seem a bit complicated just to get our 0's back, but actually, the entire process was done in 5 lines (50 through 90). SAVE the program, and when you need those 0's in your output, just include those lines! (Be careful, though, this will not work with subtraction when you get below $1!)

Setting Up Data Entry

Now that we have a firm grip on numerous commands, it is time we begin thinking seriously about organizing our programs. The first thing we must do is to arrange our data entry in a manner that we ourselves and others can understand. This involves blocking elements of our program and deciding what variables and arrays we will be using. Also, when we enter data, we want to make sure that we are entering the correct type of data; so we have to set "traps" so that any input that is over a certain length or amount can be checked against our parameters. One of the easiest ways to set traps is with the ONERR command. This command will set certain conditions when an error occurs. Try the following: (That's right, there is an ERROR if you follow instructions!)

```
10 TEXT : HOME
20 ONERR GOTO 100
30 INPUT "ENTER A LETTER FROM A-Z ->"; LE
40 PRINT : PRINT : PRINT "SEE WHAT'D I TELL YOU" : END
100 HOME : PRINT : PRINT : FLASH : PRINT " THERE IS AN
ERROR! " : NORMAL
110 PRINT : PRINT "TRY AGAIN USING A NUMBER SINCE
'LE' IS A " : PRINT "NUMERIC VARIABLE"
120 VTAB 20 : INVERSE : PRINT "PRESS ANY KEY TO
CONTINUE"
130 CLEAR : GET A$GOTO 10
```

TRAPPING YOURSELF IN ERROR TRAPS

The error messages that come with your Apple are very useful for debugging programs. The messages tell you what kind of error occurred and the line they are on. Using the ONERR statement within programs can cause difficulties in writing them since they will jump to your error routine no matter what error they encounter—even ones you don't want! To avoid this and still use the handy ONERR command, put a temporary GOTO statement around the ONERR command while you're developing your program and remove it when your program is complete. For example:

```
25 GOTO 40
30 ONERR GOTO 100
40 INPUT "ENTER NAME "; NA$
. . . ETC.
```

Now, all you have to do is to delete line 25 when you're finished and your ONERR statement can work the way it's supposed to.

The most common and useful ONERR occurs with ?OUT OF DATA errors. In setting up data entry, there will be times when there is an unknown amount of data to be READ into a program. For example, let's say you want a menu program that reads in files on your disk from DATA statements. Since you will be adding file names all the time, you do not want to bother with having to count them each time you add a new DATA element. To read in all the DATA with an unknown amount of elements, you can use a FOR/NEXT loop that reads 100 elements before exiting the loop. Since you are unlikely to have that many files on a single disk side, you will run out of data before exiting the loop. Since it is NOT generally a good idea to jump out of a loop, we will have to take another precaution that will satisfy the loop count as well. Finally, if the expected error is not an ?OUT OF DATA error, we will want our program to do something else. Let's look at an example:

```
10 REM MENU PROGRAM
20 CLEAR : TEXT : HOME
30 ONERR GOTO 200: REM BEGIN ERROR TRAP
40 DIM NA$(100)
50 FOR I = 1 TO 100: READ NA$(I)
60 N = N + 1: REM COUNTER
70 NEXT I
80 I = 100: REM RESET RESISTERS IN FOR/NEXT LOOP
90 FOR I = 1 TO N
100 PRINT I;".";NA$(I): NEXT
```

```
110 PRINT : PRINT "CHOOSE PROGRAM BY NUMBER":
INPUT " AND PRESS <RETURN>";C
120 D$ = " ": REM CTRL-D
130 PRINT D$;"RUN";NA$(C)
140 END
150 DATA FILE A, FILE B, FILE C, FILE D, FILE E : REM
ENTER THE FILES ON YOUR DISK
200 ER = PEEK (222): REM ADDRESS OF ERROR
ROUTINES
220 IF ER = 42 THEN 80: REM 42 IS THE CODE FOR ?OUT
OF DATA
230 PRINT "THERE WAS AN ERROR IN YOUR CHOICE OR IN
THE PROGRAM,": PRINT " TRY AGAIN--> HIT ANY KEY TO
RETURN TO PROGRAM OR 'Q' TO QUIT ";: GET A$
240 IF A$ < > "Q" THEN GOTO 10
250 REM SAVE PROGRAM BEFORE RUNNING
```

This program uses a PEEK statement that looks into the location where the error statement codes are stored. (We will be discussing PEEK and POKE statements in the next chapter.) If the correct code is located, then the program branches to where you want it. Otherwise, it stops and gives you another chance at INPUTing a choice or quitting.

A FUSSY BUT NICE OPTION

For whatever reason, people like to have the option of exiting a program—even at the beginning. Now it is usually possible to hit RESET to get out or CTRL–C to exit a program, but that is inelegant. That's like leaving through a wall instead of a door. Therefore, in setting up your program, always leave an option for exiting gracefully.

Now back to setting up data entry. Let's look at a way to make our strings a certain length (no shorter or longer than a length we want). We've already discussed how to keep strings to a maximum length, so let's see how to keep them to a minimum as well. This latter process is referred to as "padding."

```
10 TEXT : HOME
20 VTAB 8 : INPUT "YOUR COMPANY-->"; CO$
30 IF LEN(CO$) > 10 THEN PRINT "10 OR FEWER
CHARACTERS PLEASE" : PRINT "HIT ANY KEY TO
CONTINUE-> ";:GET A$ : HOME : GOTO 20
40 IF LEN(CO$) < 10 THEN CO$ = CO$ + "X" : GOTO 40 :
REM PADDING
```

```
50 VTAB 10 : PRINT "THE COMPUTER HAS DECIDED THAT "
: PRINT CO$; " SHOULD GIVE YOU A RAISE"
```

Now if YOUR COMPANY <CO$> is less than 10 characters, you will see some "X's" stuck on the end. These were put there to show you how padding works. Now change the "X" to " " (a space) in line 40 and see what happens. Go ahead. The second time you run the program, if your company's name was less than 10 characters, there are a lot of blank spaces after the company name. To remove the spaces, we would enter:

```
60 IF MID$(CO$,LEN(CO$,I)) = "     " THEN CO$ =
LEFT$(CO$,(LEN(CO$) - 1): GOTO 60
```

Setting Up Data Manipulation

Once you have organized your input, the next major step is performing computations on your data. There are essentially two kinds of data manipulation you will deal with:

1. NUMERIC—Manipulating numeric data with mathematical operations.
2. STRING—Manipulating strings with concatenation and substring commands.

Most of the string manipulations are for setting up input or output, and so we will concentrate on manipulating numeric data. We will use a simple example that keeps track of three manipulations: (1) additions, (2) subtractions, and (3) running balance. This will be our check book program we started earlier.

```
10 TEXT : HOME
20 REM ### BEGIN INPUT & HEADER BLOCK ###
30 CB$ = " =COMPUTER CHECK-BOOK= ": HTAB 20 -
LEN (CB$)/2: INVERSE : PRINT CB$: NORMAL : REM
=HEADER=
40 VTAB 4: INPUT "ENTER YOUR CURRENT BALANCE->
$";BA
50 VTAB 6: PRINT "1. ENTER DEPOSITS": PRINT : PRINT "2.
DEDUCT CHECKS": PRINT : PRINT "3. EXIT"
60 VTAB 20: INVERSE : PRINT " CHOOSE BY NUMBER ";:
NORMAL : GET A
70 ON A GOTO 100,200,400
80 GOTO 60: REM TRAP
90 REM END OF INPUT BLOCK
100 REM ### DATA MANIPULATION ROUTINE NO. 1 ###
110 HOME : VTAB 6: INPUT "ENTER AMOUNT OF DEPOSIT
$";DP
120 BA = BA + DP: REM RUNNING BALANCE
```

```
130 VTAB 8: PRINT "YOU NOW HAVE $";BA;" IN YOUR
ACCOUNT"
140 PRINT : VTAB 10: PRINT "MORE DEPOSITS?
(Y/N) ";: GET AN$
150 IF AN$ = "Y" THEN 110
160 PRINT : VTAB 10: PRINT "WOULD YOU LIKE TO DEDUCT
CHECKS? (Y/N) ";: GET AN$
170 IF AN$ = "N" THEN GOTO 400
180 IF AN$ = "Y" THEN GOTO 200
190 HOME : GOTO 160: REM TRAP & END OF DATA
MANIPULATION ROUTINE NO.1
200 REM ### DATA MANIPULATION ROUTINE NO. 2 ###
210 HOME : VTAB 6: INPUT "ENTER AMOUNT OF CHECK
$";CK
220 BA = BA - CK: REM RUNNING BALANCE
230 PRINT : PRINT "YOU NOW HAVE $";BA;" IN YOUR
ACCOUNT"
240 PRINT : VTAB 10: PRINT "MORE CHECKS? (Y/N) - 'Q'
TO QUIT ";: GET AN$
250 IF AN$ = "Y" THEN 210
260 IF AN$ = "Q" THEN 400
270 PRINT : PRINT "ANY DEPOSITS? (Y/N) ";: GET AD$
280 IF AD$ = "Y" THEN 100
290 GOTO 240: REM TRAP & END OF DATA MANIPULATION
BLOCK NO. 2
400 REM ### TERMINATION BLOCK ###
410 HOME : FOR I = 1 TO 400: PRINT "$";: NEXT
420 PRINT "YOU NOW HAVE A BALANCE OF $";BA
```

This program is designed to provide a simple illustration of how to block data manipulation. However, there are some problems with it in the output. We are not getting the 0's on the end of our balance! This is an "output" problem we will discuss in the following section, but before we continue, make sure you understand how we blocked the data manipulation. We used only three variables:

BA = BALANCE

CK = CHECK

DP = DEPOSIT

When we subtracted a check, we simply subtracted CK from BA, and when we entered a deposit, we added DP to BA. In this way we were able to keep a running balance and at the very end BA was the total of all deposits and checks. By keeping it simple and in blocks we were able to jump around and still keep everything straight.

Organizing Output

Let's go back to our program and repair it so that our balance will have the "0's" where they belong. This is essentially a problem of output, for all of the computations have been done, and they correctly tell us our balance, but it doesn't look right with the missing "0's". However, we don't want to have to enter the lines for converting our balance into a string variable everytime the running balance is printed. Therefore, we will put the subroutine for our conversion in a block. Looking at our COMPUTER CHECK BOOK program, it just so happens that there is a block available in the 300's—our luck is with us! We'll use that block to format our output.

```
300 REM ### FORMAT OUTPUT ###
310 BA = BA + .001:PLACE = 1:BA$ = STR$ (BA): IF BA <
.01 THEN BA$ = "0.00": GOTO 340
320 IF MID$ (BA$,PLACE,1) < > "." THEN PLACE = PLACE
+ 1: GOTO 320
330 BA$ = LEFT$ (BA$,PLACE + 2)
340 RETURN
350 REM END OF OUTPUT BLOCK
```

Now, all we have to do is to change a few lines in our program so that when there is an output of our balance, it will jump to the subroutine between lines 300 and 350 then RETURN to output BA$. The following lines in our COMPUTER CHECK BOOK program should be changed and or added:

```
125 GOSUB 300
130 VTAB 8 : PRINT "YOU NOW HAVE $"; BA$; "IN YOUR
ACCOUNT"
225 GOSUB 300
230 PRINT : PRINT "YOU NOW HAVE $"; BA$; " IN YOUR
ACCOUNT"
415 GOSUB 300
420 PRINT "YOU NOW HAVE A BALANCE OF $"; BA$
```

Now if you put everything together properly, you should have a handy little program for working with your checkbook. Just to make sure you got everything, here's the complete program with all the subroutines and changes we made:

```
10 TEXT : HOME
20 REM ### BEGIN INPUT & HEADER BLOCK ###
30 CB$ = " =COMPUTER CHECK-BOOK= ": HTAB 20 -
LEN (CB$)/2: INVERSE : PRINT CB$: NORMAL : REM
=HEADER=
40 VTAB 4: INPUT "ENTER YOUR CURRENT BALANCE->
$";BA
```

```
50  VTAB 6: PRINT “1. ENTER DEPOSITS”: PRINT : PRINT “2.
DEDUCT CHECKS”: PRINT : PRINT “3. EXIT”
60  VTAB 20: INVERSE : PRINT “ CHOOSE BY NUMBER ”;:
NORMAL : GET A
70  ON A GOTO 100,200,400
80  GOTO 60: REM TRAP
90  REM END OF INPUT BLOCK
100  REM ### DATA MANIPULATION ROUTINE NO. 1 ###
110  HOME : VTAB 6: INPUT “ENTER AMOUNT OF DEPOSIT
$”;DP
120  BA = BA + DP: REM RUNNING BALANCE
125  GOSUB 300
130  VTAB 8: PRINT “YOU NOW HAVE $”;BA$;“ IN YOUR
ACCOUNT”
140  PRINT : VTAB 10: PRINT “MORE DEPOSITS? (Y/N) ”;:
GET AN$
150  IF AN$ = “Y” THEN 110
160  PRINT : VTAB 10: PRINT “WOULD YOU LIKE TO DEDUCT
CHECKS? (Y/N) ”;: GET AN$
170  IF AN$ = “N” THEN GOTO 400
180 IF AN$ = “Y” THEN GOTO 200
190  HOME : GOTO 160: REM TRAP & END OF DATA
MANIPULATION ROUTINE NO.1
200  REM ### DATA MANIPULATION ROUTINE NO. 2 ###
210  HOME : VTAB 6: INPUT “ENTER AMOUNT OF CHECK
$”;CK
220  BA = BA – CK: REM RUNNING BALANCE
225  GOSUB 300
230  PRINT : PRINT “YOU NOW HAVE $”;BA$;“ IN YOUR
ACCOUNT”
240  PRINT : VTAB 10: PRINT “MORE CHECKS? (Y/N) – ‘Q’
TO QUIT “;: GET AN$
250  IF AN$ = “Y” THEN 210
260  IF AN$ = “Q” THEN 400
270  PRINT : PRINT “ANY DEPOSITS? (Y/N) ”;: GET AD$
280  IF AD$ = “Y” THEN 100
290  GOTO 240: REM TRAP & END OF DATA MANIPULATION
BLOCK NO. 2
300  REM ### FORMAT OUTPUT ###
310  BA = BA + .001:PLACE = 1:BA$ = STR$ (BA): IF BA <
.01 THEN BA$ = “0.00”: GOTO 340
320  IF MID$ (BA$,PLACE,1) < > “.” THEN PLACE = PLACE
+ 1: GOTO 320
330  BA$ = LEFT$ (BA$,PLACE + 2)
```

```
340 RETURN
350 REM END OF OUTPUT BLOCK
400 REM ### TERMINATION BLOCK ###
410 HOME : FOR I = 1 TO 400: PRINT "$";: NEXT
415 GOSUB 300
420 PRINT "YOU NOW HAVE A BALANCE OF $";BA$
```

Scroll Control!

One of the big problems in output occurs when you have long lists that will scroll right off the screen. For example, the output of the following program will kick the output right out the top of the screen:

```
10 TEXT : HOME
20 FOR I = 1 TO 100 : PRINT I : NEXT
```

Instead of numbers, suppose you have a list of names you have sorted or some other output you wanted to see before they zipped off the top of the screen. Depending on the desired output, screen format and so forth there are several different ways to control the scroll. Consider the following:

```
10 TEXT : HOME
20 FOR I = 1 TO 100
30 IF I = 20 THEN GOSUB 100
40 IF I = 40 THEN GOSUB 100
50 IF I = 60 THEN GOSUB 100
60 IF I = 80 THEN GOSUB 100
70 PRINT I : NEXT I
80 END
100 VTAB 23 : INVERSE : PRINT " HIT ANY KEY TO
CONTINUE " ; : GET A$ : PRINT A$ : NORMAL
110 HOME : RETURN
```

REMEMBER!! You and not the computer are in CONTROL! You can have your output anyway you want it. To use more of the screen, you could have the output tabbed to another column after the vertical screen is filled. For example:

```
10 TEXT : HOME
20 FOR I = 1 TO 40
30 IF I > 20 THEN GOSUB 100
50 PRINT I : NEXT I
80 END
100 HTAB 10 : VTAB I - 20
110 RETURN
```

You get the idea. Format your ouput in a manner that best uses the screen and your needs and get that scroll under control!

Summary

The formatting of programs makes the difference between a useful and not-so-useful application of your computer. The extent to which your program is well organized and clear, the better the chances are for simple yet effective programming. Formatting is more than an exercise in making your input/output fancy or interesting. It is a matter of communication between your Apple and you! After all, if you can't make heads or tails of what your computer has computed, the best calculations in the world are of absolutely no use.

In the same way it is important to have your computer tell you what you want, it is also important to write your programs so that you and others can understand what is happening. By using "blocks" it is easier to organize and later understand exactly what each part of your program does. Obviously, it is possible to write programs sequentially so that each command and subroutine is in an ascending order of line numbers, but to do so means that you will have to repeat simple and/or complex operations that could be better handled as subroutines. Also, it will be considerably more difficult to locate bugs and make the appropriate changes. In other words, by using a structured approach to programming, you make it simpler, not more difficult.

Finally, you should begin to see why there are commands for substrings and all the fuss about tabs. These are handy tools for organizing the various parts in a manner that gives you complete control over your computer's output. What may at first seem like a petty, even silly command in APPLESOFT BASIC, upon a useful application, can be appreciated as an excellent tool. Therefore, as we delve deeper into your computer, look at the variety of commands as mechanisms of more efficient and ultimately simpler control and not a complex "gobbleygook" of "computerese" for geniuses. After all, if you've got this far, you should realize that what you know now looked liked the work of "computer whizzes" when you first began.

CHAPTER 6
Some Advanced Topics

(But Not Too Difficult Once You Get To Know Them)

Introduction

The topics of this chapter are more "code like" and contain the kinds of commands that look "scarey." At least that's how I interpreted them when I first saw them. Many of the functions can be done with commands we already know, but many cannot. Still others, as we will see, can be accomplished better using these new commands. Like so much else you have seen in this book, what at first may appear to be "impossible" is really quite simple once you get the idea. More importantly, by playing with the commands, you can quickly learn their use.

The first thing we will learn about is the ASCII code. ASCII (pronounced ASS–KEY) stands for the AMERICAN STANDARD CODE for INFORMATION INTERCHANGE. Essentially, it is a set of numbers that have been standardized to mean certain characters. In APPLESOFT, the CHR$ (character string) command ties into ASCII and can be used to directly output ASCII. As we will see, the CHR$ command is very useful not only in disk commands but also for outputting special characters.

The next commands have to do with directly accessing locations in your computer's memory. The first, POKE, puts values into memory and the second, PEEK, looks into memory addresses and returns the values there. We will examine several different uses of these two commands.

The third command we will discuss, CALL, executes machine level routines in memory. The CALL command can be used to execute such routines from within a BASIC program. In addition, we will see how to use the BSAVE command to save binary files to the disk and BLOAD and BRUN them. Finally, we will examine the uses of the WAIT command for conditional pauses within APPLESOFT programs.

The ASCII Code And CHR$ Functions

In a couple of places we have used control characters in programs, such as CTRL-D. In the program all we saw was something like the following:

```
PRINT " ": REM CTRL – D
```

What that means is that we enter the CTRL-D between the quote marks. Unfortunately, we cannot see the CTRL-D when we list our program to printer or screen; so we have to use a REM statement to let us know what's there. Another way to access any characters we want, including control characters, is to use CHR$ commands and the ASCII code. In Appendix A there is a complete listing of ASCII from 0 to 255 in both decimal and hexadecimal. Whenever we want to access a character, all we have to do is to enter the CHR$ and the decimal value of the character we want. For example enter the following:

```
PRINT CHR$(65) <RETURN>
```

You got an "A". That's simple enough and not too interesting. On the other hand, try the following little program, and I'll bet you couldn't do it without using the CHR$ function:

```
10 TEXT : HOME
20 QU$ = CHR$(34) : REM USES ASCII VALUE FOR QUOTE
MARKS
30 VTAB 20 : PRINT "HIT ANY KEY TO CONTINUE OR "; QU$
; "Q" ; QU$ ; " TO QUIT ";
40 GET AN$
50 IF AN$ = "Q" THEN END
60 PRINT CHR$(7) : GOTO 10
```

RUN the program and look and listen carefully. Look at the quotes around the Q. If we tried to PRINT a quote mark, the computer would think it got a command to begin printing a string. However, but defining QU$ as CHR$(34) we were able to slip in the quote marks and not confuse the output! Also, did you notice the bell. Up to now, if we wanted to ring the bell, we had to put in an invisible CTRL-G, but since the ASCII value of CTRL-G is 7, by PRINTing CHR$(7) we can ring the bell and see the command that made it ring.

If you have lower case, you can use the CHR$ function to print out lower case and chracters that are otherwise unavailable directly through the keyboard. To see what different characters you have available, RUN the following program:

```
10 TEXT : HOME
20 FOR I = 32 TO 127
30 PRINT CHR$(I); : NEXT
```

Voila! There you have all of your symbols. Now, to watch funny things happen to your screen RUN the following program.

```
10 TEXT : HOME
20 FOR I = 0 TO 31
30 PRINT CHR$(I) ; : NEXT
```

Not much happened since in that range of ASCII (from 0 to 31) you ran through the control characters. To get used to your increased power over your computer, try the following little programs:

```
10 TEXT : HOME
20 LB$ = CHR$ (93) : RB$ = CHR$(91)
30 APPLE$ = "APPLE" + CHR$(32) + LB$ + RB$
40 HTAB 20 – LEN (APPLE$)/2 : PRINT APPLE$ : REM FOR
80 COLUMNS USE HTAB 40
50 VTAB 23

10 TEXT : HOME
20 FOR I = 1 TO 4 : PRINT CHR$(7);:NEXT
30 VTAB 10: PRINT CHR$(34);"WAS THAT THE PHONE OR
DOORBELL?";R$(34)

10 TEXT : HOME
20 FOR I = 65 TO 90 : PRINT CHR$(I);CHR$(I+32):NEXT
```

In the last instruction, if you have lower case on your Apple, you should have discovered that by using an "offset" of 32, it is possible to get the lower case equivalent of the upper case character.

The following program is a handly little device for printing out all of the CHR$ values to screen. The inverse "^" (carat) indicates that the character is a control character. Notice how "negative offsets" were used to print control character representations. This is because if we attempted to use the CHR$ function to print actual control characters they would have had an unusual effect on our output. Save this program to quickly look up CHR$ values. In Chapter 10 we will provide a program that you can use to print all of these characters to your printer.

```
10 TEXT : HOME
20 F = 0
30 FOR I = 1 TO 3: PRINT "CHR$/$";: NEXT
40 FOR I = 1 TO 40: PRINT "=";: NEXT : POKE 34,2
50 FOR I = 64 TO 95
60 IF I < 74 THEN PRINT " ";I – 64;". ";: INVERSE : PRINT
"^";: NORMAL : PRINT CHR$ (I):F = F + 1: GOTO 80
70 PRINT I – 64;". ";: INVERSE : PRINT "^";: NORMAL : PRINT
CHR$ (I):F = F + 1
80 IF F > 19 AND F < 40 THEN GOSUB 600
90 IF F > 39 THEN GOSUB 700
100 NEXT
110 FOR I = 32 TO 127: PRINT I;". " + CHR$(I):F = F + 1
120 IF F > 19 AND F < 40 THEN GOSUB 600
130 IF F > 39 THEN GOSUB 700
140 IF F = 60 THEN GOSUB 500
150 NEXT I
```

```
160 VTAB 21: HTAB 1: PRINT "HIT ANY KEY TO RESTART OR
" + CHR$(34) + "Q" + CHR$(34)" TO QUIT ";: GET AN$
170 IF AN$ < > "Q" THEN GOTO 10
180 VTAB 22: TEXT : END
500 F = 0: INVERSE : HTAB 1: VTAB 24: PRINT "HIT ANY
KEY TO CONTINUE OR 'Q' TO QUIT";: GET A$: NORMAL
510 IF A$ = "Q" THEN 180
520 HOME
530 RETURN
600 HTAB 17: VTAB F - 17
610 RETURN
700 HTAB 40 - 7: VTAB F - 37
710 RETURN
```

Using CHR$ With The Disk Operating System

An important control character you should become acquainted with is CTRL-D or CHR$(4). By PRINTing this character from within a program, you can access your disk system. For example, try the following program:

```
10 TEXT : HOME
20 D$ = CHR$(4)
30 PRINT D$; "CATALOG"
40 END
```

Your program CATALOGed your disk. (You may remember our HELLO program at the beginning of the book where we used that to automatically CATALOG your disk.)

An even better use of CHR$(4) is to combine it with a RETURN, or CHR$(13). Thus, change line 20 to:

```
20 D$ = CHR$(13) + CHR$(4)
```

This will function in the same way as CHR$(4), but it is a slightly better way of defining a string variable to run your DOS since it will often be necessary to put a DOS command at the end of a line with multiple commands in it. The CHR$(13) will act as a "carriage return" to bring it out of the line. For example,

```
10 TEXT : HOME : D$ = CHR$(13) + CHR$(4) : PRINT
D$;"CATALOG" : END
```

When using the definition, be sure to put the CHR$(13) BEFORE the CHR$(4).

In chapter 8 we will be going into an extensive discussion of DOS, but for now, here are a couple of programs that will show you some uses of CHR$(4) and DOS.

```
10 TEXT : HOME
20 D$ = CHR$(13) + CHR$(4)
30 PRINT D$; "CATALOG"
40 INVERSE : INPUT " WHICH PROGRAM WOULD YOU LIKE
TO RUN? "; PG$ : NORMAL
50 PRINT D$; "RUN"; PG$ :END
```

```
10 TEXT : HOME : HD$ = " FILE FIXER ": HTAB 20 -
LEN(HD$)/2 : INVERSE : PRINT HD$ : NORMAL : REM USE
HTAB 40 FOR 80 COLUMN SCREENS
20 D$ = CHR$(13) + CHR$(4)
30 VTAB 8: PRINT "1. LOCK" : PRINT : PRINT "2. UNLOCK" :
PRINT : PRINT "3. DELETE" : PRINT : PRINT "4. EXIT"
40 VTAB 20 : PRINT "CHOOSE BY NUMBER " ; : GET A
50 ON A GOSUB 100, 200, 300, 400
60 GOTO 10
100 HOME : PRINT D$ ; "CATALOG"
110 INVERSE : INPUT "LOCK WHICH FILE?"; L$ : NORMAL
120 PRINT D$; "LOCK"; L$
130 RETURN
200 HOME : PRINT D$; "CATALOG"
210 INVERSE : INPUT
"UNLOCK WHICH FILE? ";U$ : NORMAL
220 PRINT D$; "UNLOCK"; U$
230 RETURN
300 HOME : PRINT D$ ; "CATALOG"
310 INVERSE : INPUT "DELETE WHICH FILE? "; DE$ :
NORMAL
320 FLASH : PRINT " ARE YOUR SURE? (Y/N) ";: GET AN$ :
NORMAL
330 IF AN$ < > "Y" THEN RETURN
340 PRINT D$; "DELETE" ; DE$
350 RETURN
400 HOME : END
```

POKES And PEEKS: Looking Inside Your Apple's Memory

At first you won't have too many uses of POKES and PEEKS, but as you begin exploring the full range of your computer's capacity, they will be used more and more. Basically, a POKE command places a value into a given memory location and a PEEK command returns the value stored in that location. For example, try the following:

```
POKE 768, 255 : PRINT PEEK (768) <RETURN>
```

You should have gotten "255" since the POKE command entered that value into location 768 and PRINT PEEK (768). That's relatively simple, but more is going on than storage of numbers.

The key importance of POKE and PEEK involves what occurs in a given memory location when a given value is entered. In some locations nothing other than the storage of the number will occur, as in our example above. However, with other memory locations, very precise events occur. For example, we used PRINT PEEK (222) to find what type of error occurred when we used the ONERR command. So if we POKEd memory location 222, it would not be the same as POKEing locations that are "free space" available for the programs you write. What we will do in the remainder of this section is to examine some of the more useful locations for POKEing and PEEKing in your Apple. We will not be getting into the more complex elements of POKEs and PEEKs, however.

"PEEKING" INSIDE YOUR APPLE

DON'T BE SCARED

A TALE OF TWO NUMBER SYSTEMS

When using POKEs and PEEKs, we use decimal numbers for accessing locations. However, much of what is written about special locations in your *Reference Manual* that comes with your Apple is written in HEXADECIMAL, generally referred to as HEX. Since we've used decimal notations for counting all our lives, it seems to be a "natural" way of doing things. However, decimal is simply a "base 10" method of counting and we could use a base of anything we wanted. For reasons I won't get into here, "base 16," called HEXADECIMAL, is an easier way to think about using a computer's memory, and that's why so much of the notation we see is in HEX. HEX is counted in the same way as decimal except it is done in groups of 16, and it uses alphanumeric characters instead of just numeric ones. You can usually tell whether a number is HEX since they are typically preceded by a dollar sign (e.g., $45 is not the same as decimal 45), and often there are alphabetic characters mixed in with numbers (e.g., FC58, AAB, 12C). The following is a list of decimal and hexadecimal numbers.

DECIMAL	HEXADECIMAL
10	$A
11	$B
12	$C
13	$D
14	$E
15	$F
16	$10

As you can see, instead of starting with double digit numbers at 10, hexadecimal begins double digits at decimal 16 with a $10. In the major memory locations of interest in your *Apple II Reference Manual,* both the decimal and hexadecimal numbers are given.

Now let's take a look at some places to POKE. We will begin with your text screen. In our program that gives us the different CHR$ values, we used a POKE to set the text screen so that we could keep a portion of it above the new information appearing on the screen. Using POKEs we can set the left margin, width, top, and bottom of our text window. The following is an example of setting the text window and scrolling "under" our defined "window."

```
10 TEXT : HOME
20 HD$ = "THIS IS THE PROTECTED PART OF THE
SCREEN" : INVERSE : HTAB 20 – LEN(HD$)/2 : PRINT HD$
30 POKE 35, 4 : REM SET THE BOTTOM OF OUR WINDOW
TO VERTICAL POSITION 4
40 VTAB 6 : REM JUMP BELOW THE WINDOW
50 FOR I = 1 TO 100 : PRINT I : NEXT
```

The following are the POKEs for window dressing: (NOTE: Remember, to reset everything to normal use the TEXT command!)

POKE 32,N Left edge of window (0–39)

POKE 33,N	Width of text window (1–40)
POKE 34,N	Top edge of window (0–22)
POKE 35,N	Bottom of text window (1–24)

To get an idea of some different windows and their effect, try the following programs.

```
10 TEXT : HOME
20 POKE 32, 10 : REM SET LEFT EDGE TO 10
30 POKE 33, 12 : REM SET WIDTH TO 12
40 POKE 34, 8 : REM SET TOP EDGE TO 8
50 POKE 35, 15 : REM SET BOTTOM EDGE TO VERTICAL
POSITION 15
60 VTAB 9 : INVERSE : FOR I = 1 TO 6 : PRINT SPC (12); :
NEXT : REM FILL UP WINDOW WITH INVERSE SPACES
70 FOR I = 1 TO 2000 : NEXT : REM DELAY LOOP TO LOOK
AT WINDOW
80 HOME : PRINT "THIS LITTLE WINDOW IS YOUR TEXT
WINDOW – NOT MUCH ROOM, IS IT?"
90 FOR I = 1 TO 3000 : NEXT : REM DELAY
100 NORMAL : LIST
```

```
10 TEXT : HOME
20 FOR I = 1 TO 11: INVERSE : PRINT SPC(40) : NEXT I :
NORMAL
30 POKE 35,11
40 T$="TOP":B$="BOTTOM"
50 VTAB 5 : HTAB 20 – LEN(T$)/2 : PRINT T$
60 INVERSE : VTAB 17 : HTAB 20 – LEN(B$)/2 : PRINT B$ :
NORMAL
70 VTAB 23 : END :REM PREVENTS SCROLL WHEN
PROGRAM ENDS
```

REMEMBER WHEN?

When we first got started I suggested it was a good idea to begin programs with TEXT : HOME. Well, we've been able to see the advantage of having HOME at the beginning of a program since it clears the screen. Now, we can see the advantage of having TEXT since it is used to reset the text window to its full size. So after changing the text window, as we have in this section, it is convenient to RUN other programs with different sized windows and know that TEXT is waiting at the beginning to put everything right.

ANOTHER TIP

When developing programs using POKEs to change the text window, put a TEXT at the very end of the program to reset it to full size before LISTing and editing. In fact, if you want to be all set for editing, add the following line:

```
62000 GET A$ : PRINT A$ : TEXT : HOME : POKE 33,33 :
LIST
```

This is a way to automatically reset your text window, clear the screen, set the screen width to the width of program lines and list your program. The GET statement simply holds whatever you have on the screen until you are ready to edit it. When the program is completed remember to delete line 62000. The TEXT statement at the beginning of your program will reset the POKE 33,33.

Poking The Text Screen

Another use of POKEs is to enter a character to a location on your text screen. Each character has a different value between 0 and 255. Unlike the CHR$ values, values POKEd into memory and displayed on the screen are inverse, flashing, control, normal, upper case, and lower case. That is, a flashing "A" is decimal value 65 while a normal "A" is 193. Your screen can be envisioned as a set of addresses on a 40 (or 80) by 24 grid beginning with decimal location 1024. However, the addresses are not contiguous, and you should check your *Reference Manual* for a map of your text screen to see exactly where a given address will place a character. To get an idea of what you will see, try the following POKEs:

```
HOME :POKE 1190, 65 : POKE 1191, 193 <RETURN>
HOME : FOR I = 1880 TO 1890 : POKE I, 101 : NEXT
<RETURN>
HOME : FOR I = 1240 TO (1240 + 255) : POKE I, I – 1240 :
NEXT <RETURN>
```

The first line showed different addresses for flashing and normal "A" located at adjacent addresses. The next exercise used a sequence of addresses from 1880 to 1890 and put in a flashing "%" at each location. Finally, the third exercise used adjacent memory locations to insert a sequence of ASCII characters.

Now, since you know how to use the HTAB and VTAB commands, along with FLASH, INVERSE, and NORMAL, this may seem like a very difficult way to display text to the screen. If you think that, you're absolutely right!

It is much simpler and just as efficient to use the commands you alreay know for displaying text. Rarely will you need to use POKEs to display information to the screen. However, it is interesting to know, and if you like to "encode" secret messages in your programs and amaze your friends, POKEing the text screen can be a lot of fun. The following program will give you a handy little utility for determining the values for all the different characters:

```
10 TEXT : HOME
20 X = PDL(0) : REM PADDLE 0. IF YOU DO NOT HAVE
PADDLES, CHANGE THIS LINE TO -> VTAB 2 : HTAB 1 :
CALL -868 : INPUT "ENTER A NUMBER FROM 0 TO 255->
"; X : IF X > 255 THEN 20
30 HTAB 5 : VTAB 10
40 IF X < 10 THEN PRINT "POKE <1024 TO 2047>,";
X;"=   " : GOTO 70 : REM 2 SPACES AFTER "="
50 IF X < 100 THEN PRINT "POKE <1024 TO 2047>,"; X ;
"=  " : GOTO 70 : REM 1 SPACE AFTER "="
60 PRINT "POKE <1024 TO 2047>," ; X ; "="
70 POKE 1220, X
80 GOTO 20
```

LABEL IT!

If you do have paddles, it is a good idea to label them PADDLE 0 and PADDLE 1. (PADDLE 2 and 3 also, if you have 4 paddles.) If you don't know which paddle is PADDLE 0 or PADDLE 1, simply run the above program, and if the numbers change then you have PADDLE 0. While you're at it, use labels as reminders for all kinds of POKEs & PEEKs as well. Using those label makers that produce little plastic strips with adhesive on them, punch in handy POKEs and PEEKs and stick them on your computer. Don't over-do it, but if you find yourself constantly looking up POKE and PEEK numbers, save yourself some time by making a little label.

A Little Sound

Another area of interest involving PEEKs and POKEs is your Apple's speaker. By using a series of PEEKs and POKEs it is possible to produce entire tunes. However, here we will simply look at some basic ways to make your speaker produce sounds. The most elementary way of kicking on your speaker is with PEEK (-16336). Try the following:

```
FOR I = 1 TO 10 : SS = PEEK (-16336) : NEXT <RETURN>
```

That should have given you a little buzz. Now enter the following program and listen carefully as the sounds change.

```
10 TEXT : HOME
20 N = −16336
30 FOR I = 1 TO 100 : S = PEEK (N) : NEXT
40 FOR I = 1 TO 100 : S = PEEK (N) + PEEK(N) : NEXTI
50 FOR I = 1 TO 100 : S = PEEK (N) − PEEK (N) : NEXTI +
PEEK (N)
```

By experimenting with adding and subtracting combinations of PEEK (N) you can arrive at a limited set of sound subroutines. The following program, however, will provide an even fuller range of sounds.

```
10 TEXT : HOME
20 FOR I = 768 TO 795: READ J: POKE I,J: NEXT
30 POKE 1013,76: POKE 1014,0: POKE 1015,3
40 VTAB 5: HTAB 1: PRINT "ENTER TWO NUMBERS LESS
THAN 256": CALL −868: INPUT "SEPARATED BY A COMMA
−> ";I,K
50 VTAB 10: HTAB 1: CALL −868: PRINT "TONE VALUE: =
";K
60 VTAB 12: HTAB 1: CALL −868: PRINT "DURATION = ";I
70 & I,K: GOTO 40
80 DATA 32,70,231,134,81,164,80,152,170,202,208,253,44,
48,192,69,81,170,202,208,253,44,48,192,136,208,236,96
```

Now, the above program has a lot of material in it you should not be expected to know about at this stage of the game, and it was included only to show you the tones that can be produced on the Apple. The "&" in line 70 calls a machine-level subroutine that was POKEd in with the loop on line 20 and data on line 80. For an excellent discussion of how all of this works, and the source of the locations that were POKEd, see David Lingwood's article "Amplifying APPLESOFT" in *All About APPLESOFT* (Renton, WA: A.P.P.L.E., 1981). In the meantime don't worry about knowing what's going on! Just play with the sounds and read David Lingwood's article when you finish this book for an advanced understanding of APPLESOFT.

A MUSICAL PLUS FOR INTEGER USERS

If you've been struggling along trying to understand how to convert INTEGER BASIC into APPLESOFT, when it comes to music you get a real break. Most INTEGER machines come with a PROGRAMMER'S AID chip that has all kinds of simple musical note generating routines. Look at the PROGRAMMER'S AID manual and you will find a chapter on generating musical notes using INTEGER BASIC.

CALLing A Monitor Subroutine

You should have noticed that we have been using a CALL command in various programs. For example, in the last program there was a CALL −868. What a CALL does is to "run" a machine – level subroutine in your monitor (not your TV, but the system monitor within your computer) or another machine program in memory. In the REFERENCE MANUAL that comes with your computer, there is a listing of the AUTOSTART ROM. Along the far left side are the starting addresses of the various subroutines that can be CALLed from your APPLESOFT program. The problem is that the listing is in HEXADECIMAL and you have to make the CALLs with decimal values. There are a lot of programs and charts available for converting hexadecimal to decimal. However, for the beginner, it would probably be more confusing than enlightening to go into either the conversion process or explain the monitor listing. Instead, we will make a list of some handy CALLs, and when you are more advanced, you can see how these CALLs jumped to a machine-level subroutine.

CHART IT!

In addition to having labels stuck all over my computer, I have a number of charts. The nice thing about a chart is that it has everything from a single category together in one place. This book has charts in it and so do other books available for the Apple, but you have to go riffling through books to find the right chart. You should make or buy or somehow get your hands on charts that will summarize CALLs, POKEs, and other handy locations and addresses. A couple of commerical charts I can recommend are the Beagle Bros. charts: (1) Command Chart and (2) Peeks & Pokes Chart (Beagle Bros., 4315 Sierra Vista, San Diego, CA 92103). Another source of charts is from (would you believe) Cut The Bull Software (Box 82761, San Diego, CA 92138). Also, in several computer magazines, you can find charts. Make copies of the charts and using rubber cement, paste them to cardboard and keep them handy.

MINI CALL CHART

CALL −151	Enter the monitor
CALL −936	Same as HOME
CALL −868	Clear from cursor to end of line
CALL −875	Clears entire line of text
CALL −958	Clear from cursor to end of screen
CALL −1184	Puts Apple II at top of screen
CALL −1401	Boots system and resets pointers
CALL −912	Scrolls up a line
CALL −756	Waits for keypress

CALL −678 Waits for RETURN to be pressed
CALL 42350 CATALOGs disk

Try some of the above CALLs in your programs to see their effect. If you CALL −151, use CTRL-C or type in 3D0G to get back to APPLESOFT. Here are some programs to play with CALL.

```
10 TEXT : HOME : FOR I = 1 TO 800 : PRINT "X"; : NEXT :
REM SOMETHING TO FILL THE SCREEN
20 FOR I = 1 TO 24 : HTAB 20 : VTAB I : CALL -868 : FOR J
= 1 TO 50 : NEXT J : NEXT I
30 FOR I = 1 TO 24 : HTAB 1 : VTAB 25 - I : CALL -868 :
FOR J = 1 TO 50 : NEXT J : NEXT I

10 TEXT : CALL -936
20 FOR I = 1024 TO 2039 : POKE I, 102 : NEXT
30 FOR PAUSE = 1 TO 2000 : NEXT PAUSE : REM PAUSE
LOOP
40 FOR I = 1 TO 24 STEP 2 : VTAB I : CALL -875 : NEXT :
```

```
PRINT : CALL -875
50 FOR PAUSE = 1 TO 2000 : NEXT PAUSE
60 FOR J = 2 TO 23 STEP 2 : HTAB 1 : VTAB J : INVERSE :
PRINT SPC(40): NORMAL : NEXT J
70 FOR PAUSE = 1 TO 2000 : NEXT PAUSE
80 FOR K = 1 TO 24 : CALL -912 : NEXT
```

BSAVEing A Binary File

We won't be writing any machine- or assembly-level programs, but often you will want to load and save a binary file. For example, FID on your SYSTEM MASTER is a handy program to have on different disks. If you wanted to load it and save it to another disk (without using the FID program to do so!) you would have to first use the BLOAD command to load the file since it is a binary one. Once it is BLOADed, you will have to BSAVE it. Unlike APPLESOFT and INTEGER files, binary files have to be BSAVEd with the starting address and length of the program. For example, we might have a program named SUPER JET that begins at hex $300 and is hex $1A5 long. (Remember the $ indicates the number is in hexadecimal.) To save the program we would write in

```
BSAVE SUPER JET, A$300, L$1A5
```

The problem is in finding the beginning address and length of the file. Fortunately, the process is relatively simple. Here's how.

1. BLOAD a binary file. (We'll use FID for our example.)
2. Get into the monitor with CALL -151. When you arrive, you will get the asterisk (*) prompt.
3. Enter AA72.AA73   AA60.AA61
4. You will get two sets of numbers looking something like this:
   ```
   AA72-   03 08
   AA60-   4E 12
   ```
5. Reverse the pairs of bits:
   ```
   03 08  to ->  08 03
   4E 12  to ->  12 4E
   ```
6. Now you have the starting address of $0803 (or simply $803) and the length of $124E.
7. BSAVE FID, A$803, L$124E (on another disk).
8. Use CTRL-C or 3DØG (that's 3D-ZERO-G) to return to APPLESOFT.

You might want to make a label with AA72.AA73 and AA60.AA61 on it as a reminder. There are a lot of times you will want to transfer a binary file without having to BRUN FID or some other file copy program, and this will be very handy information.

WAITing Without A Cursor

The final command we will examine is the WAIT command. Essentially, what WAIT does is to halt execution of your program until a given key(s) is hit. Unlike the GET command, you will not have a cursor on your screen, and it makes your program that much neater. For example, try the following two programs to compare the differences in using GET and WAIT.

```
10 TEXT : HOME
20 FOR I = 1 TO 800 : PRINT "#"; : NEXT
30 PP$= "HIT ANY KEY TO CONTINUE" : HTAB 20 -
LEN(PP$)/2 : PRINT PP$
40 GET A$ : HOME
```

Now change line 40 to:

```
40 WAIT -16384,128 : HOME
```

That is relatively simple, but you can see the difference between using GET & WAIT. Sometimes you will want to use GET in order to "get" a value for a variable, or the program looks better with a flashing cursor to remind the user that input is required. It is also a good idea to clear the keyboard buffer when using WAIT. Here's how:

```
10 TEXT : HOME
20 VTAB 10 : PRINT "HIT ANY KEY TO CONTINUE: " : WAIT
-16384, 128 : POKE -16386,0 : REM POKE TO CLEAR
KEYBOARD
30 HOME : HTAB 1 : VTAB 10 : PRINT "THANKS, I NEEDED
THAT"
```

If you want to use the WAIT command with a selected key input, think of WAIT as a special kind of POKE. That is, when you press a key, the ASCII screen value of that key is put into the address of −16384, almost in the same manner as a POKE. Now, since we've been using WAIT −16384,128, it would seem that the value (128) is stored in location −16384. However, the 128 refers to an ASCII value greater than 128 when used with WAIT. If you look at the ASCII screen values, you will find that 128 is the beginning value of characters that can be entered from the keyboard—the CTRL and NORMAL characters. (To test this, try entering a control character on the above program using WAIT −16384,128.) Now to see WAIT can be used with a selected character, try the following program:

```
10 TEXT : HOME
20 W = -16384 : P = -16368 : REM USING VARIABLES
INSTEAD OF WRITING IN VALUES EACH TIME
30 VTAB 10 : PRINT "HIT ANY KEY TO CONTINUE OR 'Q' TO
QUIT->"
40 WAIT W,128 : IF PEEK (W) = 209 THEN POKE P,0 : END :
REM 209 IS THE ASCII SCREEN VALUE OF "Q"
50 POKE P, 0 : HOME : FOR I = 1 TO 800 : PRINT "*"; : NEXT
60 GOTO 10
```

Remember, PEEK simply looks into an address and sees what value is stored there. The address (−16384) is the keyboard data location and −16369 is the clear keyboard strobe. By PEEKing into the keyboard data address we can find what key was pressed last. By POKEing −16368,0 we clear the keyboard so that we do not have anything on the screen or in memory once we have finished using it. (In Appendix B you will find an ASCII Screen Chart with the values to be POKEd in for the different ASCII characters.)

Summary

This chapter has ventured into the Apple's memory, and while you are not expected to understand all of the nuances of our discussion, it is hoped that you have a general idea of how ASCII values work and a little about addresses and locations. Most important is that you have tried out some of the commands introduced and attempt to use them in your programs.

The more you use different commands, the more you begin to understand what is happening.

The CHR$ function introduced ASCII values. Some of the uses of CHR$ allows us to access characters not available from the keyboard directly, while others can be used to visually write CTRL characters in a program. This is especially useful in writing disk commands from within a program.

The POKE command enters a value to a decimal address and the PEEK command retrieves a value from an address. Special locations in your Apple's memory have special functions, such as the screen window setting and ASCII screen values. More advanced uses of POKE and PEEK can provide a way of virtually writing machine-level subroutines from APPLESOFT.

The CALL command allows the user to run a machine program or subroutine from within an APPLESOFT program. Many of the CALL commands can be written with APPLESOFT commands, but others are only accessible with the CALL function. We also learned how to locate the beginning address and length of binary files and use them with BSAVE and BLOAD commands. Finally, we saw how to stop a program with WAIT, branch on a keyboard character with PEEK, and clear the keyboard strobe with a POKE. These commands perform similar functions of earlier commands we have discussed, but these added commands provide us with added understanding and control over our computer.

CHAPTER 7
Using Graphics

Introduction

One of the nicest features of the Apple is its graphics capability. Basically, there are two kinds of graphics: (1) Low Resolution, and (2) High Resolution—referred to as Lo-Res and Hi-Res, respectively. Parts of the Apple's memory are set up to provide graphics in 8 different combinations of lo-res, hi-res and text. The command to access lo-res graphics is GR, giving the user the lo-res graphics screen with 4 lines of text at the bottom. The HGR command does the same for hi-res graphics, and the HGR2 command accesses page 2 of hi-res. In order to get to the other 5 "screens" of graphics and graphics/text, it is necessary to use POKEs. Further on in this chapter, we will discuss the POKEs required to access all 8 screens, but to get started, we will concentrate on using GR and HGR access graphics and the commands for using graphics.

LOW RESolution GRaphics

Low resolution graphics are produced with little "blocks" on the screen. They are referred to as "low resolution" since the blocks can only produce rough figures due to the size of the blocks in relation to the screen size. Think of low-res graphics as a mosaic picture. It is possible to represent a wide variety of two dimensional shapes, but they have a mosaic texture to them; hence a "low resolution."

The main advantage of low-res graphics is the wide variety of colors available. There are 16 colors, numbered from 0 to 15. To get the color you want, the command COLOR = N (N representing the color number you want). The following are the color values:

0	Black	8	Brown
1	Magenta	9	Orange
2	Dark Blue	10	Gray
3	Purple	11	Pink
4	Dark Green	12	Green
5	Gray	13	Yellow
6	Blue	14	Aqua
7	Light Blue	15	White

LO-RES AND HI-RES

If you do not have a color TV or monitor, the colors will appear as different shades of black and white or green (if you have a green screen monitor). The different color patterns will create different density in the lines and figures you create. If you have something other than a color TV or monitor, it is best to experiment with white (COLOR = 15) until you get used to the commands. Later when you get used to the line patterns created on a non-color screen, you can mix them for different effects.

Assuming you have a color screen, it might be necessary to adjust your TV/monitor to get the proper colors. On your SYSTEM MASTER, there is a handy program called COLOR DEMOSOFT that will provide a set of color bars with their color names at the bottom of the screen. RUN COLOR DEMOSOFT and the menu program called, "STANDARD COLOR NAMES." Adjust your "color," "tint" and possibly "contrast" dials on your TV until the colors are correct.

GOOD GRAPHICS AND BAD TEXT

One of the problems that users often run into when using graphics is the intensity of the color and the quality of the text. In programming with color graphics, we tend to intensify the color to get the best results. This is as it should be. However, you will notice that when you go from graphics back to text that the intensified color will result in blurred text. To solve this problem, once you have set your colors properly, only change the "color" dial—not the "tint," though. By turning the "color" dial "up" when using graphics and turning it "down" when using text (e.g., when writing programs), you can keep your color settings correct and have clear text.

Now that the color is all set, let's take a look at some commands and replicate some of the bar chart on the COLOR DEMOSOFT program. We will first get into low-res graphics with a GR command. Then, using a FOR/NEXT loop we will generate the different colors and positions on the screen for our color bars. The command VLIN will provide a vertical line for us beginning at a given starting point and terminating at an ending point at a given horizonal position.

```
10 TEXT : HOME
20 GR
30 FOR I = 0 TO 15
40    COLOR = I
50    VLIN 5, 35 AT I + 3
60 NEXT I
```

Now, let's take a closer look at what we have done. Our FOR/NEXT loop gave us our different colors by changing the value of COLOR from 0 to 15. That's simple enough. Our VLIN command drew a line from vertical position 5 to vertical postion 35 at horizontal position I + 3. That would be horizontal positions 3 to 18 on your screen. That's how we got them to line up neatly. (We used an "offset" of 3 so that our bars would not be jammed up against the left side of the screen.)

We can do the same thing with horizontal lines using the command HLIN. Let's stack our bars on top of one another.

```
10 TEXT : HOME
20 GR
30 FOR I = 0 TO 15
```

```
40    COLOR = I
50    HLIN 5, 35 AT I + 10
60 NEXT I
```

As you probably figured out, HLIN works exactly like VLIN except the lines are horizontal rather than vertical. Now, let's draw a frame around our screen in white using both HLIN and VLIN.

```
10 TEXT : HOME
20 GR : COLOR = 15
30 HLIN 0 , 39 AT 0 : REM HORIZONTAL LINE AT TOP OF
SCREEN
40 HLIN 0 , 39 AT 39 : REM HORIZONTAL LINE JUST ABOVE
TEXT PORTION
50 VLIN 0 , 39 AT 0 : REM VERTICAL LINE DOWN LEFT SIDE
60 VLIN 0 , 39 AT 39 : REM VERTICAL LINE DOWN RIGHT
SIDE
```

It's easy to make good looking, clear horizontal and vertical lines, but what about diagonal lines? Since there is no command to draw diagonal lines, we will have to use another command, PLOT, to put a little box or plot at a series of points. Let's add the following command to our last program:

```
70 FOR I = 0 TO 39 : PLOT I, I : NEXT : REM DRAWS A
DIAGONAL LINE FROM THE UPPER LEFT TO LOWER RIGHT
80 FOR I = 39 TO 0 STEP -1 : PLOT I, 39 - I : NEXT : REM
DRAWS A DIAGONAL LINE FROM THE UPPER RIGHT TO
LOWER LEFT
```

So far so good. We have made straight and diagonal lines, but other than an amusing exercise, what practical applications do lo-res graphics have? Besides games, which we will get to in a bit, we can easily make graphs and charts. We'll make a simple bar graph using a combination of lo-res graphics and the little text we have at the bottom of the screen.

```
10 TEXT : HOME
20 VTAB 10: INPUT "NAME OF PLOT -> ";NP$: HOME
30 VTAB 10: PRINT "HOW MANY PLOTS?(1-7) ";: GET P%:
PRINT P%: PRINT
40 PRINT : FOR I = 1 TO P%
50    PRINT "PLOT VALUE (0-39) FOR PLOT ";I;" ->";:
INPUT " ";V(I): IF V(I) > 39 THEN PRINT CHR$ (7): GOTO 50
60 NEXT
70 GR : COLOR = 10
80 VLIN 0,39 AT 0: HLIN 0,39 AT 39
90 FOR I = 0 TO 39 STEP 4: PLOT 1,I: NEXT
100 COLOR = 15: FOR I = 1 TO P%: VLIN 39,(39 - V(I)) AT
(I * 5): NEXT
```

```
110 HOME : FOR I = 1 TO P%: VTAB 21: HTAB (I * 5) + 1:
PRINT I: NEXT I
120 PRINT : HTAB 20 - LEN (NP$)/2: PRINT NP$
130 WAIT -16384,128: TEXT : HOME : END : REM HOLDS
GRAPH ON SCREEN UNTIL KEY IS HIT THEN CLEARS
SCREEN AND GOES BACK TO TEXT
```

RUN the program and see how nicely you can present data graphically. The program is severely limited in that it only does a maximum of 7 plots and values from 0 to 39. It is simple to change the number of plots above 7. All you have to do is to change the trap value to a higher number and the offset in line 80 to less than I * 5. You can go as low as the values of I, but then all of the bars would be adjacent. Changing the values to above 39 requires more sophisticated manipulations, however. This is because 39 represents the maximum length of a vertical plot. Using a 2 bar plot, we will examine how to enter any range of numbers we want.

```
10  TEXT : HOME
20  INPUT "MAX VALUE ->";MV
30  N = 1:NN = MV : REM FOR MORE PRECISE
    CALCULATIONS LET N = .1
40  IF NN > 39 THEN N = N + 1:NN = MV/N: GOTO 40
50  FOR I = 1 TO 2
60     INPUT "PLOT VALUE -> ";PV(I)
70     PV(I) = INT(PV(I)/N)
80  NEXT
90  GR : COLOR = 15
100 VLIN 0,39 AT 0: HLIN 0,39 AT 39
110 FOR I = 0 TO 39 STEP 4: PLOT 1,I: NEXT
120 FOR I = 1 TO 3: VLIN 39,(39 - PV(1)) AT 10 + I: NEXT
130 FOR I = 1 TO 3: VLIN 39,(39 - PV(2)) AT 20 + I: NEXT
140 WAIT -16384,128 : TEXT : HOME : REM CLEARS
    GRAPHICS MODE AND SCREEN
```

In order to understand what happened, we will go over the significant lines and explain what happened.

1. In line 30 the variable NN was defined to equal the maximum value (MV) entered in line 20.
2. In line 40, the crucial line for creating a proportional scale, NN was compared with 39 to find if the maximum value was greater than 39. If it was greater then the counter variable N was incremented by 1 and NN was re-defined to be the value of MV divided by N and looped back to the beginning of the line for another comparison. As soon as the value of N increased to a point where the maximum value, MV, divided by N was not greater

than 39, the loop is exited. Whatever the value of N is at that time will be used in the rest of the program to divide any value entered.

For example—The value of MV is established to be 100. Since 100 is greater than 39, 1 is added to N and 100 is divided by 2 resulting in the value of NN equaling 50. Since 50 is still larger than 39, N is incremented to 3. When MV is divided by 3, the result is 33.33. This time, when the comparison to 39 is made, it is found that NN is not larger than 39 and so the line is exited and the value of N is established at 3. No matter what value is entered, as long as it does not exceed the maximum value, there will be no errors since all plot values, PV (1) etc., will be divided by 3. Since 100 is the maximum value to be entered, 33 is the maximum value that will be charted.

3. Two values for PV (I) are entered in line 60, and in line 70, PV(I) is divided by N. The INT command is introduced to provide an integer (whole) number for charting.
4. In lines 90 through 110 the chart outline is set up.
5. In lines 120 and 130 our charts are plotted, using 3 vertical lines to make each bar. This is done using a FOR/NEXT loop of 3 incrementing the horizontal placement by 1 each time through the loop.

FOR THE PERFECTIONIST WITH SOME TIME

We incremented N by 1 each time we passed through our test loop in line 40. If we wanted to get a finer value, we could have incremented N by .1 or .01 or even .00001! This would give us a nearer minimum value by which to divide PV(I) and still keep it proportional. However, it would take longer for the loop to find the minimum value of N. Change the program to see the different results in the charts. The smaller the increment, the closer to the top of the chart the maximum value will appear, but the longer the program will take to execute.

We have spent a good deal of time working on charts in lo-res graphics, but it is important to see the practical applications of such graphics. Often users simply see lo-res graphics as something to draw mosaic pictures on and nothing else, but as we have seen, it is possible to make very good practical use of them as well. Now let's have a little fun before going on to hi-res graphics.

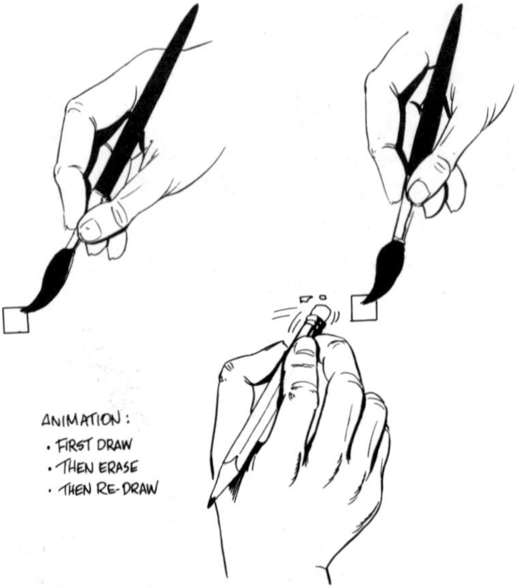

Animation in lo-res can be used in games and special effects. However, we will only touch upon some elementary examples to provide you with the concepts of how animation works. Basically, you plot a position in any color except black and then plot a new position and cover up the old position in black. This gives the appearance of a "block" moving since it is plotted from one adjacent position to another, its previous position being "erased" with a black plot. For example, from the immediate mode, enter the following:

```
GR : COLOR = 15 : PLOT 20, 20 : <RETURN>
COLOR = 0 : PLOT 20, 20 : COLOR = 15 : PLOT 21, 20
```

If you watched carefully, you saw what appeared to be a moving "block." However, we can see from what we entered, that it is really a matter of plotting a block in one position, erasing it and drawing it in an adjacent position. For a more dramatic example, the following program will start in the upper right hand corner of your screen and "bounce" a white block around your screen:

```
10 TEXT : HOME : GR
20 FOR I = 1 TO 38: PLOT I,I : COLOR = 15 : PLOT I + 1, I
+ 1 : COLOR = 0 : NEXT
30 COLOR = 0 : PLOT 39,39 : REM CLEAR THE BLOCK IN
```

```
THE CORNER
40 FOR I = 39 TO 1 STEP −1 : PLOT I, 38 : COLOR = 15:
PLOT I − 1,38 : COLOR = 0 : NEXT
50 COLOR = 0 : PLOT 0,38
60 FOR I = 1 TO 39 : PLOT I, 39 − I : COLOR = 0 : PLOT
I,39 − I : COLOR = 15 : NEXT
70 COLOR = 0 : PLOT 39, 0
80 FOR I = 39 TO 1 STEP −1 : PLOT I,0 : COLOR = 15 :
PLOT I − 1,0 : COLOR = 0: NEXT
```

By experimenting with different algorithms, you can do anything from making letters and numbers to animated games.

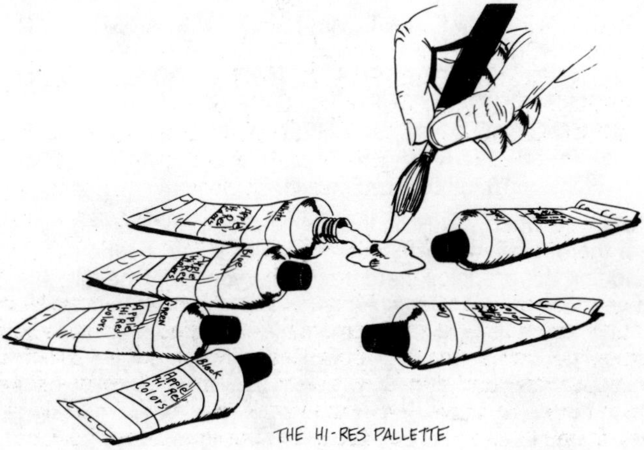

THE HI-RES PALLETTE

HIgh RESolution GRaphics

Once you understand lo-res graphics, you will understand most of hi-res graphics. However, there are some important differences. The following chart summarizes the differences:

LO-RES	HI-RES
16 Colors	8 Colors
40 by 48 Matrix	280 by 192 Matrix
Line Commands	HPLOT Commands only

The above are the main differences, but there are other differences that are not so easily summarized. One of the differences has to do with preserving a graphics screen. If you exit a lo-res drawing and enter TEXT and HOME, the graphics you have drawn are destroyed. You can test this by drawing a simple lo-res graphics and then returning to the graphics "page" with POKEs. For example, the following program will draw a simple lo-res graphics, clear back to the text page and then return to the graphics with POKES.

```
10 TEXT : HOME
20 GR : COLOR = 15
30 FOR I = 0 TO 39 : PLOT I, I : NEXT : REM DRAWS A
DIAGONAL LINE
40 PRINT "HIT ANY KEY TO CONTINUE"; : WAIT -16384,128
: POKE -16368,0
50 TEXT : HOME : LIST : REM SHOW YOU ARE BACK IN THE
TEXT SCREEN
60 POKE -16304,0 : POKE -16300,0 : POKE -16298,0 :
REM POKES TO RETURN TO LO-RES GRAPHICS
DESTROYING WHAT IS CURRENTLY THERE
70 PRINT "HIT ANY KEY TO CONTINUE"; : WAIT -16384,128
: POKE -16368,0 : TEXT : END
```

As you can see when you RUN the above program, the diagonal line is no longer there. However, with hi-res graphics if you did the same thing, you would find the graphics there waiting for you. RUN the following program to see:

```
10 TEXT : HOME
20 HGR : HCOLOR = 3 : REM COLOR FOR WHITE
30 HPLOT 0,0 TO 279, 155 : REM DRAWS DIAGONAL LINE
40 VTAB 22 : PRINT "HIT ANY KEY TO CONTINUE";: WAIT
-16384,128 : POKE -16368,0
50 TEXT : HOME : LIST
60 HTAB 1 : VTAB 22 : PRINT "HIT ANY KEY TO CONTINUE";:
WAIT -16384,128 : POKE -16368,0
70 POKE -16304,0 : POKE -16301,0 : POKE -16300,0 :
POKE -16297,0 : REM POKES FOR HI-RES PAGE 1
WITHOUT DESTROYING CURRENT GRAPHICS
80 HTAB 1 : VTAB 22 : PRINT "HIT ANY KEY TO CONTINUE";:
WAIT -16384,128 : POKE -16368,0
90 TEXT : END
```

This time, you saw the diagonal line. For most applications, as long as you do not enter HGR, your graphics will remain on the graphics page. In larger programs, it is possible for APPLESOFT to "crash" into the hi-res memory area and destroy or distort your graphics. Normally, however, you can put up a hi-res graphics picture and it will stay there, even if you type in NEW or FP. To see for yourself, key in the POKEs in line 70. Your hi-res graphics should still be there. (If they are go tell all your friends.) We'll return to the POKEs later in more detail.

Now that we've seen an important difference between hi-res and lo-res in terms of keeping graphics in memory, let's draw some. The HPLOT command will put a "dot" (called a "pixel") in the coordinates you specify in a range of 0 to 279 horizontally and 0 to 191 vertically. The syntax is HPLOT X,Y with "X" being the horizonal position and "Y" being the vertical. We'll start with a dot in the upper left hand corner. From the immediate mode, key in:

```
HGR : HCOLOR = 3 : HPLOT 0,0 : VTAB 22
```

You should be able to see a little white dot. To draw lines, you HPLOT from X,Y to X',Y'. For example:

```
HGR : HCOLOR = 3 : HPLOT 0,0 TO 279,0 : VTAB 22
```

That drew a line across the top of your screen. Now, you may be wondering why there is a VTAB 22 at the end of the line. That's because, only the bottom 4 lines are in text, and if you did not put in the VTAB 22 you would not be able to see your cursor. It would be "behind" the graphics screen.

With HPLOT it is possible to begin at a point and draw all over the screen with a single HPLOT command and several TO commands. For example, try the following program:

```
10 TEXT : HOME
20 HGR : HCOLOR = 3
30 HPLOT 0,0 TO 279,0 TO 0,150 TO 279, 150
40 Z$ ="THE MARK OF ZORRO!": VTAB 22: HTAB 20 –
LEN(Z$)/2 : PRINT Z$
50 WAIT –16384,128 : TEXT : HOME
```

Experiment with different plots and colors until you're comfortable with them.

One function of the Apple we have not yet explored is the RND function. It is a random number generator, and it will generate a range of random numbers. It is introduced here since it is fun to use with graphics. The basic syntax is RND (N) giving a number less than 1 but greater than 0. Usually, we are looking for a range of numbers greater than 1 and numbers that have no fractional parts. The following is a handy little formula for generating a range of numbers from 1 to N, with N being the upper limit of random numbers to be generated:

```
INT (RND (1) * (N) + 1)
```

To see how it works, key in the following program:

```
10 TEXT : HOME
20 FOR I = 1 TO 66
```

```
30 PRINT INT (RND (1) * (10) + 1), : REM GENERATES
RANDOM NUMBERS FROM 1 TO 10
40 NEXT
```

Now, let's use the random number generator in a program with hi-res graphics. The random number generator will be used to make the computer "create" a picture for us, using different colors and lines. In other words, we will have a program that does the graphics drawing, with each one being different.

```
10 TEXT : HOME
20 REM HI-RES RANDOM GRAPHIC GENERATOR **
STARBURST **
30 N = 0
40 X = 100 : Y = 100 : REM X,Y AXIS FOR CENTER OF
'STARBURST'
50 HGR
60 RC = INT (7 * RND (1)) + 1 : REM GENERATES RANDOM
COLOR VALUES
70 REM GENERATE RANDOM MAXIMUM X AND Y AXIS
POINTS
80 X2 = INT (279 * RND (1))
90 Y2 = INT (158 * RND (1))
100 HCOLOR = RC
110 HPLOT X,Y TO X2,Y2
120 N = N + 1 : IF N = 100 THEN 140
130 GOTO 60
140 A$ = "STARBURST" : VTAB 22 : FLASH : HTAB 20 –
LEN(A$)/2: PRINT A$: NORMAL : WAIT –16384,128 : TEXT :
HOME
```

By now you should be able to see the different ways it is possible to draw lines on the hi-res screen. Sometimes, though, we may want to draw on some other background other than black. Wouldn't it be nice to draw on a blue or green background? Well, if you think that's what we're going to do next, you're absolutely right! To clear the screen to the most recent HCOLOR we have used to plot lines, we use the CALL 62454 command. That command CALLs a monitor subroutine that will flood the screen with the most recent HCOLOR. The following program draws a rough "hourglass" (actually an "X" with horizontal lines on the top and bottom) in the color of your choice and then clears the screen to that color. Notice that instead of using a CALL 62454, we define the variable C to be 62454 and then use a CALL C. This is done to show you that in programs where you would be using CALL 62454 in several different places, it's a lot easier to simply write in CALL C. (It's only used once in our program, but you get the idea.)

```
10 TEXT : HOME : REM **CLEAR TO COLOR**
20 HGR
30 VTAB 21 : PRINT "ENTER COLOR (0 TO 7)" : INPUT
"(COLORS 0 AND 4 ARE BLACK) " ; HC
40 HCOLOR = HC
50 HPLOT 0,0 TO 279,155 TO 0,155 TO 279,0 TO 0,0
60 VTAB 22 : CALL -875 : PRINT "HIT ANY KEY TO
CONTINUE" : REM CALL -875 CLEARS THE LINE OF
PREVIOUS TEXT
70 WAIT -16384,128 : POKE -16368,0
80 C = 62454: REM ADDRESS FOR CLEARING SCREEN TO
MOST RECENT HCOLOR
90 CALL C
100 WAIT -16384,128 : TEXT : HOME : LIST
```

GRAPHICS PACKAGES CAN TURN YOU INTO A COMPUTER ARTIST!

The power of the Apple's graphics are considerable. There are several commercial programs available to allow you to write in hi-res fonts, draw several different figures and generally use your computer as an artist would use a canvas or a draftsman a drafting board. Of course, you can write a program yourself to allow you to do the same thing. To give you an idea of how such programs work, we have provided the "Very, Very Poor Person's Drawing Board." Key it in and play with it.

```
10 TEXT : HOME
20 ONERR GOTO 10
```

```
30  HOME : HGR : HCOLOR = 3: VTAB 23
40  PRINT "LINES OR FIGURES?(L/F)": INVERSE : PRINT
"'C'";: NORMAL : PRINT " TO CLEAR";: VTAB 23: HTAB 38:
GET AZ$: IF AZ$ = "F" THEN 130
50  IF AZ$ = "C" THEN 30
60  HOME : VTAB 23: INPUT "HOR PLOT, VERT PLOT
BEGIN- -> ";H,V
70  INPUT "HOR PLOT, VERT PLOT END - -> ";HE,VE
80  HPLOT H,V TO HE,VE
90  HOME : VTAB 23: PRINT "ANOTHER?(Y/N) ";: GET AN$
100  IF AN$ = "N" THEN INVERSE : PRINT " CLEAR
SCREEN?(Y/N)? "; : NORMAL : GET CL$: IF CL$ = "Y" THEN
TEXT : HOME : END
110  IF CL$ = "N" THEN END
120  GOTO 40
130  HOME : VTAB 21: PRINT "(S)QUARE,(T)RIANGLE": PRINT
"(R)ECTANGLE,(P)ARALLELOGRAM": PRINT "CHOOSE BY
LETTER-> "; : GET L$:
140  IF L$ = "S" THEN HPLOT 0,0 TO 255,0 TO 255,150 TO
0,150 TO 0,0
150  IF L$ = "T" THEN HPLOT 127,0 TO 255,150 TO 0,150 TO
127,0
160  IF L$ = "R" THEN HPLOT 0,20 TO 255,20 TO 255,90 TO
0,90 TO 0,20
170  IF L$ = "P" THEN HPLOT 20,20 TO 200,20 TO 180,80 TO
0,80 TO 20,20
180  GOTO 90
```

As you can see, the "Very, Very Poor Person's Drawing Board" allows you to enter different figures simply by going to subroutines. This saves a lot of HPLOTting every time you want a simple figure. However, wouldn't it be nice if you could INPUT the size of the figure you wanted and the computer did everything else. As we saw in the above program, we were able to INPUT different line sizes and angles, but we were stuck with a single figure size. The following program shows you how to INPUT a figure of different sizes. Again, it is relatively simple and always begins the figure in the upper left hand corner and only draws a square, but it will give you an idea how such graphics can be done.

```
10  TEXT : HOME : REM **INPUT SQUARE**
20  INPUT "SIZE OF SQUARE (1 TO 155)-> "; SS
30  HGR : HCOLOR = 3
40  HPLOT 0,0 TO SS,0 TO SS,SS TO 0,SS TO 0,0 : REM
HPLOTS A SQUARE TO YOUR SPECIFICATIONS
50  HTAB 1: VTAB 22: CALL -875 : PRINT "ANOTHER
```

```
SQUARE?(Y/N) "; : GET AN$: IF AN$ = "N" THEN TEXT :
HOME :END
60  IF AN$ = "Y" THEN 10
70  GOTO 50 : REM A TRAP FOR NOT GETTING A "Y" OR "N"
```

So far, we've only dealt with figures that have straight lines, HPLOTting the sides of the figures. That limits us, but when we start getting into making curves and circles, we have to make a quantum leap in com-

mands. Using the SIN command, which gives us a sine value, and COS command, for cosine, we can make curves and even circles. At this point, if you have a good math background, you probably understand how these calculations are used. However, if you do not, simply make a note of the algorithm used, and whenever you need a circle, you can use it. Since there are several calculations occurring, it will take a while for the circle to be completely drawn. Be patient, though, your Apple will patiently draw it before your eyes.

```
10  TEXT : HOME : HGR : HCOLOR = 3 : REM **HGR
CIRCLE**
20  FOR I = 0 TO 6.3 STEP .01
30  R = 40 : XPLACE = 100 : YPLACE = 75 : REM R =
RADIUS – XPLACE = HOR START – YPLACE = VERT
START
40  X = R * COS (I) + XPLACE
```

```
50 Y = (R/4) * SIN (I)/.3 + YPLACE
60 HPLOT X,Y
70 HPLOT TO X,Y
80 NEXT
90 VTAB 22 : HTAB 1 : PRINT "HIT ANY KEY TO CLEAR"; :
WAIT -16384,128 : TEXT : HOME
100 REM TRY CHANGING THE VALUE OF R, XPLACE AND
YPLACE
```

It is important that you experiment, even with commands such as SIN and COS that you may not understand. Also, you might want to want to take a look at an old geometry or trigonometry book to brush up on what sine and cosine do. Just for fun, of course. . . .

Keeping Your Graphics Intact: Looking Without Losing

Suppose you spend a lot of time with a graphics drawing, made with a program you've slaved over. As you develop your graphics, you may not want to wait while it slowly draws circles and puts your masterpiece on the screen every time you edit your program. However, with so little room at the bottom of the hi-res screen for you to examine your listing, you need to TEXT the screen to see your listing. To get back to the hi-res screen, you have to HGR, and as you know by now, that will blast anything on the screen. In order to keep your graphic drawing intact after you have left hi-res, you will need to POKE in certain values that put you on the hi-res screen(s). As we saw in our comparison of hi-res and lo-res, we can keep our pictures in memory. The following POKEs are handy to know for doing that:

POKE	WHAT IT DOES
POKE −16304,0	Goes to graphics
POKE −16302,0	Full graphics
POKE −16301,0	Text & graphics
POKE −16300,0	Page 1
POKE −16299,0	Page 2
POKE −16298,0	Lo-res
POKE −16297,0	Hi-Res

To use these POKEs, you can either enter them from the immediate mode or within a program. It is better to have them somewhere in a program since it is necessary to enter at least 4 POKEs to access a hi-res screen.

The following program shows how they can be used to draw on the hi-res screen, enter the TEXT mode and then re-enter the hi-res screen without destroying the graphics there.

```
10 TEXT : HOME : HGR : HCOLOR = 3
20 HPLOT 0,70 TO 279,70
30 HPLOT 140,0 TO 140,155 : REM DRAWS A CROSS
40 HTAB 1 : VTAB 22 : PRINT "HIT ANY KEY FOR TEXT –> ";
: WAIT –16384,128 : POKE –16368,050 TEXT : HOME : VTAB
10 : PRINT "THIS IS THE TEXT SCREEN!!!"
60 VTAB 22 : INVERSE : PRINT "HIT ANY KEY TO RETURN
TO YOUR PICTURE –> "; : NORMAL : WAIT –16384,128 :
POKE –16368,0
70 POKE –16304,0 : POKE –16301,0 : POKE –16300,0 :
POKE –16297,0 : REM POKES TO RETURN TO PAGE 1 HI-
RES GRAPHICS WITH TEXT AT BOTTOM
80 HOME : VTAB 22 : HTAB 1 : PRINT "WE'RE BACK TO
GRAPHICS!!"
```

When you RUN this program, you will first see the graphics "cross," then the text in the middle of the screen, and finally the cross again.

In discussing lo-res graphics we saw how we could create animation by PLOTing a "block," then drawing over it with black, and then PLOTing another point. The same can be done in hi-res as well to create animation. However, there is something else we can do with hi-res and animation that we did not do in lo-res. We can "toggle" the two hi-res screens. So far, we've only used hi-res screen 1 (or page 1). By using both screens 1 and 2 of hi-res, it is possible to draw images on both, and then by using POKE –16300,0 (Page 1) and POKE –16299,0 (Page 2), we can alternate the graphics. The following program illustrates how this is done:

```
10 TEXT : HOME : HGR2 : HGR : HCOLOR = 3: REM
CLEARS EVERYTHING!
20 HPLOT 50,70 TO 100,70
30 HPLOT 55,70 TO 95,50 TO 95,70
40 HGR2
50 HPLOT 50,70 TO 100,70
60 HPLOT 55,70 TO 95,60 TO 95,70
70    FOR I = 1 TO 30: FOR J = 1 TO 100: NEXT J: POKE –
16300,0: FOR K = 1 TO 100: NEXT K: POKE – 16299,0:
NEXT : REM TOGGLES HI-RES PAGE 1 AND 2
1000 WAIT – 16384,128: TEXT : LIST
```

In line 70, there are 3 loops. The "I" loop sets the number of times the screens will be toggled at 30. The "J" and "K" loops simply delay the screen toggles long enough so that it does not appear that a single combined picture of HGR and HGR2 images is on the screen all by itself. By changing the HPLOTs in lines 20 and 30 and 50 and 60, you can create your own animations.

BSAVING YOUR GRAPHICS

In chapter 6, we saw how to BSAVE binary files. Graphics can also be saved to the disk as 34 sector binary files. However, rather than having to determine the starting address and length of your binary graphics file, it is possible to remember two simple addresses and lengths. They are:

```
HI-RES PAGE 1      A$2000,L$2000
HI-RES PAGE 2      A$4000,L$2000
```

Graphics on Page 1 start at hex address $2000 and have a length of $2000, while those on Page 2 start at $4000 and have a length of $2000. Therefore, all you have to remember is $2000 and $4000. If you don't want to do that, use the following program to do it for you.

```
10 TEXT : HOME : REM **PICTURE CAPTURE**
20 D$ = CHR$(13) + CHR$(4)
30 HOME : VTAB 4 : INPUT "WHAT NAME DO YOU WANT
FOR THIS PICTURE? "; NA$
40 HOME : VTAB 4 : INPUT "WHAT DRIVE? "; R%
```

```
50  HOME : VTAB 4: INPUT "PAGE 1 OR PAGE 2? "; PG%
60  IF PG% = 2 THEN PRINT D$; "BSAVE " NA$ ",A$4000,
L$2000,D"R%
70  IF PG% < > 1 THEN GOTO 50
80  PRINT D$ "BSAVE"; NA$; ",A$2000, L$2000,D"R%
90  INPUT " DO YOU WANT TO CONTINUE? "; AN$: IF AN$ =
"Y" THEN GOTO 10
100  HOME : VTAB 10: PRINT "DONE FOR NOW" : END
```

To use the above program, draw your graphics on the screen, TEXT back to the text screen and RUN the program. It will save your graphics on disk.

Now, to get your graphics back! You can simply BLOAD your picture (e.g., BLOAD <FILE NAME>) or, you can BLOAD your graphics to Page 1 or Page 2. Since a picture BSAVEd from Page 1 or Page 2 will automatically BLOAD to the appropriate screen, you do not have to include an address (e.g., A$2000 or A$4000), but if you want to load a picture to a screen other than the one to which it was BSAVEd, then the loading address must be included. For example, if you BSAVEd a file named "PICTURE" from hi-res screen 1 and wanted to bring it up on HGR2, you would have to:

```
BLOAD PICTURE, A$4000
```

To view your pictures, you can either POKE in the appropriate addresses after the picture is loaded, or use HGR or HGR2 and BLOAD them "in the dark." That's simple enough, but the following little program will do it all for you.

```
10  TEXT : HOME : D$ = CHR$(13) + CHR$(4) : REM
**PICTURE LOADER**
20  L$ = "= = = = = = = = = = = = = = = = = = = = = = =;
eq= = = = = = = = = ":VTAB 20 : PRINT L$: VTAB 22 : PRINT L$
: VTAB 21 : INPUT "NAME OF PICTURE -> "; PIC$
30  VTAB 23 : PRINT "PAGE 1 OR 2 " ; : GET P%
40  IF P% = 2 THEN 110
100  POKE -16304,0 : POKE -16302,0: POKE -16300,0:
POKE -16297,0 : REM PAGE 1 POKES
105  GOTO 200
110  POKE -16304,0 : POKE -16302,0: POKE -16299,0:
POKE -16297,0 : REM PAGE 2 POKES
120  GOTO 210
200  PRINT D$;'BLOAD" PIC$ ",A$2000"
205  GOTO 300
210  PRINT D$;'BLOAD" PIC$ ",A$4000"
300  END
```

Using the above program, you will be able to see your picture as it is loaded to either hi-res screen.

Other Aspects Of Graphics And Graphic Packages

Everything we have discussed in this chapter you have been able to do without any special hardware using the simple BASIC programming commands on your Apple. However, there is a great deal more possible with advanced programming techniques and/or special hardware and commercial programs. In this section, I would like to briefly point out some of these other graphic capabilities and tools.

> **A WORD FROM OUR SPONSOR**
>
> There are numerous commercial programs and hardware devices for the Apple. In fact, one of the major advantages of owning an Apple is that you can purchase many different packages to do just about anything. In chapter 10, besides some handy little programs to help you get started, there is a section on various commercial programs to do different things. One area of application in which you will find such programs and hardware very useful is in graphics. Take a look at the section on graphics programs in Chapter 10 to get an idea of what is available.

Shapes

Shape tables are special binary tables that create hi-res images on the screen. They can be moved, rotated and changed in scale. Once the shape is constructed, and BSAVEd on disk, it is relatively simple to have all kinds of animation, using commands such as DRAW, XDRAW, ROT, and SCALE. To make shapes without special programs requires a lot of patience and programming skills beyond the novice level. It is far simpler to purchase one of several commercial programs available to make shapes than construct your own shape tables from scratch. The program package, "APPLE MECHANIC" by Beagle Bros. Micro Software, not only has an excellent routine for making shapes, it comes with an outstanding "Tip Book" that explains how shapes are constructed.

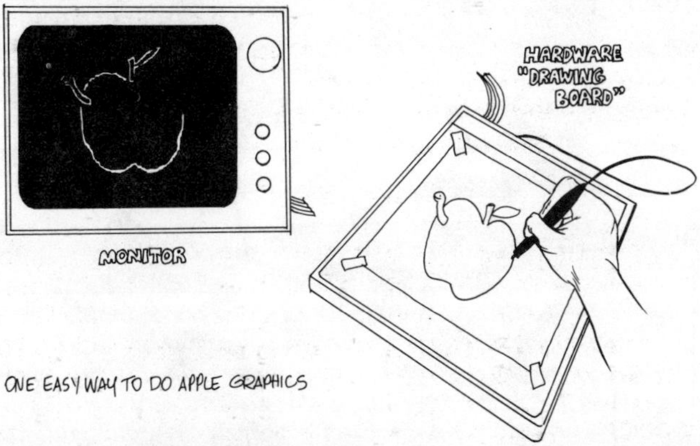

ONE EASY WAY TO DO APPLE GRAPHICS

Hardware And Software Drawing Devices

If HPLOTting pictures is too confining for your artistic skills, you may want to purchase either a hardware "drawing board" or software package that provides drawing capabilities with the game paddles, joystick or keyboard. Using "electronic pens," and drawing either on a drawing board or on the screen, there are devices for easily making two or three dimensional drawings, just as you would on canvas or with mechanical drawing tools. However, these items tend to be expensive. For a lot less money, and a little less convenience, there are numerous software packages that do essentially the same things. About the only thing that you cannot easily do with the software that can be done with the hardware is to "trace" over images to be drawn on the screen.

Fonts

If you want to create interesting messages on your screen, you will find the many hi-res fonts available to be a lot of fun and very practical. "Fonts" are the different styles of lettering, such as art-deco, Old English, gothic and similar artistic alphabetic and numeric characters. They have practical uses in easily creating fancy letterheads, advertisements, and labeling hi-res graphs and charts. (You may have noticed that other than the 4 lines at the bottom of your screen, you do not have the capability to write alphanumeric characters on the screen.) Most commercial font programs come with "font editors" to allow you to create your own fonts.

YOU CAN USE YOUR APPLE AS A CAMERA

Computer Photography

Whenever we see a "photograph" of other planets, or even photographs of earth from weather satellites, we are actually viewing computerized representations. With the right equipment, consisting of a small television camera and a hardware adaptation, it is possible to take "photographs" with your Apple and save them to disk in a manner very similar to satellite "photography." You can "dump" (or print) your "photos" from disk to a printer. Since the "photos" are simply a configuraton of dots on the hi-res screen, it is a simple matter to crop, change and enhance them either with drawing programs or HPLOTs.

Summary

This chapter has explored the many different graphic capabilities of the Apple. Beginning with lo-resolution graphics, we saw that it is possible to program mosaic-like images on the screen in 16 colors. Using the four lines of text at the bottom of the screen, it was possible to create very crisp bar charts with labels. Also, we saw how, using black to "erase" images, animation was possible.

Hi-resolution graphics, while decreasing our choice of colors, increased the choice of shapes we could make. The HPLOT command was used to create lines, figures and even circles. The RND function was introduced to add random drawings (or anything else) to our warehouse of commands. We also saw how to use special POKEs to switch from HGR to HGR2 without erasing our graphics and then create animation by switching the two screens. Finally, we learned how to BLOAD, and BSAVE graphics from and to the disk. All in all, while we saw that graphics can be a lot of fun, there are numerous practical applications as well.

CHAPTER 8

Text Files And The Disk System

Introduction

In this chapter we are going to learn more about how to work with the disk system and also how to create data files. We will be covering three types of files: (1) EXEC files, (2) Sequential Text files, and (3) Random Access files. All of the files we will be discussing are one type of text file or another, but while they are similar, they do different things in somewhat different ways. What we are calling "EXEC" files are actually text files that we want to access or execute, while sequential and random access files are types of data storage systems.

You are going to find the functions in this chapter to be extremely practical. First, we will see how an EXEC file can be used to "key in" commands for you and save programs and subroutines in text files. Its like having a robot at the keyboard! Secondly, we are going to make simple sequential text and random access files. These files are very useful for storing information you have entered, and rather than having to enter the data all over again, you simply OPEN the data file and READ it. We will make a simple program for keeping and updating names, cities and states to show how these files work.

"MON" COMMANDS LET YOU "OVERHEAR" COMMUNICATION BETWEEN YOUR COMPUTER AND THE DISK SYSTEM

Before we get started, though, two useful commands we should know are MON and NOMON. Usually, we are left out of the communication between our computer and disk system. However, using the MON command, we can see what's going on between the computer and the disk. We can view disk (C)ommands, (I)nput and/or (O)utput. For example, if we write in,

MONCIO (or MON C,I,O)

we could see the disk commands (input and output between our computer and disk drive). Usually, there is no reason to do this, but if you wish to debug a program that accesses the disk system a good deal, it is a handy tool to have, for it allows you to detect any possible bugs between your computer and disk. Once you "turn on" your MON command, it will stay on until you enter

NOMONCIO (or NOMON C,I,O)

Therefore, if you want to watch computer-disk communication for a while, use MON and when you're finished, enter the NOMON command.

TEXT FILES

TO EXCESS OR NOT TO EXCESS

One of the more confusing aspects of the Apple computer for beginners is the different options available for performing a single function. In the DOS manual that comes with your Apple drives, the format for MON and NOMON includes spaces and commas separating MON and C,I,O. Well, you don't need the spaces and commas and it's less work to enter MONCIO or NOMONCIO than MON C,I,O or NOMON C,I,O. My own inclination is to omit excess entries wherever possible, and elsewhere in this chapter we will take shortcuts that may appear to conflict with your manual, but they work perfectly well. However, if you like the added spaces, commas, etc. for clarity, then by all means use them.

Create EXEC Files (And Leave The Driving To Them)

EXEC files are text files that you can EXECecute with the DOS command EXEC. Depending on what's in the files, you can either put a program into memory or have your computer "key in" several commands as though the computer took over the keyboard. First, we will examine how to put a program into a text file and then how to have the program "key in" commands.

Snatching A Program In Mid-air

The purpose of this section is to show how to place a program or subroutine into a text file. Now, you may well ask yourself, "Why in the world would you want to do that?" After all, it is a lot simpler to SAVE a program to the disk. That's is a good point, except whenever you LOAD or RUN a program, it wipes out whatever program is in memory. However, using text files and the EXEC command, it is possible to LOAD one program and then append another program to it by EXECing its text file. For example, key in the following two partial programs and save them both to the disk under the names "ENTER STRINGS" and "CENTER STRINGS":

```
10 TEXT : HOME : REM ENTER STRINGS
20 VTAB 10 : INPUT "HOW MANY STRINGS TO ENTER
(1-20) "; N%
30 DIM S$(N%)
40 HOME: FOR I = 1 TO N%
50 PRINT "STRING #"; I; " -->"; :INPUT " "; S$(I)
60 NEXT I : HOME
70 FOR J = 1 TO N% : GOSUB 1000
80 NEXT J
90 END
```

Now SAVE the above part as a program called "ENTER STRINGS," and write in NEW to clear it out of memory (AFTER you have SAVEd it to the disk). Next key in the following:

```
1000 HTAB 20 - LEN(S$(J))/2 : PRINT S$(J)
1010 RETURN
```

Now save lines 1000 and 1010 to the disk as "CENTER STRINGS." If you want to put these two pieces together, you will find it to be impossible without a special program or by re-entering the lines by keying them in. However, if one part or the other is written as a text file, it is a simple matter to LOAD one part and EXEC the other. So let's do that. To create a text file, we use the commands, OPEN, WRITE, and CLOSE. We first issue OPEN and WRITE commands using CHR$(13) and CHR$(4). Then we enter the contents of the text files, and finally, using CHR$(4), we close the text file. (We have defined CHR$(13) + CHR$(4) as D$ and CHR$(4) by itself as

D1$. We could have used D$ for all three commands (OPEN, WRITE, and CLOSE) but when we start writing sequential and random access files, there is a good reason to use D$ and D1$, and we might as well get in the habit of doing it this way.

First, LOAD CENTER STRINGS. Next, DELETE CENTER STRINGS. (This will delete CENTER STRINGS as an 'A' file, but you will see that CENTER STRINGS is still in memory.) Now, write in the following BUT DO NOT TYPE IN "NEW"!:

```
1 TEXT : HOME
2 D$ = CHR$(13) + CHR$(4) : D1$ = CHR$(4)
3 PRINT D$ "OPEN CENTER STRINGS" : PRINT D$ "WRITE
CENTER STRINGS"
4 POKE 33,30
5 LIST 1000,1010
6 PRINT "NOMONCIO"
7 PRINT D1$ "CLOSE CENTER STRINGS"
8 END
```

When you LIST the program now it should look like this:

```
1 TEXT : HOME
2 D$ = CHR$(13) + CHR$(4) : D1$ = CHR$(4)
3 PRINT D$ "OPEN CENTER STRINGS" : PRINT D$ "WRITE
```

```
CENTER STRINGS"
4 POKE 33,30
5 LIST 1000,1010
6 PRINT D1$ "CLOSE CENTER STRINGS"
7 END
1000 HTAB 20 - LEN(S$(J))/2 : PRINT S$(J)
1010 RETURN
```

Now, RUN the program. You will hear your disk whirling. It is writing a 'T' file called "CENTER STRINGS." When the disk stops, CATALOG your disk and you will now see the file CENTER STRINGS.

Now, write in NEW and FP to make sure everything is cleared from memory. First, LOAD the program "ENTER STRINGS," LIST the program to make sure it does NOT have lines 1000 and 1010. (If it does, DEL 1000,1010.) Everything is all set to EXEC CENTER STRINGS. Do it. Your disk should whirl and soon stop. Now, LIST your program, and voila! There is your complete program. Lines 1000 and 1010 were placed into a text file and then "released" with an EXEC statement. This is a very handy way to store little subroutines you use in a lot of your programs. Rather than having to re-write your common or lengthy subroutines every time you want them in a program, all you have to do is EXEC them into the program portion you have keyed in. However, you must be careful as to what line numbers you use, for if you have two subroutines in text files with the same range of line numbers, you'll get strange results! By blocking your important subroutines within 1000 range blocks (e.g., 1000–1999, 2000–2999) and keeping track of what subroutines are in what blocks, you will not have conflicts when they are EXECed.

Making EXEC Files Do The Work: Robot EXECs

Another important use of EXEC files is in their ability to issue commands as though they were coming from the keyboard. We saw how to issue DOS commands using CTRL-D or CHR$(4) from within a program, and we can use EXEC files to do the same thing but much more. To make a "ROBOT" EXEC file that will take over the keyboard, it is necessary to set up special formats, using PRINT statements to issue the correct commands. For example, the following little ROBOT EXEC file will catalog your disk:

```
10 TEXT : HOME
20 D$ = CHR$(13) + CHR$(4) : D1$ = CHR$(4)
30 PRINT D$ "OPEN CAT": PRINT D$ "WRITE CAT"
40 PRINT "CATALOG"
50 PRINT D1$ "CLOSE CAT"
```

RUN the program to create a text file called "CAT." Now, EXEC CAT and your disk drive should spin and CATALOG your diskette. When it does, notice that the file CAT is there.

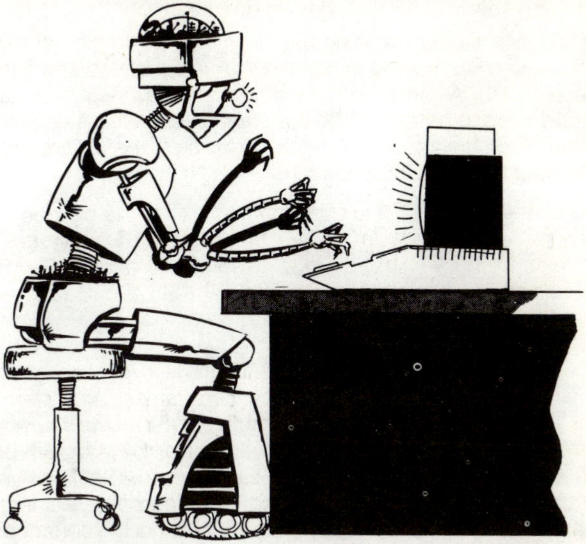

ROBOT EXEC

In some programs it is necessary to load different "supporting" files to get the program to work properly. Using a ROBOT EXEC is useful since rather than having to type in all the LOADs, BLOADs, and EXECs yourself, you can have a ROBOT EXEC do it for you. For example, let's create a ROBOT EXEC to put ENTER STRINGS and CENTER STRINGS together for us and LIST and RUN it as well. Additionally, we are using the MON and NOMON commands so that you can see what's happening between the computer and disk system.

```
10 TEXT : HOME
20 D$ = CHR$(13) + CHR$(4) : D1$ = CHR$(4)
30 PRINT D$ "OPEN COMBINE": PRINT D$ "WRITE
COMBINE"
40 PRINT "MONCIO"
50 PRINT "LOAD ENTER STRINGS"
60 PRINT "LIST"
70 PRINT "EXEC CENTER STRINGS"
80 PRINT D1$ "CLOSE COMBINE"
```

First RUN the above program to create the file COMBINE. Make sure your disk has the Applesoft file "ENTER STRINGS" and the text file "CENTER STRINGS" on it and then EXEC COMBINE. Watch what happens as the ROBOT EXEC takes control of your computer. Now enter RUN.

As a final demonstration of using EXEC files, we will reach back to Chapter 6 where we showed how to locate the starting address and length of the most recently BLOADed or BRUN binary file. It was necessary to have the starting address in order to BSAVE a binary file. Well, instead of having to remember all of the steps in doing that (do you?), we will create a ROBOT EXEC to do it for us. Here's how:

```
10 TEXT : HOME
20 D$ = CHR$(13) + CHR$(4) : D1$ = CHR$(4)
30 PRINT D$ "OPEN BINARY FINDER": PRINT D$ "WRITE
BINARY FINDER"
40 PRINT "HOME"
50 PRINT "CALL -151"
60 PRINT "AA72.AA73 AA60.AA61"
70 PRINT "3D0G"
80 PRINT D1$ "CLOSE BINARY FINDER"
```

First, RUN the program to set up the text file, BINARY FINDER. Then BLOAD a binary program, such as FID on your SYSTEM MASTER, and EXEC BINARY FINDER to see the beginning address and length of the program. (Remember to reverse to 2-digit sets to get the correct addresses. See Chapter 6 if you forgot.) As you become more experienced you will find BINARY FINDER to be extremely useful.

Sequential Text Files

Of the two kinds of text files we will discuss, sequential text files are simpler to work with and use less memory. Random access files, which we will discuss in the next section, are a little trickier but they can be accessed faster than sequential files. Using sequential and random-access text files, it is possible to enter data from a program and store it as a text file. You can add to the file, change it, and retrieve data from it.

Creating Sequential Text Files

The first step is to write a "formatting" program, or a program that will create a sequential text file. Essentially, the program will look almost identical to the programs we wrote to create EXEC files. There's a good reason for that—EXEC files are a type of sequential text file. To create a file we use:

```
OPEN
WRITE
```

```
PRINT *****(PORTION THAT GOES IN TEXT FILE)****
CLOSE
```

These commands take care of everything we need in a sequential text file.

Now to begin using sequential text files, we will write a formatting program for our text file. We will begin with a simple example that will store the names of a known number of people who sent us Christmas cards. (Then next Christmas we can check the file to see to whom we should send cards.)

```
10 TEXT : HOME : REM ** SIMPLE SEQUENTIAL FILE WRITER **
20 D$ = CHR$(13) + CHR$(4) : D1$ = CHR$(4)
30 VTAB 10 : HTAB 1 : INPUT "HOW MANY ENTRIES? "; N%
40 DIM NA$(N%)
50 FOR I = 1 TO N%
60 VTAB 10 : HTAB 1 : CALL -868 : PRINT "NAME #" ; I ; "->";
: INPUT " "; NA$(I)
70 NEXT I
100 REM ** CREATE SEQUENTIAL TEXT FILE 'CHRISTMAS CARDS'
**
110 PRINT D$ "OPEN CHRISTMAS CARDS" : PRINT D$ "WRITE
CHRISTMAS CARDS"
120 FOR I = 1 TO N% : PRINT NA$(I) : NEXT : REM ** ENTERS
ALL THE NAMES **
130 PRINT D1$ "CLOSE CHRISTMAS CARDS"
140 END
```

After you enter the program, RUN it; remember the number of names that you entered. SAVE the program under the name CC WRITER, for we will come back to it later. CATALOG your disk and make sure there is a file called CHRISTMAS CARDS that was created by our CC WRITER program.

The next step is to READ our files using,

```
OPEN
READ
INPUT ** TAKES DATA OUT OF FILE **
CLOSE
```

The following program will OPEN CHRISTMAS CARDS, READ the file, CLOSE the file and then PRINT out the contents to the screen. Notice the similarities and differences between it and our program for writing files.

```
10 TEXT : HOME : REM ** SIMPLE SEQUENTIAL FILE
READER **
20 D$ = CHR$(13) + CHR$(4) : D1$ = CHR$(4)
```

```
30  VTAB 10 : HTAB 1 : INPUT "HOW MANY ENTRIES? "; N%
40  DIM NA$(N%)
100  REM ** READ SEQUENTIAL TEXT FILE 'CHRISTMAS
CARDS' **
110  PRINT D$ "OPEN CHRISTMAS CARDS" : PRINT D$
"WRITE CHRISTMAS CARDS"
120  FOR I = 1 TO N% : INPUT NA$(I) : NEXT : REM **
READS ALL THE NAMES **
130  PRINT D1$ "CLOSE CHRISTMAS CARDS"
140  FOR I = 1 TO N% : PRINT NA$(I) : NEXT : REM **
PRINTS TO SCREEN ALL NAMES **
150  END
```

After you RUN the program, SAVE it under the file name CC READER. If you forgot the number of names you put in the CHRISTMAS CARDS file, you might get a OUT OF DATA ERROR. By entering too many names to be read, you went beyond the limits of the file. Later, we will look at a way to make sure that doesn't happen.

So far so good. We have a program that will WRITE a list of names in a data file and one that will READ those names back to us. What happens, though, if we want to add some names to our file? Well, we could make a new file under another name, but a better way is to APPEND our current CHRISTMAS CARDS file. Using the APPEND command, we write our additional files to the bottom of the data list we have in our existing file. It is IMPORTANT to remember that when using APPEND, that there is an existing file to which we can APPEND our data. To do that, we use the following format:

```
APPEND
WRITE
PRINT ** ENTER OUR APPENDED DATA **
CLOSE
```

Since we will need only a slightly different program than our CC WRITER, simply LOAD CC WRITER, make some changes, and SAVE the program under the name CC APPENDER.

Look at the following program carefully, and note the changes made from CC WRITER.

```
10 TEXT : HOME : REM ** SIMPLE SEQUENTIAL FILE
APPENDER **
20 D$ = CHR$(13) + CHR$(4) : D1$ = CHR$(4)
30 VTAB 10 :HTAB 1 : INPUT "HOW MANY ENTRIES? "; N%
40 DIM NA$(N%)
50 FOR I = 1 TO N%
60 VTAB 10 : HTAB 1 : CALL -868 : PRINT "NAME #" ; I ;
"->"; : INPUT " "; NA$(I)
70 NEXT I
100 REM ** APPEND SEQUENTIAL TEXT FILE 'CHRISTMAS
CARDS' **
110 PRINT D$ "APPEND CHRISTMAS CARDS" : PRINT D$
"WRITE CHRISTMAS CARDS"
120 FOR I = 1 TO N% : PRINT NA$(I) : NEXT : REM **
ENTERS ALL THE APPENDED NAMES **
130 PRINT D1$ "CLOSE CHRISTMAS CARDS"
140 END
```

Now that didn't take much did it? All you had to do was to change WRITE to APPEND and once you SAVE the program as CC APPENDER, you have programs that will WRITE, READ and APPEND sequential text files.

Finally, we may want to examine only one entry or record in our sequential text file. To do this we use the POSITION command. This command will allow you to go to a certain record and examine it. Since POSITION rec-

THE "POSITION" COMMAND

ognizes only numbers, you will have to inspect any entry by its number. The following program will let you examine any of the entries you have in your CHRISTMAS CARDS text file:

```
10 TEXT : HOME : REM ** CC POSITIONER **
20 D$ = CHR$ (13) + CHR$ (4) : D1$ = CHR$(4)
30 VTAB 10 : HTAB 1 : INPUT "READ WHICH ENTRY # -> ";
N
40 PRINT D$ "OPEN CHRISTMAS CARDS"
50 PRINT D$ "POSITION CHRISTMAS CARDS,R"; N
60 PRINT D$ "READ CHRISTMAS CARDS"
70 INPUT NA$
80 PRINT D1$ "CLOSE CHRISTMAS CARDS"
90 PRINT NA$
```

(Just for fun, you could make this into a guessing game for your kids. "Who's #5? It's Uncle Willie!" Well, maybe not. . . .)

Now we've seen how to WRITE, APPEND, READ, and POSITION elements of a single text file. However, since text file names are essentially nothing but strings, we could use variables to do a lot of the work automatically. Remember, if we can write a program that will do most of the work for us, then we can save a lot of time writing several little programs. The following program, FILE MANAGER, will create, append, read and position any file you want. It only handles a single string element, but you can change that if you want. It's main purpose is to provide an example of a program that deals will all the basic aspects of sequential text file handling in one place.

```
10 TEXT : HOME : REM ** FILE MANAGER **
20 D$ = CHR$ (13) + CHR$ (4):D1$ = CHR$ (4):L = 200:
DIM NA$(L)
30 GOTO 1000
100 REM ** CREATE A FILE **
110 HOME : VTAB 10: INPUT "HOW MANY NAMES TO
ENTER-> "; N%
120 HOME : PRINT : PRINT : FOR I = 1 TO N%: INPUT
"ENTER NAME-> "; NA$(I): NEXT
130 HOME : VTAB 10: INPUT "NAME OF FILE TO CREATE->
";CF$
140 PRINT D$"OPEN";CF$: PRINT D$"WRITE";CF$
150 FOR I = 1 TO N%: PRINT NA$(I): NEXT
160 PRINT D1$"CLOSE";CF$
170 GOTO 1000
200 REM ** APPEND A FILE **
210 HOME : VTAB 10: INPUT "HOW MANY NAMES TO
APPEND-> "; N%
220 HOME : PRINT : PRINT : FOR I = 1 TO N%: INPUT
"ENTER NAME-> "; NA$(I): NEXT
230 HOME : VTAB 10: INPUT "NAME OF FILE TO
APPEND-> ";CF$
240 PRINT D$"APPEND";CF$: PRINT D$"WRITE";CF$
250 FOR I = 1 TO N%: PRINT NA$(I): NEXT
260 PRINT D1$"CLOSE";CF$
270 GOTO 1000
300 REM ** READ A FILE **
310 ONERR GOTO 390
320 NR = 0: HOME : VTAB 10: INPUT "NAME OF FILE TO
READ-> ";RF$
330 PRINT D$"OPEN";RF$: PRINT D$"READ";RF$
340 FOR J = 1 TO L: INPUT NA$(J):NR = NR + 1: NEXT
350 PRINT D1$"CLOSE";RF$
360 FOR I = 0 TO NR: PRINT NA$(I): NEXT
370 VTAB 24: INVERSE : PRINT " HIT ANY KEY TO
CONTINUE ";: NORMAL : GET AN$: PRINT AN$
380 GOTO 1000
390 J = L:J = 0: GOTO 350
400 REM ** POSITION FILE ENTRY **
410 HOME : VTAB 10: INPUT "POSITION # ";X%
```

```
420 VTAB 12: INPUT "NAME OF FILE -> ";PF$
430 PRINT D$"OPEN";PF$: PRINT
D$"POSITION";PF$;",R";X%: PRINT D$"READ";PF$
440 INPUT NA$
450 PRINT D1$"CLOSE";PF$
460 PRINT NA$
470 VTAB 24: INVERSE : PRINT "HIT ANY KEY TO CONTINUE
"; : NORMAL : GET AN$: PRINT AN$
1000 HOME :H$ = " FILE MANAGER ": INVERSE : HTAB 20
- LEN (H$)/2: PRINT H$: NORMAL : RESTORE : FOR I = 1
TO 5: READ M$(I): NEXT
1010 VTAB 6
1020 FOR J = 1 TO 5: PRINT J;". ";M$(J): PRINT : NEXT
1030 PRINT : PRINT : INVERSE : PRINT " CHOOSE BY
NUMBER "; : NORMAL : GET A%: IF A% < 1 OR A% > 5
THEN PRINT CHR$ (7): GOTO 1000
1040 ON A% GOTO 100,200,300,400,1200
1100 DATA  CREATE A FILE, APPEND A FILE, READ A FILE,
POSITION/READ FILE, EXIT
1200 TEXT : HOME : END
```

Before we go on to random access files, I want to remind you that there are several more aspects to sequential data files, and there is a great deal more you can do with them than the simple things we've covered in this section. At the end of the chapter, I have recommended some books that go into great detail on text file applications. So, if you want to go beyond the elementary stage with this very important aspect of the Apple II computer, I strongly suggest you take a look at one of these other sources.

Random Access Files

Random access files are like containers of equal size into which you store data. If you are familiar with containers in shipping, using standardized boxes, you will have some idea of how random access files work. Basically, you first decide how big a container you will need, based on the maximum size of the material you will be entering. Since all we can put into a random access file is either numbers or strings, the problem is greatly simplified. Each character in a number or string takes 1 byte and there is a 1 byte "housekeeping" or "overhead" required for each string or number. Therefore, if your maximun for a given string is 10, it will be necessary to allocate a total of 11 bytes : *one* for each of the *ten* characters and *one* for the housekeeping. (As you remember, a "byte" is a unit of measurement in the Apple's memory.) With numbers, everything, including the decimal point counts. For example, 99.95 would take 6 bytes: *one* for each of the *four* numbers, *one* for the decimal point and *one* for housekeeping.

For the most part creating and reading random access files looks very much like sequential text files, but there are very important differences as well. First, when you OPEN a random access file, you must include the (L)ength of the file. First, as we did with sequential text files, we PRINT D$ (composed of CHR$(14) + CHR$ (4)) and then place the OPEN command and the name of the file in quotes. However, then it is necessary to put a comma (,) and an 'L' along with the maximum length of our file. The following example shows the format for OPENing a random access file:

```
PRINT D$ "OPEN NAME FILE, L40"
```

The next step in creating a random access file is to enter the WRITE command, but we must include the (R)ecord number with it, such as,

```
PRINT D$ "WRITE NAME FILE, R1"
```

To illustrate how to use random access files, we will make a series of programs to store the names, cities and states of people. We will call the file we create HOMETOWN using 3 strings:

NA$ for a person's name

CT$ for the city

SC$ for the state's mailing code

Since people and cities have different length names, we are going to have to decide on a maximum size name, and longer names will simply be truncated to our desired size. This process is extremely important in working with random access files since we are limited to the number of bytes specfied when we OPEN a file. If our entries go over the length, they will spill over into the next record. Therefore, we will limit the length of a name to 20, a city to 10 and states to 2-character abbreviations employed by the post office. If a string is longer than the specified length, we will convert the string using LEFT$. (A bit brutal, I admit, but it serves the purpose of illustration and reminds you to keep track of name lengths.) Now we can calculate the (L)ength to OPEN our file:

NA$ = 20 + 1 (housekeeping) = 21

CT$ = 10 + 1 (housekeeping) = 11

SC$ = 2 + 1 (housekeeping) = 3

TOTAL = 35

Using these values, we will write a program that will enter a single record into a random access file:

```
10 TEXT : HOME : REM ** RANDOM ACCESS FILE **
20 D$ = CHR$ (13) + CHR$ (4):D1$ = CHR$ (4)
30 VTAB 4: HTAB 1: INPUT "NAME-> "; NA$: IF LEN (NA$)
> 20 THEN NA$ = LEFT$ (NA$,20): REM REQUIRES 21
BYTES - 20 FOR THE NAME AND 1 EXTRA
40 PRINT : INPUT "CITY-> ";CT$: IF LEN (CT$) > 10 THEN
CT$ = LEFT$ (CT$,10): REM 11 BYTES
50 PRINT : INPUT "STATE CODE-> ";SC$: IF LEN (SC$) < >
2 THEN VTAB 8: HTAB 1: CALL -875: VTAB 7: GOTO 50:
REM 3 BYTES
60 PRINT : PRINT "NAME REQUIRES 21 BYTES": PRINT "CITY
REQUIRES 11 BYTES": PRINT "STATE CODE REQUIRES 3
BYTES": FOR I = 1 TO 27: PRINT "-";: NEXT : PRINT " ":
PRINT "TOTAL BYTES = 35"
70 PRINT : PRINT : INVERSE : PRINT " HIT ANY KEY TO
CONTINUE ";: NORMAL : WAIT -16384,128: POKE -16368,0
100 REM ** CREATE RANDOM ACCESS RECORD **
110 PRINT D$"OPEN HOMETOWN,L35"
120 PRINT D$"WRITE HOMETOWN,R1"
130 PRINT NA$: PRINT CT$: PRINT SC$
140 PRINT D1$"CLOSE HOMETOWN"
```

That was a lot of work to get in one crummy record, but be patient and we will do more. Now, we will READ a record from a random access file. Like WRITEing random access files, we must OPEN them with a specified (L)ength and READ them in terms of a specified (R)ecord. The following program will read the HOMETOWN file:

```
10 TEXT : HOME : REM ** RANDOM ACCESS FILE READER
**
20 D$ = CHR$(13) + CHR$(4) : D1$ = CHR$(4)
30 PRINT D$ "OPEN HOMETOWN,L35" : PRINT D$ "READ
HOMETOWN, R1"
40 INPUT NA$
50 INPUT CT$
60 INPUT SC$
70 PRINT D1$ "CLOSE HOMETOWN"
80 HOME : VTAB 7 : PRINT NA$ : PRINT CT$; ", ";SC$
```

Now that was a lot of work just to WRITE and READ a single record. However, you can see how random access files operate. Now, as you may have guessed, we will examine how to deal with multiple records. We will stick with our HOMETOWN example, though, since dealing with multiple random access records is a bit more involved than with sequential text files. We will even begin our program with a reminder of how many bytes we are using and the strings.

Lines 10 through 150 are very much like our original program used to create a file, but notice the "counter" variable RN in line 120. We will use the counter to keep track of the number of records in our file HOMETOWN. By storing the value of the counter (renamed RZ in line 200 once we have entered all our records) in R0 (record zero), we will have a way of knowing how many records there are in our file. Then, when we READ our files, we will first read R0 and then make a FOR/NEXT loop with the value of RZ as the maximun records to read. Now, since we have another value to store, we will have to increase the (L)ength of HOMETOWN to 39. (999 as the maximum number of records—1 byte for each number and the added 1 byte for housekeeping.) Also notice we have PRINTed D1$ in line 180. This is to leave the WRITE mode to query if the user wants to enter another record.

```
10 TEXT : HOME : REM ** RANDOM ACCESS MULTIPLE
FILES **
20 D$ = CHR$ (13) + CHR$ (4):D1$ = CHR$ (4)
60 PRINT : PRINT "NAME REQUIRES 21 BYTES": PRINT "CITY
REQUIRES 11 BYTES": PRINT "STATE CODE REQUIRES 3
BYTES": PRINT "COUNTER REQUIRES 4 BYTES": FOR I = 1
TO 27: PRINT "–";: NEXT : PRINT " ": PRINT "TOTAL BYTES =
39"
70 PRINT : PRINT : INVERSE : PRINT " HIT ANY KEY TO
CONTINUE ";: NORMAL : WAIT –16384,128: POKE
–16368,0: HOME
100 REM ** MAKE MULTIPLE RANDOM ACCESS RECORDS
```

```
110 PRINT D$"OPEN HOMETOWN,L39"
120 RN = 0: REM INITIALIZE COUNTER FOR RECORD
NUMBER
130 RN = RN + 1: VTAB 4: HTAB 1: INPUT "NAME->
";NA$: IF LEN (NA$) > 20 THEN NA$ = LEFT$ (NA$,20): REM
REQUIRES 21 BYTES - 20 FOR THE NAME AND 1 EXTRA
140 PRINT : INPUT "CITY-> ";CT$: IF LEN (CT$) > 10 THEN
CT$ = LEFT$ (CT$,10): REM 11 BYTES
150 PRINT : INPUT "STATE CODE-> ";SC$: IF LEN (SC$) <
> 2 THEN VTAB 8: HTAB 1: CALL -875: VTAB 7: GOTO 150:
REM 3 BYTES
160 PRINT D$"WRITE HOMETOWN,R";RN
170 PRINT NA$: PRINT CT$: PRINT SC$
180 PRINT D1$
190 INVERSE : INPUT "ANOTHER RECORD?(Y/N) ";AN$:
NORMAL : IF AN$ = "Y" THEN HOME : GOTO 130
200 RZ = RN: REM RECORD 0 TO INDICATE NUMBER OF
FILES 4 BYTES
210 PRINT D$"WRITE HOMETOWN,R0"
220 PRINT RZ
230 PRINT D1$"CLOSE HOMETOWN"
240 HOME : VTAB 10:
PRINT "HOMETOWN CLOSED"
```

Now that we have several records in our file, we will need to get them out again. Here's where our "counter variable" RZ, stored in R0, comes in handy. First, we will read R0 to see how many records there are, and then loop through the records to READ them all. Notice that in line 40, we first read HOMETOWN,R0 and after INPUTing it into memory, it is used in the FOR/NEXT loop in line 70 to pull all the records out.

```
10 TEXT : HOME : REM ** MULTIPLE RANDOM ACCESS FILE
READER **
20 D$ = CHR$ (13) + CHR$ (4):D1$ = CHR$ (4)
30 PRINT D$"OPEN HOMETOWN,L39"
40 PRINT D$"READ HOMETOWN,R0"
50 INPUT RZ
60 PRINT D1$
70 FOR G = 1 TO RZ: PRINT D$"READ HOMETOWN,R"G
80 INPUT NA$
90 INPUT CT$
100 INPUT SC$
110 PRINT D1$
120 PRINT NA$: PRINT CT$;",";SC$: PRINT : NEXT
130 PRINT D1$"CLOSE HOMETOWN"
```

Now that you have seen how to build a random access file, here's a little problem for you to solve. By adding a few lines and calculating a few more bytes, you can create a very useful "Address List." You already have a program that enters Names, Cities and States. All you have to add is address and zip code, and there you have it! By attaching a little subroutine to kick it out to your printer, which will be discussed in the next chapter, you could generate your own mailing list program!

Further Extensions Of Sequential And Random Access Files

There is a great deal more you can do with text files, and this introductory look at them just scratches the surface. To a beginner it might look like a lot, but it is only an introduction. It is possible to make "Data Base" systems to search for individual records, change individual records, sort records and do all kinds of other things with them. Entire books are written just for the Apple and its uses of text files. There are three I can recommend:

1. *Apple Files* by David Miller (Reston Publishing Co.).
2. *Apple BASIC: Data File Programming* by LeRoy Finkel and Jerald R. Brown (Wiley & Sons).
3. *Apple BASIC For Business* by Alan Parker and John Stewart (Reston Publishing Co.).

So, if you want to use the full potential of your Apple's text file handling, take a look at one of the above books, and in the meantime, experiment and extend the programs provided here.

Summary

We began this chapter by examining ways in which we could capture a program in a text file and ended up creating individual records in random access files. Most of what we have covered in this chapter has been very rudimentary, and there are several tricks and techniques needed to fully use text files. Nevertheless, you are off to a start, and by refining and extending what you have learned in this book, it is possible to vastly extend your knowledge.

First, we saw how to "catch" a program or subroutine in a text file that can be brought into memory with EXEC. This allows the user to load several programs simultaneously or to attatch useful subroutines onto programs. Also, we found that we could create ROBOT EXEC files that take over the keyboard. These are handy when a series of operations are needed to execute a program.

Second, we learned how to OPEN, WRITE, APPEND, POSITION, and CLOSE sequential text files to store data. These files are very useful for storing data in the form of numbers or strings to be accessed for later use by programs that READ data from text files.

Finally, we saw how to begin using random access files. These files, while taking up more memory and being trickier to deal with than sequential text files, have speed advantages and uses for multiple record handling that make them practical for certain applications. With more advanced understandings of these files, just about any data base program can be created.

CHAPTER 9
You And Your Printer

DON'T BE SURPRISED IF IT'S ALL GREEK TO YOU

Introduction

Until recently, when an Apple owner bought a printer, he or she had to have a good bit of luck to have a manual that would give the user the slightest hint on how to use it. Some printer manufacturers decided upon a certain brand of computer, other than the Apple, and explained how to use their printer with that particular brand. Other manuals were written for people with high-level printer operation understanding, simply providing the hardware specifications to be applied to any computer. Needless to say, there were a lot of frustrated Apple users and printers were only used to their minimum capacity. Things have improved somewhat, and now it is possible to obtain good manuals for printer operation either supplied free with the printer or from independent sources; however, just in case your manual does not tell you how to work it specifically with the Apple, there are some things you should know.

In this chapter we will discuss printers both in general terms and in terms of specific popular printers. The general discussion will cover how your

Apple communicates with the printer. This will give you a chance of deciphering some of the manuals that come with your printer, allowing you to enter the correct code in BASIC to get your printer to do your bidding. Once you get the idea of how a printer works, it is really quite simple to operate them, but until you learn a few "secrets" (seemingly kept so by the manuals), they usually cannot be used to their full capacity.

WHY THE MANUALS ARE SO BAD

Normally, it is in very bad taste to criticize another's manual from the pages of one's own. However, I have encountered so many frustrated beginners with printer manuals that only provide vague hints as to their operation that I felt compelled to explain why the manuals are, in general, so bad. In the brief history of computers, they have only just recently come into the home with the printers not far behind. Printers developed for businesses had technical manuals for the company technicians who set up the printers. Likewise, many printers were simply hooked up to a word processor that had all the code for operating printers already installed in the program. Furthermore, the small, inexpensive printers that came on the market at the beginning of the 1980's and were intended for home or small business use were designed to be used with any number of different computers. (After all, if you were selling printers, you would not want it to be for only a single brand of computer.) Rather than having separate manuals for different computers, the manuals were written for the technicians who could get them to work on any computer. As of this writing, some printer companies have provided manuals that explain how to use them on several different computers, including the Apple, but others do not for the above cited reasons.

Printing Text On Your Printer

In chapter 1, you have a simple example of how to print something out to your printer. As you remember, we put the interface card to your printer in Slot #1; and by entering PR#1 and a PRINT statement, you were able to print text to your printer. To return to your screen simply enter PR#0. This will "disconnect" your printer. However, your printer will not always be in Slot #1, and in writing programs for the Apple, there should be a choice of which slot the printer will be connected to. (PR#0 will always "disconnect" your printer, no matter what slot it is in—except Slot #0, where it should NOT ever be!) The following little program allows you to enter text and print it to the printer in any slot used by the printer or to the screen (Slot #0):

```
10 TEXT :HOME : D$ = CHR$(13) + CHR$(4)
20 VTAB 10 : INPUT "ENTER STRING -> "; MS$
30 GOSUB 1000
40 PRINT MS$
50 PRINT D$; "PR#0"
60 VTAB 22 : INVERSE : PRINT " ANOTHER ENTRY?(Y/N) "; :
NORMAL : GET AN$ : PRINT AN$
70 IF AN$ = "N" THEN END
80 IF AN$ = "Y" THEN 10
90 PRINT CHR$(7) : PRINT " PLEASE ENTER 'Y' OR 'N' " :
GOTO 60
1000 HOME : VTAB 10 : PRINT "PRINTER SLOT # (0 TO
PRINT TO SCREEN ): "; : GET S% : PRINT S%
1010 IF S% > 7 THEN PRINT CHR$(7) : GOTO 1000
1020 PRINT D$; "PR#";S%
1030 RETURN
```

The subroutine in Lines 1000 to 1030 is handy to have, and you might want to save it as a text file and EXEC it into programs that require using the printer. (If you have a special interface that uses a binary driver routine, you should use a different subroutine. See your interface manual for instructions on that.)

Over 40

Using the above program, type in a string that has more than 40 characters. For example, key in "THIS PRINTER HAS AT LEAST 80 COLUMNS AND IT SHOULD PRINT THIS IN ONE LINE." When your printer prints this out it will do one of two things: (1) print it on one line, or (2) print it up to 40 characters (including spaces) and start a new line. If your printer put the entire string on one line, its default width is probably 80 columns. That is, it will print 80 characters/spaces before issuing a carriage return (CR). However, since your Apple's screen is 40 columns, some printers will read the end of the screen line as the point at which they should issue a carriage return. Since you don't want to have to go through life in 40 columns on a printer, it is necessary to change the width on the printer's CR. Here's how:

1. First issue a PR# 1 (or # whatever your slot your printer is in).
2. Enter CTRL-I 80N.
3. Now your entries will be 80 columns until you turn off your printer, computer or reset the column-width to something other than 80.

Since we really would not have a great deal of use for a printer command in the immediate mode, let's turn our command into a program line and insert it into our program that prints out strings:

```
35 PRINT CHR$(9) + "80N"
```

Now, RUN the program, and if your printer only printed up to 40 columns in our first test, it should now print 80. Be sure to notice that our command to kick the printer up to 80 columns came AFTER you turned on the printer (PR# 1). Your printer has its own microprocessor chips, and when you issue it commands, it "remembers" what it was told. However, like your computer, it has to be turned on and have the link to it from your computer enable for it to work. (In the same way that PR#6 sets up a communication link between your computer and disk drive, PR#1 sets up the link to your printer.)

Assuming that all is well, we will run another test for 80 columns. LOAD a program into memory that has lines over 80 characters/spaces. (The program we've been using to test the printer will work fine.) Now, enter PR#1 (or whatever slot # your printer is in) and LIST the program to the printer. If your program LISTs up to only 40 columns, it requires another "kick" to set up 80 column format. PR#0 to get out of the printer mode and attach the following lines to your program:

```
1 POKE 33,33 :D$ = CHR$(13) + CHR$(4)
2 PRINT D$; "PR#1" : REM CHOOSE THE CORRECT SLOT
FOR PRINTER IF NOT 1
3 PRINT CHR$(9) + "80N" : REM FOR PARALLEL PRINTERS
4 LIST 10,
5 PRINT D$ "PR#0" : END
```

Now RUN the program, making sure your printer is turned on and is "ON LINE', and your listing should be in 80 columns and only include lines 10 to the end of the program. If you attach those 6 lines to any program, it will list it in 80 columns for you. (However, your program must begin on Line 10 or all of it will not be listed.)

Since listing programs to one's printer is a good way to de-bug a program or simply sending it to a friend, it would be convenient to have a utility program with which we do just that! Since it is a nuisance to key in the little 6 liner above, let's make a ROBOT EXEC file that will not only list our program in 80 columns but also provide a title for it and "break" the listing at spaces after 70 columns. In straight 80 column listings, often there will be a carriage return in the middle of a variable or word. To avoid that we enter

```
PRINT CHR$(9) + "70R" + "80N"
```

The "70R" means that as soon as there is a space after 70 columns, start a new line. Thus if the command HTAB began at line 69, instead of breaking it at the H, it would print the entire command and then issue a carriage return. Of couse, if you have no spaces between line 69 and line 80, you'll still get broken words and commands, but not too many. To create the ROBOT EXEC file, first key in the program and then RUN 10. If you run the program from Line 0 (i.e., the beginning), it will not create the text file PROGRAM LISTER. Remember, key it in and enter from the keyboard 'RUN 10.' (If you save the entire program, use the name 'PROGRAM LISTER SETUP'—DO NOT SAVE it as an Applesoft program under the name PROGRAM LISTER!!) We begin at LINE ZERO!

```
0 HOME : VTAB 10 : PRINT "PRINTER SLOT# -> ";:GET
PR%: VTAB 10 : HTAB 1 : INPUT "PROGRAM NAME -> ";PG$
1 POKE 33,33 : D$ = CHR$(13) + CHR$(4) : PRINT
D$;"PR#";PR% : PRINT CHR$(9) + "70R" + "80N": PRINT
PG$ : FOR I = 1 TO LEN (PG$) : PRINT "*"; : NEXT : PRINT
2 LIST
5  PRINT D$; "PR#0" : END
10 REM ** PROGRAM LISTER **
20 D$ = CHR$(13) + CHR$ (4)
30 PRINT D$"OPEN PROGRAM LISTER"
40 PRINT D$"WRITE PROGRAM LISTER"
50 POKE 33,30
60 LIST 0,2
70 PRINT "RUN"
80 PRINT CHR$(4); "CLOSE PROGRAM LISTER"
90 TEXT : END
```

Just for fun, load one of your programs, make sure your printer is turned on and "ON LINE" and then enter EXEC PROGRAM LISTER. Enter the slot number of your printer and then the program's name. Your printer should chug out a listing of your program with a title that looks a lot better than ones all jammed together in 40 columns. (Note: Different printers and interfaces may react differently to this listing program. If it doesn't work, try taking out the "70R." If that doesn't work, check to see if the line length sequence in your printer uses "CTRL-I XXN" as the column setting sequence.)

Special Characteristics Of Your Printer

As was pointed out in Chapter 1, there are 3 kinds of printers: (1) dot matrix, (2) letter quality (daisy wheel), and (3) thermal. We will focus our discussion on dot matrix printers, since they have the most characteristics to be controlled by your computer, but we will also explain various options available in daisy wheel type printers. Thermal printers are both limited in their use and tend to have sufficient documentation not to require any elaboration here.

CHR$ To The Rescue

The secret to using printers is in understanding what their control codes mean and how to use those codes. For example, the following is a partial list of codes provided with a CENTRONICS 737 printer:

MNEMONIC	DECIMAL	OCTAL	HEX	FUNCTION
ESC,SO	27,14	033,016	1B,0E	Elongated Print
ESC,DC4	27,20	033,034	1B,13	Select 16.7 cpi
ESC,DC1	27,17	033,021	1B,11	Proportional Print

Now for most first-time computer owners, that could have been written by a visitor from another planet for all the good it does. However, there is important information in those codes, and once you get to know how to use them, it is relatively easy.

To get started, forget everything except the "DECIMAL" and "FUNCTION" columns. Now taking the first row, we have decimal codes 27 and 14 to get elongated print. To "tell" your printer you want elongated print you would use CHR$(27) + CHR$(14). To kick that into your printer you would do the following:

1. PR#1 (or whatever slot your printer is in)
2. PRINT CHR$(27) + CHR$(14) + "MESSAGE"

If you have a Centronics 737 or 739 printer that would have printed the string "MESSAGE" in an elongated print. Likewise, for the condensed printing 16.7 cpi (characters per inch), you would have entered CHR$(27) + CHR$(20) and for the proportional type face, CHR$(27) + CHR$(17). Once you get the decimal code, all you have to do is to enter that code to the printer and it will do anything from changing the type-face to performing a backspace function.

Let's take a look at another printer, the MX-80 and it's control codes. However, rather than keying in all of the codes, we will write a program that will give us different type faces, underlining and other tricks with the MX-80. The first thing we will do is define string variables as printer codes; then enter messages we want to go to our printer.

```
10 TEXT : HOME : REM ** MX-80 CONTROLLER **
20 D$ = CHR$ (13) + CHR$ (4)
30 LF$ = CHR$ (10) : REM LINE FEED
40 VT$ = CHR$ (11) : REM VERTICAL TAB
50 FF$ = CHR$ (12) : REM FORM FEED
60 CR$ = CHR$ (13) : REM CARRIAGE RETURN
70 EL$ = CHR$ (14) : REM ELONGATED TYPE
80 CD$ = CHR$ (15) : REM CONDENSED TYPE
90 CC$ = CHR$ (18) : REM CANCEL CONDENSED TYPE
100 CE$ = CHR$ (20) : REM CANCEL ELONGATED TYPE
110 CB$ = CHR$ (24) : REM CLEAR PRINT BUFFER
```

```
200 HOME : VTAB 10 : PRINT "PRINTER SLOT # -> "; : GET
S% : IF S% > 7 THEN 200
210 HOME : VTAB 3 : INPUT "ENTER MESSAGE -> ";MS$
220 PRINT : PRINT "1. NORMAL TYPE" : PRINT "2.
ELONGATED TYPE" : PRINT "3. CONDENSED TYPE"
230 PRINT : PRINT "CHOOSE TYPE FACE BY NUMBER -> ";
: GET TF% : PRINT TF%
240 ON TF% GOSUB 500,600,700
250 PRINT : INPUT "HORIZONTAL TAB -> "; HT%
260 INPUT "VERTICAL TABS TO SHIFT -> "; VT%
270 PRINT "FORM FEED AT END? (Y/N) "; : GET AN$ : PRINT
AN$
300 REM ** PRINT THE MESSAGE ON THE PRINTER **
310 PRINT D$ "PR#";S%
320 FOR I = 1 TO VT% : PRINT VT$ ; : NEXT : REM
VERTICAL TAB
330 PRINT TAB (HT%); TF$ + MS$ : REM PRINT
HORIZONTAL TAB, TYPE FACE AND MESSAGE
340 PRINT CB$ : REM CLEAR BUFFER
350 IF AN$ = "Y" THEN PRINT FF$ : REM FORM FEED IF
DESIRED
360 PRINT CC$; : PRINT CE$ : REM CANCEL CONDENSED
AND ELONGATED MODE
370 PRINT D$ "PR#0"
380 VTAB 22 : PRINT "ANOTHER MESSAGE? (Y/N) "; : GET
AM$ : PRINT AM$
390 IF AM$ = "Y" THEN 210
400 END
500 RETURN
600 TF$ = EL$ : RETURN
700 TF$ = CD$ : RETURN
```

There is a good deal more that can be done by way of controlling the type face of your MX-80, especially if you have the GRAFTRAX or GRAFTRAX-PLUS options. However, the above program should give you a simple example of how to control your type faces from within a program. Experiment with it and then add control codes or write your own program to make your printer do your bidding.

From CHR$ To HEX In Your Printer

Since most of us think in decimal it is simple to understand how CHR$ commands work in terms of the ASCII code. If a given character has a decimal value, we can get that character by putting the decimal value into the CHR$ parentheses (e.g., A = decimal value 65 and so CHR$(65) =

A). By examining a DECIMAL-HEX conversion chart, it is equally simple to find the HEX value for a character. For example, 65 = $41 (the "$" means a HEX value or number). Therefore, $41 also would equal "A." (In Appendix B, the ASCII Screen Chart contains both decimal and hex values of ASCII.)

Now you may be wondering why this is interesting since all you have to do is to enter the CHR$ in decimal. Why bother yourself with HEXADECIMAL. Well, there will be times when you are asked to provide a HEXADECIMAL value for your printer control. For example, word processors sometimes will require the user to enter a HEX number for some special function (such as the backspace HEX character) for a specified printer. Usually, your printer manual will include a HEXADECIMAL listing of what HEX values are required. If it does not, then use the ASCII SCREEN VALUE or APPLESOFT TOKEN charts in Appendix A to look up the values.

However, there is one problem to be aware of. There are actually two "sets" of ASCII on your Apple, we will refer to these sets as "high" and "low" ASCII. Low ASCII is from 0 to 127 ($0 to $7F), and high ASCII is from 128 to 255 ($80 to $FF). For the most part, the high ASCII simply repeats low ASCII, but in some cases word processors will employ the high ASCII as special screen characters. If your manual is unclear as to which ASCII set to use (e.g., it simply indicates to use "ESC E" but not the decimal or hexadecimal code), try both the high and the low sets to see what happens. For example, let's say that your manual indicates that the sequence "ESC E" will provide a special print you desire. The following are the combinations in both HEX and DECIMAL: (NOTE: The "low ASCII" value for ESC works with both high and low ASCII of other characters.)

"ESC E" LOW ASCII

DECIMAL: CHR$ (27) + CHR$ (69)
HEX: $1B $45

"ESC E" HIGH ASCII

DECIMAL: CHR$ (27) + CHR$ (197)
HEX: $1B $C5

To convert in decimal from low to high ASCII all you have to do is to add 128 to the low ASCII value. Like your computer though, you cannot destroy your printer with a program. Therefore, experiment with your printer code commands until you get what you want. The worst that can happen is the use of a lot of paper and ribbon, and even if everything locks up, just turn off your system and turn it on again.

Daisy Wheel Printers

Daisy wheel and dot matrix printers have a good deal in common when it comes to the use of codes to make the printer do something special. However, with daisy wheel printers, you change the type-face on the printer by changing the wheel and not some special command. Depending on the kind of daisy wheel printer you own, there are several different wheels available, but once you put a printer wheel on, only the characters on the wheel can be printed.

Different daisy wheels have different sized print, referred to in terms of 10, 12 or 15 "pitch." The "pitch" refers to the characeters per inch (cpi). The larger the type the lower the pitch. A 10 cpi wheel is equivalent to "pica" type on a typewriter and the 12 cpi wheel is the same as "elite." When changing wheels of different sized pitch, it is necessary to change the pitch. This can be done either by code sequences from the computer or by flipping switches on the printer. Using the former method, the same techniques used for issuing commands described above in our discussion of changing type face on dot matrix printers changes horizontal pitch on daisy wheel printers. The second method, flipping hardware switches, will be described in the next section.

Another consideration with daisy wheel printers is in the number of characters on a single wheel. Some printers have 96 character wheels, and others have wheels with a different number of characters. Therefore, make sure the number of characters on your print wheel is compatible with your printer when buying new wheels. If you get one with the incorrect number of characters or "arms," your print-out will not have the correct characters. Usually, you will be looking for "brand compatible" wheels. So if you have a Diablo brand daisy wheel, for example, you will want to either purchase wheels made by the Diablo company or ones that are "Diablo Compatible." Likewise, Qume brand printers require either Qume or Qume compatible print wheels, but even when buying wheels for the same brand, make sure of the number of characters.

Internal Hardware Switches On Printers

In addition to enabling or disabling special characteristics on either dot matrix or daisy wheel printers through software commands, it is also possible to set your printer with hardware switches. In some cases, if you do not make switch adjustments on your printer, it will not work with the Apple. This is because, many manufacturers set their switches for a particular brand of computer other than the Apple. For example, the F-10 "Starwriter" daisy wheel printer made by C. Itoh works extremely well with the Apple once the switches are set correctly. The following settings are needed using the 10 horizontal pitch wheel that comes with the printer:

F-10 STARWRITER (C. ITOH) 40 CPS SWITCH SETTINGS

Line Mode:

1. Set Switches 2, 3, 5, 7, and 8 of switch set 40 (left bank of 8 switches) to open position.
2. Set switches 1, 4, and 6 of switch set 40 to closed position.
3. Set switches 2, 6, 7, 9, 10 of switch set 41 (right bank of 10 switches) to open position.
4. Set switches 1, 3, 4, 5, and 8 of switch set 41 to closed position.

Serial Mode:

1. Set all switches of switch set 40 to open postion except switch 4.
2. Set all switches of switch set 41 to open except 3, 5, and 8.

With the number of switches and options, these "combinations" are critical, and since most manuals are highly technical, it can be difficult for the novice. Probably your best strategy is to get the people at the store where you buy your printer to demonstrate the printer for you on an Apple and have them set the switches. If they cannot do it, then DON'T BUY IT FROM THEM! Find a store that supports its products to be used with the Apple and helps the user.

There is an extremely important switch on many models of dot matrix printers. It is the switch that prints out the "zero" character with a slash through it. When you use your printer to make program listings, it is often essential that you can easily differentiate between "O's" and "0's'. For example, if you have a variable "O" and you want to have a FOR/NEXT LOOP from the variable "O" to 255, you would enter

FOR I = O TO 255

Most people reading that would assume that the "O" was a "0" and enter the wrong character. By flipping the appropriate switch on your printer, all zeros can be differentiated from "Oh's." On Epson MX-100 printers, for example, when switch SW1–7 is in the "on" position, the zeros have slashes through them, and when it is "off" the zeros have no slashes.

DON'T USE "O" AS A VARIABLE

Since there are enough problems in getting programs correctly copied from printed listings in the first place, there is no reason to make it more difficult by using the "O" (Oh) character as a variable. Even if your zeros have slashes through them, if you have an "O" for a variable, when it comes time to PRINT O, chances are, you will enter "PRINT Ø" (slash and all). Use other characters—you have plenty!

Before we go on to examine printer graphics, the following program will give you single or multiple address labels. Use it to experiment with your printer's special characteristics. See if you can re-write portions of it to get interesting effects on your print-out.

```
10  TEXT : HOME : REM ** MULTIPLE LABEL MAKER **
20  D$ = CHR$ (13) + CHR$ (4)
30  RESTORE
40  FOR I = 1 TO 5: READ LB$(I): NEXT
50  FOR I = 1 TO 5: VTAB I + 7: PRINT LB$(I): NEXT
60  FOR I = 1 TO 5: HTAB 11: VTAB I + 7: INVERSE : PRINT
SPC( 25): NEXT : NORMAL
70  HTAB 11: VTAB 8: INPUT " ";NA$: HTAB 11: INPUT
" ";AD$: HTAB 11: INPUT " ";CI$: HTAB 11: INPUT " ";ST$:
HTAB 11 + (LEN(ST$) + 1): INPUT " ";ZI$
80  GOSUB 7000
90  GOSUB 9000
100  GOSUB 8000
200  PRINT D$"PR# 0"
210  HOME : VTAB 9: PRINT "DO YOU WISH TO CONTINUE?";
: GET AN$: IF AN$ = "Y" THEN GOTO 10
220  HOME :EN$ = "UNTIL THE POSTMAN RINGS AGAIN
. . .": VTAB 8: HTAB 20 - LEN (EN$)/2: PRINT EN$: VTAB 23:
TEXT : END
230  END
1000  DATA  NAME,ADDRESS,CITY,STATE,ZIP
7000   VTAB 22: PRINT "IS THIS CORRECT?(Y/N) "; : GET A$
7010  IF A$ = "N" THEN 10
7020  PRINT : INPUT "HOW MANY LABELS WOULD YOU
LIKE? ";N
7030  RETURN
8000  FOR I = 1 TO N
8010  PRINT NA$: PRINT AD$: PRINT CI$;", ";ST$;"  ";ZI$:
PRINT
8020  PRINT : PRINT : NEXT
8025 IF PR = 0 THEN PRINT : PRINT "HIT ANY KEY TO
CONTINUE"; : WAIT -16384,128: POKE -16368,0
8030  RETURN
9000  HOME : PRINT "ENTER PRINTER SLOT OR BINARY
DRIVER CALL (0 DISPLAYS TO SCREEN)": INPUT "  ";PR
9010  IF NOT PR THEN RETURN
9020  IF PR > 7 THEN CALL PR: RETURN
9030  PRINT D$"PR#"PR: RETURN
```

Printer Graphics

In this section, we will discuss your printer and graphics. Before you begin, it is important to understand that not all printers do graphics, and while daisy wheel printers can print graphics, they are very slow. Furthermore, to print graphics on most printers, special programs (or hardware) beyond the programming skill of novices are required. Therefore, we will discuss programs and interfaces you can purchase to get your printer to do all kinds of tricks with graphics. Some printers come with the software/hardware so that it is unnecessary to buy additional or special devices. Likewise, some "graphics dump" programs operate only with certain printers and not with others. Therefore, I will try and use illustrations with graphics programs that work on most popular printers and provide some illustrations of what can be done with them.

Dumping Your HI-RES Screen

When you print out graphics, your computer sends a series of bytes to your printer reflecting the pixels on your hi-res screen. Since most printers only print graphics in black and white (black on white paper), the colors would not seem to matter, however, as we can see from the following dump, different colors give different textures on the printer:

By using different colors, it is possible to get interesting effects and "shading" in graphics on your printer even though all your printer is doing is printing "dots" in black ink. Unfortunately, this cannot be done with the same ease you can print out text.

One graphics printing program found to work very well on every printer tested, including daisy wheel printers, was THE PRINTOGRAPHER by Southwestern Data Systems. For ease of use, cropping, different magnification and horizontal and vertical printing, it was found to be excellent. Two other popular graphics dump programs are ZOOM GRAPHICS by Phoenix Software and GRAPHTRIX by Data Transforms, Inc. There are others as well, and I suggest you examine any one you intend to purchase first and consider the following points:

1. Will it work on my printer?
2. Will it crop pictures easily?
3. Is it easy to use?
4. Will it magnify graphics?
5. Will it place graphics in different horizontal locations on the printout?
6. Will it condense graphic files on the disk?
7. Will it access either drive?
8. Will it print both inverse and normal?
9. Can it be used within a program?

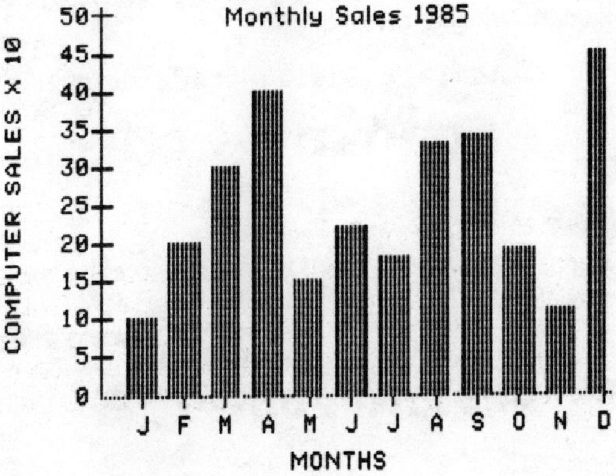

Hardware Devices For Graphics

Many users prefer a hardware interface to their printer that will include graphics printing capabilities. The GRAPPLER+ by Orange Micro and WIZARD-BPO (Buffered Parallel Output) are two printer interface cards that provide special chips on the cards for graphics. Using one of these cards instead of a regular printer interface, it is possible to have printer graphics without any special software. For example, with the WIZARD card, all the user does is enter CTRL-I G and the graphics on hi-res screen 1 will be dumped to the printer, centered on the page. Since you have to buy a printer interface card for your printer anyway, it may be worth the little extra cost to purchase an interface card that includes a graphics dump. However, even though they are more convenient to use, the cards do not provide all the options of the better software graphics dump programs. Also, the cards only work with certain printers for which they are especially configured, and so if you buy one, make certain it is the one for your printer. (Both the GRAPPLER and WIZARD-BPO, and presumedly other such cards, are configured for several types of printers, but each configuration works only on a single type.)

Printing Fonts

One of the more useful, and just plain fun, aspects of printing graphics is the special graphics fonts. There are several font programs available, including HIGHER TEXT PLUS & HIGHER FONTS (Synergistic and CALL -A.P.P.L.E.), THE COMPLETE GRAPHICS SYSTEMS II (Penguin), DOS TOOL KIT (Apple Inc.), I.A.C. FONTS (International Apple Core) and APPLE MECHANIC (Beagle Bros.). Most font programs involve loading a font, and then with PRINT statements from within a program, printing out various messages. HIGHER TEXT PLUS has a "Billboard" program for scrolling messages entered from a prompt, and APPLE MECHANIC has an XTYPER program that works something like a little "word processor" for hi-res fonts. Also, hi-res fonts are useful for labeling hi-res graphics. The following are some examples of graphic fonts:

This is a small Circus font

Broadway Font

Three-D Font

Stencil Font

This is a small Square Font
[Note proportonal spacing]

Western Font

Using some graphics dump programs, such as GRAPHTRIX, it is possible to integrate word processing and graphics together!

Printing "Photographs"

A final use of hi-resolution printing is for printing computer photographs. However, instead of using photographic paper and chemicals to reproduce your pictures, you use your printer dump program and regular paper. The following is an example of a photo that has been "touched up" with a graphics font/drawing package, ALPHA PLOT by Beagle Bros.:

Summary

In this chapter, we have covered the many aspects of working with your printer. It is important to understand that we have only touched upon a few of the printers that work with the Apple and some printers are far more flexible than others. However, you should now have a good idea of how your computer sends messages to your printer to get it to print using different type faces as well as any other special feature available on your particular machine and interface card.

Since printer manuals are often too technical for the beginning user, it is important to know how to "translate" them so that you can use all their special features. Basically, all that is required is a chart in the manual that provides that decimal codes for "turning on" the various printer devices—from type faces to line feed. If you can find these codes in your manual, then it is a relatively simple matter to encase them in CHR$ commands to "communicate" your desires to the printer. Sometimes this will involve using HEXADECIMAL code, but that too is simply a matter of knowing what the code is for a particular feature.

For printing graphics, you will need to purchase a special program, hardware interface, or learn a higher level of programming than is covered in this book. However, with many software and hardware packages avaiable for the Apple and printer graphics, it is easiest to begin with a commercial graphics dump routine. With a printer capable of doing graphics, it is possible to print out anything on your hi-res screen.

CHAPTER 10
Programs, Hints, And Help

Introduction

Well, here we are at the last chapter. We've covered most of the commands used for programming in APPLESOFT BASIC on the Apple and many tricks of the trade. However, if you are seriously interested in learning more about your computer and using it to its full capacity, there's more to learn. In fact, this last chapter is intended to give you some direction beyond the scope of this book.

First, we will introduce you to the best thing since silicone—Apple Users Groups. These are groups that have interests in maximizing their computer's use. Second, I would like to suggest some periodicals with which you can learn more about your Apple computer. Third, we will examine some languages other than BASIC that you can use on your Apple. BASIC has many advantages, but like all computer languages it has its limitations, and you should know what else is available.

Next, we will examine some more programs. First, there will be several listings of programs that you may find useful, fun or both. The ones included were chosen to show you some applications of what we have learned in the previous nine chapters, enhancing what you already know. Then we will look at different types of programs you can purchase. These are programs written by professional programmers to do everything from making your own programming simpler to keeping track of your taxes. Finally, we will examine some hardware peripherals to enhance your Apple.

Apple User Groups

Of all of the things I did when I bought my Apple, the most helpful, economical, and useful was joining an Apple User Group. Not only did I meet a great group of people with Apple computers, but I was taught how to program and generally what to do and not to do. My club, The Apple Corps of San Diego, has a "Disk-Of-The-Month," with programs on both sides of the disk from all over the world each month. The programs are contributed by members in the International Apple Core. At monthly general meetings, speakers inform us about everything from new peripherals for the Apple to programming techniques. A "Beginner's Group" meets monthly to teach novices how to program and several other special interest groups meet to discuss hardware, various programming languages, or whatever else people want to learn more about in using their Apple.

We receive a monthly magazine with club news, tutorials and programs. The club also makes group buys on various supplies, programs, etc. for the Apple, saving members a good deal of money.

APPLE USER GROUPS

Usually the best way to contact your local Apple User Group is through local computer stores. Often stores selling Apple computers will have application forms, and some even serve as the meeting site for the clubs. If your computer store sells the magazine *Apple Orchard,* it has a listing of all of the Apple clubs affiliated with the International Apple Core. Also, you can write to:

Apple Orchard
910 George St.
Santa Clara, CA 95050

The Apple Orchard is the publication of the International Apple Core, Inc. Other microcomputer clubs in your area may also have Apple users in them, and if there is not an Apple club, join a general computer group. The help you will get will be worth it.

To start your own Apple User's group, post a notice and meeting time and site in your local computer store. Write to the International Apple Core (at the Apple Orchard address), and they will supply you with disks from their library at a nominal fee to get you started. Your club will then be listed in the Apple Orchard, and other people in your area will soon join up.

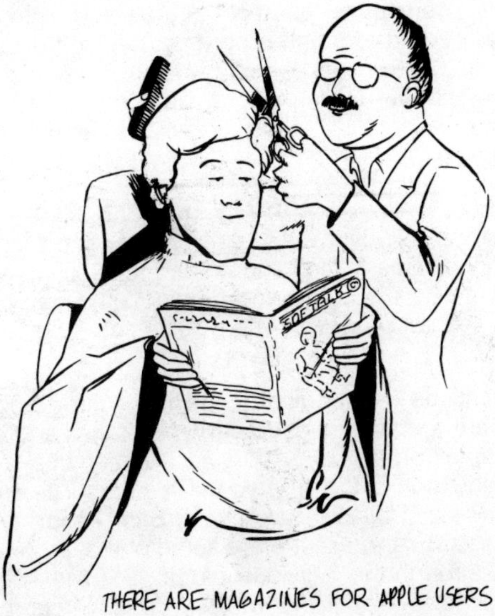

THERE ARE MAGAZINES FOR APPLE USERS

Apple Magazines

There are several periodicals with information about the Apple. Some microcomputer magazines are general and others are for the Apple only. When you're first starting, it is a good idea to stick with the ones dedicated to the Apple since there are different versions of BASIC for non-Apple computers. When you become more experienced, you can choose your own, but to get started there are several good ones with articles exclusively on the Apple. These are as follows:

***Softalk*, 11021 Magnolia Blvd., North Hollywood, CA 91601** — *Softalk* is a monthly publication with a wide variety of articles and programs for the Apple. Their "Beginner's Corner" is an excellent way to learn how to get started, and other tutorial columns will help you in other languages as well. Roger Wagner's "Assembly Lines" is an outstanding tutorial for machine/assembly level programming. The best part is that for the first year a subscription is free! Just send in your Apple serial number and a request for subscription to the above address and you will begin receiving *Softalk* in the mail.

Call -A.P.P.L.E., **304 Main Ave. S., Suite 300, Renton, WA 98055, (206)271-4514** — Some of the best articles and programs to be found are in *Call -A.P.P.L.E.* The monthly magazine is a professionally produced club magazine with over 10,000 members nationwide. For beginners there is a column entitled "A is for Apple," but most of the publication is filled with slightly more advanced articles and programs. Next to the excellent articles, programs and tips, the best aspect of belonging to CALL -A.P.P.L.E. (Apple Pugetsound Program Library Exchange) is the savings on software and hardware. In addition, CALL -A.P.P.L.E. provides a "Hotline" to call for help with your Apple.

***Nibble,* P.O. Box 235, Lincoln, MA 01773, (617)259-9710** — *Nibble* has tutorial series such as "Nibbling at Applesoft," designed for beginners. Also, it has very good "Tips & Techniques" and (interestingly) "Letters to the Editor" columns where you can find helpful comments on using the Apple. It also has several programs, many extremely long, and so it can be useful for building up a program library.

Other Useful Publications — In addition to the above three magazines and *Apple Orchard,* there are several good club magazines and newsletters. None have quite as much as *Call -A.P.P.L.E.,* but many have issues that are excellent. Washington D.C.'s *Apple PI,* Chicago's *The Harvest,* San Francisco's *Cider Press,* Dallas' *Apple Gram,* San Diego's *Sandy Apple Press,* and Los Angeles' *Applesauce* are some of the larger club magazines you can get through the individual clubs. (See the *Apple Orchard* for addresses.) For reviews, *Peelings II* (945 Brook Circle, Las Cruces, NM 88001) magazine is considered the best. They exclusively review software for the Apple, and many consider it to be a "Consumer's Guide" to Apple software. For more general reviews of software Addison-Wesley's *Red Book* is the most complete.

Apple Speaks Many Languages

Besides BASIC, your computer can be programmed and run programs in several other languages. In some cases, special hardware devices are required to run the languages, and there is special software required as well. We'll look at some of these other languages.

Assembly Language

Assembly language is a "low level" language, close to the heart of your computer. It is quite a bit faster than BASIC and virtually every other language we will discuss. To write in assembly language, it is necessary to have an "assembler" to enter code. (The mini-assembler in INTERGER BASIC on your Apple will work, but it is very limited.) This language gives you far more control over your Apple than BASIC, but it is more difficult to

learn, and a program takes more instructions to operate than BASIC. (However, the object code is more compact, taking up fewer sectors on your disk.) Some popular assemblers include:

1. BIG MAC (Call -A.P.P.L.E.)
2. MERLIN (Southwestern Data Systems)
3. LISA 2.5 (On-Line Systems)
4. TED II+ (I.A.C.)

To learn how to program in assembly language, the following two books were found to be the most useful:

1. *Using 6502 Assembly Language: How Anyone Can Program The Apple II* by Randy Hyde. This book can be purchased from your local book or computer store or from:

   Datamost Inc.
   9748 Cozycroft Ave., Unit ABC
   Chatsworth, CA 91311
   (213)709-1202

This is a most useful book for programming with the LISA 2.5 assembler.

2. *Assembly Lines: The Book—A Beginner's Guide To 6502 Programming On The Apple II* by Roger Wagner. This book can be purchased from your local book or computer store or from:

   Softalk Publishing Inc.
   11021 Magnolia Blvd.
   North Hollywood, CA 91601

   This is an excellent book for programming the MERLIN, BIG MAC and TED II+ assemblers.

Other books are available for learning assembly level programming, but the above two are the best for novices.

HIGH AND LOW LEVEL LANGUAGES

When computer people talk of "high" and "low" level languages, think of high level being close to talking in normal English and low level in terms of machine language, e.g., binary and hexadecimal.

PASCAL

PASCAL is a high-level language originally developed for teaching students structured programming. It is faster than BASIC, but it is not as difficult to master as assembly language. However, it is necessary to have a "language card" or 16K RAM card to use it. Apple Inc. markets a version of UCSD PASCAL along with manuals on how to use it. However, other versions of PASCAL are available. LAZAR PASCAL, for example, (Ark Computing, P.O. Box 2025, Corona, CA 91720) is one other source of PASCAL on the market. There are several books on PASCAL available, and the following two were found to be good beginner's books.

1. *Apple PASCAL: A Hands-on Approach* by Arthur Luehrmann and Herbert Peckham. (New York: McGraw-Hill.) This is a step-by-step introduction to Apple PASCAL, showing how to program in PASCAL using a single disk drive. Many books assume the user has 2 drives. Highly recommended.
2. *Elementary PASCAL: Learning To Program Your Computer In PASCAL With Sherlock Holmes* by Henry Ledgard and Andrew Singer. (New York: Vintage Books.) This is a fun way to learn PASCAL since the authors use Sherlock Holmes-type mysteries to be solved with PASCAL. It is based on the draft standard version for Pascal called X3J9/81-003 (!?) and may be slightly different from the version you have, but only slightly so.

FORTH

FORTH is a very fast high-level language, developed to create programs that are almost as fast as assembly language but take less time to program. Faster than PASCAL, BASIC, FORTRAN, COBOL, and virtually every other high-level language, FORTH is programmed by defining "words" that execute routines. New words incorporate previously defined words into FORTH programs. The best part of FORTH is that several versions are public domain. Many Apple clubs have a FORTH language system in their disk libraries based on George Lyons' Fig- (FORTH Interest Group) FORTH, and no special hardware is required to run it since it is an extremely compact language. Likewise, several commercial versions are available for the Apple as well. The following is a sample:

1. **FORTH-79 Ver. 2 (MicroMotion)**—Enhancement package with floating point and hi-res Turtle Graphics available as well. A 79 Standard FORTH system.
2. **LAZAR FORTH (Ark Computing)**—Fig-FORTH using the ANIX operating system.
3. **MVP-FORTH (Mountain View Press, Inc.).**
4. **OGI Fig-FORTH (On-Going Ideas)**—An inexpensive Fig-FORTH with 6502 assembler, editor, and decompiler.

Good books on learning FORTH are only just now becoming available. For learning FORTH, the following are recommended:

1. *Starting FORTH* by Leo Bodie (Englewood Cliffs: Prentice-Hall).

Well written and illustrated work on FORTH for beginners. Uses a combination of words from Fig, 79-Standard, and polyFORTH.

2. *FORTH Dimensions*. Journal of FORTH INTEREST GROUP., P.O. Box 1105, San Carlos, CA 94070. This periodical has numerous articles on FORTH and tutorial columns for persons seriously interested in learning the language.

CP/M

For the Apple, there are several excellent CP/M programs available. In fact, CP/M has one of the largest available public domain libraries of any language. In order to get CP/M for your computer, it is necessary to have a card with a Z-80 microprocessor, of which there are several available. Many business programs, including word processors and data base programs are available in CP/M, and for those primarily interested in business and professional applications, CP/M is certainly something you will want to look into.

Miscellaneous Languages And Compilers

Besides the above languages, it is possible to get disks with COBOL, FORTRAN, LOGO, and other languages for specialized and general applications. Before you spend time, money, and effort on another language, it is highly recommended that you carefully examine your needs. If your main interest is in developing your own programs, first learn BASIC thoroughly and see what you can do with it. If it fits your needs, and its relatively slow speed is sufficient for your uses, then your time will be better spent improving your programming skills in BASIC. If your main interest is in using application programs, then the language capability depends on the programs you are using. Most importantly in this context is whether or not you use CP/M. If you do, then you will need some kind of Z-80 card. Just about all other professionally produced programs will run on a 48K Apple without any other added hardware (this includes programs written in PASCAL, FORTH, etc.).

Finally, if you find that programming in BASIC is most suitable for you, but you would like to speed up your programs, a simple way to do that is with a compiler. Essentially, a compiler is a program that transforms your code into a binary file that will run 4 to 5 times faster than APPLESOFT. All you do is write the program in BASIC, compile it, and then BSAVE the compiled program. From then on, you BRUN your compiled program. The following are some APPLESOFT compilers.

1. SPEED-STAR (Southwestern Data Systems)
2. EXPEDITER (On-Line Systems)
3. BASIC COMPILER (Microsoft)

There are some limitations to compilers, and certain conventions to be followed in writing APPLESOFT programs to be compiled. However, they can significantly reduce your program's run-time.

Some Useful And Fun Programs

This section consists of programs that contain many of the programming practices we have discussed throughout this book. The ones that are included here do something useful either in terms of applications or learning about your computer.

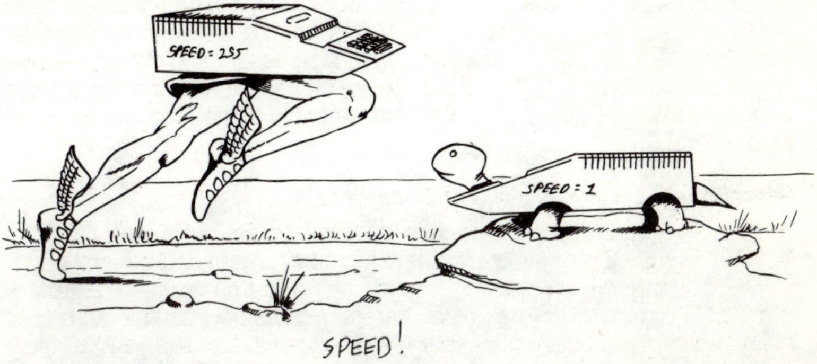

Quick Apple-betize

This program sorts a list of strings (words) for you. It uses the Quick-Sort 2 algorithm for the sort. It is a fairly limited program in that it only accepts single strings and you cannot enter commas, but if you ever want to sort a list of names, recipes or anything else, you will find it handy.

```
10 D$ = CHR$ (13) + CHR$ (4)
20 Z = 0:F = 0
30 TEXT : HOME
40 DIM A$(1000)
50 FOR N = 1 TO 1000
60 INPUT "ENTER WORD ";A$(N)
70 IF A$(N) = " / " THEN 100
80 Z = Z + 1
90 NEXT N
100 I = 1000: REM QUICKSORT 2
110 CALL -936:MS$ = "ALPHABETIZING": FLASH : VTAB 9:
HTAB 20 - LEN(MS$)/2: PRINT MS$: NORMAL
120 S1 = 1
```

```
130 L(1) = 1
140 R(1) = N
150 L1 = L(S1)
160 R1 = R(S1)
170 S1 = S1 - 1
180 L2 = L1
190 R2 = R1
200 X$ = A$(INT ((L1 + R1)/2))
210 C = C + 1
220 IF A$(L2) > = X$ THEN 250
230 L2 = L2 + 1
240 GOTO 210
250 C = C1
260 IF X$ > = A$(R2) THEN 290
270 R2 = R2 - 1
280 GOTO 250
290 IF L2 > R2 THEN 360
300 S = S + 1
310 T$ = A$(L2)
320 A$(L2) = A$(R2)
330 A$(R2) = T$
340 L2 = L2 + 1
350 R2 = R2 - 1
360 IF L2 < = R2 THEN 210
370 IF L2 > = R1 THEN 410
380 S1 = S1 + 1
390 L(S1) = L2
400 R(S1) = R1
410 R1 = R2
420 IF L1 < R1 THEN 180
430 IF S1 > 0 THEN 150
440 REM SORT COMPLETE
450 HOME
460 GOSUB 9000
470 FOR N = 2 TO Z + 1
480 F = F + 1
490 IF F > 22 THEN GOSUB 1000
500 PRINT A$(N)
510 NEXT N
520 PRINT CHR$ (4);"PR#0"
530 END
1000 INVERSE : PRINT "HIT ANY KEY TO CONTINUE ": GET
AN$: NORMAL
1005 F = 0
```

```
1010  RETURN
9000  CALL -936: PRINT "ENTER PRINTER SLOT OR BINARY
DRIVER CALL (0 DISPLAYS TO SCREEN)": INPUT "  ";PR
9010  IF NOT PR THEN RETURN
9020  IF PR > 7 THEN CALL PR: RETURN
9030  PRINT D$;"PR#";PR: PRINT RV$ + RV$: RETURN
```

Sort Menu

This menu program uses the Shell Sort algorithm instead of the Quick Sort. To use this program, it is necessary to enter the files on your disk as DATA statements within the program. It will automatically RUN any APPLESOFT or INTEGER BASIC program but not binary or text files. Of course with your newly acquired programming skills you can fix that.

```
10  TEXT : HOME
20  MU$ = " SORTING MENU ": VTAB 10: HTAB 20 -
LEN(MU$)/2: FLASH : PRINT MU$
30  DIM A$(40):L$ = CHR$ (91):R$ = CHR$ (93)
40  ONERR GOTO 70
50  FOR I = 1 TO 40: READ A$(I)
60  N = N + 1: NEXT
70  I = 40
100  REM SHELL SORT
110  L = (2 ^ INT(LOG (N)/LOG (2))) - 1
120  L = INT(L/2)
130  IF L < 1 THEN 260
140  FOR J = 1 TO L
150  FOR K = J + L TO N STEP L
160  I = K
170  T$ = A$(I)
180  IF A$(I - L) < = T$ THEN 220
190  A$(I) = A$(I - L)
200  I = I - L
210  IF I > L THEN 180
220  A$(I) = T$
230  NEXT K
240  NEXT J
250  GOTO 120
260  NORMAL : REM SORT DONE
270  ONERR GOTO 310
310  HOME : FOR I = 1 TO N
320  IF I < 10 THEN INVERSE : PRINT L$;"  ";I;R$; : NORMAL :
PRINT "  ";A$(I): NEXT
325 IF N < 10 THEN 360
```

```
330  IF I > 20 THEN GOTO 350
340  INVERSE : PRINT L$;I;R$; : NORMAL : PRINT "  ";A$(I):
NEXT
345 IF N < 20 THEN 360
350  VTAB (I − 20): HTAB 20: PRINT "  "; : INVERSE : PRINT
L$;I;R$; : NORMAL : PRINT "  ";A$(I): NEXT
360  GOSUB 600
370  IF C = 99 THEN END
380  PRINT CHR$ (4);"RUN";A$(C)
400  DATA : REM ***ENTER FILES NAMES HERE SEPARATED
BY A COMMA***
500  REM
BY ADDING FILES TO DATA LIST, YOU CAN UPDATE MENU
AUTOMATICALLY
510  REM
THIS ONLY WORKS WITH 40 FILES OR LESS AND IT ONLY
RUNS "A" OR "I" FILES
520  REM
SEE IF YOU CAN FIX IT UP TO RUN WITH ANY KIND OF FILE
AND MORE THAN 40
530  REM
BY ENTERING YOUR FILES AS DATA STATEMENTS THIS CAN
BE USED ON ANY DISK
600  VTAB 22: INVERSE : PRINT " ENTER 99 TO EXIT ":
NORMAL
610  VTAB 23: FOR W = 1 TO 500: NEXT : FOR I = 38 TO 1
STEP − 1: FOR J = 1 TO 10: NEXT : HTAB I: PRINT "  "; :
NEXT : HTAB 2: INPUT "CHOOSE FILE BY NUMBER− −> ";C:
RETURN
```

Disk Locator

This program incorporates the Shell Sort again, but it does it with a sequential text file. When you begin to accumulate disks, it is sometimes difficult to remember where everything is, but using DISK LOCATOR, you can keep track of everything on both sides of your disk. (NOTE: You must first CREATE a file before READing or APPENDing a file!)

```
10  TEXT : HOME : VTAB 7
20  HD$ = " DISK LOCATOR BY BILL SANDERS "
30  SPEED = 150: FOR I = LEN(HD$) TO 1 STEP − 1: PRINT
MID$(HD$,I,1); : NEXT
40  INVERSE : FOR W = 1 TO 1000: NEXT : VTAB 7: HTAB 1:
FOR I = 1 TO LEN(HD$): PRINT MID$(HD$,I,1);: NEXT :
```

```
NORMAL
50  MD$ = CHR$ (13) + CHR$ (4):D$ = CHR$ (4):S$ = " / "
60  DIM DI$(200), D1$(200), D2$(200), ST$(200)
70  SPEED = 255: PRINT : VTAB 10
80  FOR R = 1 TO 4: READ R$(R): NEXT
90  FOR R = 1 TO 4: PRINT CHR$ (91);R; CHR$
(93);"  ";R$(R): PRINT : NEXT
100  FOR I = 38 TO 1 STEP - 1: FOR J = 1 TO 10: NEXT :
HTAB I: PRINT "  ";: NEXT : HTAB 2: PRINT "CHOOSE BY
NUMBER-->";: GET A%: PRINT A%
110  IF A% = 3 THEN PRINT "DO YOU WANT THIS ON THE
PRINTER?(Y/N) ";: GET AA$: PRINT AA$
120  IF A% = 3 THEN 450
130  IF A% = 4 THEN END
140  TEXT : HOME : REM DISK STORAGE DATA BASE
150  N = 0
160  FOR I = 1 TO 200
180  HOME : VTAB 10: INVERSE : PRINT "FILE #';N + 1;:
NORMAL :: PRINT SPC(5);: INVERSE : PRINT "ENTER 'XX' TO
QUIT": NORMAL : PRINT
190  INPUT "SIDE 1 --> ";D1$(I)
200  IF D1$(I) = "XX" THEN 280
210  INPUT "SIDE 2 --> ";D2$(I)
220  INPUT "LOCATION --> ";ST$(I)
230  DI$(I) = D1$(I) + S$ + D2$(I) + S$ + ST$(I)
240  PRINT : PRINT DI$(I): INVERSE : PRINT : PRINT
"CORRECT?(Y/N)";: NORMAL : GET AN$
250  IF AN$ = "N" THEN 180
260  N = N + 1
270  NEXT I
280  I = 200:I = 0
290  HOME :MS$ = " SORTING ": FLASH : VTAB 10: HTAB 20
- LEN(MS$)/2: PRINT MS$
300  GOSUB 610
310  IF A% = 2 THEN 380
320  PRINT MD$"OPEN DISK FILES": PRINT MD$"WRITE DISK
FILES"
330  FOR I = 1 TO N
340  PRINT DI$(I)
350  NEXT I
360  PRINT D$"CLOSE DISK FILES"
370  GOTO 430
380  PRINT MD$"APPEND DISK FILES": PRINT MD$"WRITE
DISK FILES"
```

```
390  FOR I = 1 TO N
400  PRINT DI$(I)
410  NEXT I
420  PRINT D$"CLOSE DISK FILES"
430  HOME : VTAB 10: PRINT "DISK FILES CLOSED": VTAB
23: END
440  DATA "CREATE DISK FILES","APPEND DISK FILES","READ
DISK FILES","EXIT"
450  PRINT MD$;"OPEN DISK FILES": PRINT MD$"READ DISK
FILES"
460  N = 0
470  ONERR GOTO 520
480  FOR I = 1 TO 200
490  INPUT DI$(I)
505 N = N + 1
510  NEXT I
520  I = 200:I = 0
530  HOME : FLASH : VTAB 10:MS$ = " SORTING ": HTAB 20
- LEN(MS$)/2: PRINT MS$
540  GOSUB 610
550  HOME
560  IF AA$ = "Y" THEN GOSUB 810
570  FOR I = 1 TO N: PRINT I;". ";DI$(I): NEXT
580  IF AA$ = "Y" THEN PRINT MD$;"PR#0"
590  PRINT D$"CLOSE DISK FILES"
600  END
610  REM SHELL SORT
620  L = (2 ^ INT(LOG (N)/LOG (2))) - 1
630  L = INT(L/2)
640  IF L < 1 THEN 790
650  FOR J = 1 TO L
660  FOR K = J + L TO N STEP L
670  I = K
680  T$ = DI$(I)
690  C = C + 1
700  IF DI$(I - L) < = T$ THEN 750
710  DI$(I) = DI$(I - L)
720  S = S + 1
730  I = I - L
740  IF I > L THEN 690
750  DI$(I) = T$
760  NEXT K
770  NEXT J
780  GOTO 630
```

```
790  NORMAL : REM SORT DONE
800  RETURN
810  HOME : PRINT "ENTER PRINTER SLOT OR BINARY
DRIVER CALL (0 DISPLAYS TO SCREEN)": INPUT "  ";PR
820  IF NOT PR THEN RETURN
830  IF PR > 7 THEN CALL PR: RETURN
840  PRINT D$;"PR#";PR: RETURN
```

PROGRAM HEADER

This program is simply for fun and adding a little interest to your program (or disk) headers. After playing with it for a while, rather than INPUTing the title of your program, simply define YP$ as the title of your program and GOSUB to it as a subroutine at the beginning of your own program. It will put an end to boring program headers.

```
10000  TEXT : HOME :F$ = "=": PRINT "ENTER PROGRAM
NAME:": PRINT "(MUST BE EVEN # OF CHARACTERS.)":
INPUT "-->";YP$:YP$ = "**" + YP$ + "**":P = LEN(YP$)
10010  HOME :LM = 20 - LEN(YP$)/2
10020  IF LEN(F$) <> 40 THEN F$ = F$ + "=": GOTO
10020
10030  PRINT F$;: FOR I = 1 TO 15: PRINT "I"; SPC(38);"I";:
NEXT : PRINT F$
10040  INVERSE : FOR I = 2 TO 16: HTAB 2: VTAB I: PRINT
SPC(38): NEXT : NORMAL : FOR PAUSE = 1 TO 1000: NEXT
10050  FOR K = 2 TO 16: FOR W = 20 TO 21: VTAB K: HTAB
W: PRINT SPC(1): NEXT : NEXT : FOR I = 2 TO LEN(YP$)/2
10060  FOR J = 2 TO 16: VTAB J: HTAB I + 20: PRINT
SPC(1): VTAB J: HTAB 21 - I: PRINT SPC(1): NEXT : NEXT
10070  VTAB 22
10080  SS$ = "*"
10090  IF LEN(SS$) < 40 THEN SS$ = SS$ + "*": GOTO
10100  FLASH : HTAB 1: VTAB 18: PRINT SS$: NORMAL
10110  SPEED = 150
10120  L$ = LEFT$(YP$, LEN(YP$)/2)
10130  R$ = RIGHT$(YP$, LEN(YP$)/2)
10140  FOR V = 1 TO (LEN(YP$)/2)
10150  VTAB 9: HTAB 20 + V: PRINT MID$(R$,V,1): GOSUB
10160  IF V = (LEN(L$)) + 1 THEN 10180
10170  VTAB 9: HTAB 21 - V: PRINT MID$(L$,
LEN(L$)-(V-1),1): GOSUB 10230
10180  NEXT : SPEED = 255
10190  INVERSE : VTAB 22:H$ = " <HIT ANY KEY TO
CONTINUE> ": HTAB 20 - LEN(H$)/2: PRINT H$: NORMAL :
```

```
WAIT -16384,128: POKE -16368,0
10200 VTAB 16: HTAB LM: POKE 32,LM: POKE 35,16: POKE
33,P: POKE 34,2
10210 FOR I = 1 TO 16: FOR J = 1 TO 50: NEXT J: CALL
-912: NEXT
10220 VTAB 22: TEXT : FOR I = 1 TO 24: FOR J = 1 TO 50:
NEXT J: CALL -912: NEXT : END
10230 BZ = 49200: FOR I = 1 TO 15: FOR J = 1 TO I *
(J-1): NEXT :B = PEEK (BZ): NEXT
10240 RETURN
```

Calendar Plot

This program is an extension of what we learned in Chapter 7 about using lo-res graphics for plotting. It will allow you to enter a maximum above 39 and then translate the data you INPUT into proportional graphing on a monthly basis. You can begin and end with any month you wish, but you have to keep it within the confines of a single year.

```
10 TEXT : HOME
20 VTAB 8: INPUT "MAXIMUM VALUE TO BE ENTERED ->
";MV
30 N = 1:NN = MV: FLASH : PRINT " CALCULATING ":
NORMAL
40 IF NN > 39 THEN N = N + .1:NN = MV/N: GOTO 40
50 HOME : VTAB 10: INPUT "NAME OF PLOT-> ";NP$
60 HTAB 1: VTAB 10: CALL -868: INPUT "YEAR-> ";Y
70 VTAB 1: HTAB 20 - LEN(NP$)/2: INVERSE : PRINT NP$:
NORMAL : POKE 34,2
80 HTAB 1: VTAB 10: CALL -868: INPUT "BEGIN WITH
WHAT MONTH?(1-12) ";B%:: PRINT
90 HTAB 1: VTAB 10: CALL -868: INPUT "END WITH WHAT
MONTH?(1-12) ";P%: HOME
100 DIM V(P%)
110 CA$ = "JFMAMJJASOND"
120 FOR I = B% TO P%: PRINT "PLOT VALUE (MAX=";MV;")
FOR ";: GOSUB 230: INPUT "  ";V(I): PRINT
130 V(I) = INT(V(I)/N): NEXT
140 GR : COLOR = 10
150 VLIN 0,39 AT 0: HLIN 0,39 AT 39
160 FOR I = 0 TO 39 STEP 4: PLOT 1,I: NEXT
170 COLOR = 15: FOR I = B% TO P%: VLIN 39,(39 - V(I))
AT (I * 3): NEXT
180 HOME : FOR I = B% TO P%: VTAB 21: HTAB (I * 3) + 1:
PRINT MID$(CA$,I,1): NEXT I
```

```
190  PRINT "HATCH MARKS=";MV/10
200  HTAB 20 - LEN(NP$)/2: PRINT NP$;: PRINT "  ";:
INVERSE : PRINT SPC(1);Y; SPC(1): NORMAL
210  WAIT -16384,128
220  TEXT : HOME : END
230  INVERSE : ON I GOSUB
250,260,270,280,290,300,310,320,330,340,350,360
240  NORMAL : RETURN
250  PRINT "JANUARY";: RETURN
260  PRINT "FEBRUARY";: RETURN
270  PRINT "MARCH";: RETURN
280  PRINT "APRIL";: RETURN
290  PRINT "MAY";: RETURN
300  PRINT "JUNE";: RETURN
310  PRINT "JULY";: RETURN
320  PRINT "AUGUST";: RETURN
330  PRINT "SEPTEMBER";: RETURN
340  PRINT "OCTOBER";: RETURN
350  PRINT "NOVEMBER";: RETURN
360  PRINT "DECEMBER";: RETURN
```

ASCII Hex/Dec

This little program lists ASCII in both HEX and DECIMAL either to your printer or the screen. It only lists the first 128 (0 to 127) codes, but it is handy for looking up CHR$ codes and it will give you an idea of one way to translate decimal into hexadecimal.

```
10  TEXT : HOME
20  GOSUB 400
30  HOME : PRINT
40  GOSUB 300
50  DIM H$(127)
60  FOR H = 0 TO 127
70  READ H$(H): NEXT H
80  FOR I = 0 TO 63
85 IF PEEK (-16384) > 128 THEN GOSUB 500
90  J = I:K = I + 64
100  IF I < 27 THEN J = I + 64
105 IF I < 10 THEN PRINT "$0";H$(I);: HTAB (5): PRINT "  ";I;:
HTAB 11: PRINT CHR$ (J); CHR$ (99);: GOTO 150
110  IF I < 27 THEN PRINT "$";H$(I);: HTAB (5): PRINT I;:
HTAB 11: PRINT CHR$ (J); CHR$ (99);: GOTO 150
120  PRINT "$";H$(I);: HTAB (5): PRINT I;: HTAB (11): IF I > 26
AND I < 32 THEN PRINT "ESC";: GOTO 150
```

```
130  IF I = 32 THEN PRINT "SPACE";: GOTO 150
140  HTAB (11): PRINT CHR$ (J);
150  HTAB (17): PRINT "$";H$(K);: HTAB (23): PRINT K;: HTAB
(29): PRINT CHR$ (K)
160  NEXT
170  PRINT CHR$ (4);"PR#0"
180  END
200  DATA  0,1,2,3,4,5,6,7,8,9,0
A,0B,0C,0D,0E,0F,10,11,12,13,14,15,16,17,
18,19,1A,1B,1C,1D,1E,1F,20,21,22,23,24,25,26,27,28,29,2A,
2B,2C,2D,2E,2F,30,31,3
2,33,34,35,36,37,38,39,3A,3B,3C,3D,3E,3F,40,41,42,43,44,45,4
96,47,48,49
210  DATA  4A,4B,4C,4D,4E,4F,50
220  DATA  51,52,
53,54,55,56,57,58,59,5A,5B,5C,5D,5E,5F,60,61,62,63,64,65,66,
67,68,69,6A,6B,6C,6D,6E,
6F,70,71,72,73,74,75,76,77,78,79,7A,7B,7C,7D,7E,7F
300  HEX$ = "HEX":DEC$ = "DEC":CH$ = "CHAR"
310  L$ = "======================;
=============="
320  PRINT HEX$; SPC( 1);DEC$; SPC(2);CH$;"  ";: INVERSE :
PRINT " / ";: NORMAL : PRINT "  ";HEX$; SPC(3);DEC$;
SPC(2);CH$: PRINT L$
330  POKE 34,3: IF PR < > 0 THEN RETURN
340  VTAB 10: HTAB 33: PRINT "HIT": HTAB 33: PRINT "ANY":
HTAB 33: PRINT "KEY": HTAB 33: PRINT "TO STOP": HTAB 33:
PRINT "OR START": POKE 33,32: VTAB 4: RETURN
400  CALL -936: PRINT "ENTER PRINTER SLOT OR BINARY
DRIVER CALL (0 DISPLAYS TO SCREEN)": INPUT "  ";PR
410  IF NOT PR THEN RETURN
420  IF PR > 7 THEN CALL PR: RETURN
430  D$ = CHR$ (13) + CHR$ (4)
440  PRINT D$;"PR#";PR: RETURN
500  GET A$: GET B$: RETURN
```

Screen View

This program was written by Richard Myers to show the 10 screens of your Apple. Notice the POKE addresses used to access all the screens. When you RUN it, it will take you on a tour of your Apple's screens.

```
10 REM THIS PROGRAM WAS INSPIRED BY ERIC GOEZ.
20 TEXT : HOME : PRINT : INVERSE
30 FOR I = 1 TO 200: PRINT "  ";: NEXT
```

```
40 VTAB 3: HTAB 14: PRINT "SCREEN VIEW"
50 PRINT TAB(18)"BY"
60 PRINT TAB(14)"R. H. MYERS": PRINT : NORMAL
70 PRINT : PRINT : PRINT : PRINT "THIS PROGRAM
DISPLAYS EACH OF THE TEN"
80 PRINT "SCREENS AVAILABLE ON THE APPLE
COMPUTER"
90 PRINT : PRINT : PRINT "PRESS ANY KEY TO BEGIN";: GET
A$: TEXT : HOME
100 A0 = 49232:A1 = 49233:A2 = 49234:A3 = 49235:A4
= 49236:A5 = 49237:A6 = 49238:A7 = 49239
110 PRINT "SCREENS AVAILABLE FOR VIEWING": PRINT
120 PRINT "A   TEXT SCREEN #1"
130 PRINT "B   TEXT SCREEN #2": PRINT
140 PRINT "C   LO-RES SCREEN #1"
150 PRINT "D   LO-RES SCREEN #2": PRINT
160 PRINT "E   HI-RES SCREEN #1"
170 PRINT "F   HI-RES SCREEN #2": PRINT
180 PRINT "G   TEXT & LO-RES SCREEN #1"
190 PRINT "H   TEXT & LO-RES SCREEN #2": PRINT
200 PRINT "I   TEXT & HI-RES SCREEN #1"
210 PRINT "J   TEXT & HI-RES SCREEN #2"
220 PRINT : PRINT : PRINT "PRESS LETTER FOR DESIRED
SCREEN": PRINT
230 PRINT "SPACE BAR WILL CYCLE THROUGH ALL
SCREENS"
240 PRINT "PRESS 'Q' TO QUIT"
250 FOR I = 1 TO 10
260 ON I GOSUB 430,440,450,460,470,480,490,500,510,520
270 GET A$
280 IF A$ = "A" THEN : FLASH : PRINT "THIS IS TEXT
SCREEN #1": FOR J = 1 TO 2000: NEXT J: NORMAL : TEXT :
HOME : GOTO 110
290 IF A$ = CHR$ (32) THEN 410
300 IF A$ = "B" THEN GOSUB 440: GET A$: GOTO 250
310 IF A$ = "C" THEN GOSUB 450: GET A$: GOTO 250
320 IF A$ = "D" THEN GOSUB 460: GET A$: GOTO 250
330 IF A$ = "E" THEN GOSUB 470: GET A$: GOTO 250
340 IF A$ = "F" THEN GOSUB 480: GET A$: GOTO 250
350 IF A$ = "G" THEN GOSUB 490: GET A$: GOTO 250
360 IF A$ = "H" THEN GOSUB 500: GET A$: GOTO 250
370 IF A$ = "I" THEN GOSUB 510: GET A$: GOTO 250
380 IF A$ = "J" THEN GOSUB 520: GET A$: GOTO 250
390 IF A$ = "Q" THEN GOTO 530
```

```
400  IF A$ < > CHR$ (32) THEN GOTO 250
410  NEXT I
420  GOTO 250
430  POKE A4,1: POKE A1,1: RETURN
440  POKE A5,1: POKE A1,1: RETURN
450  POKE A4,1: POKE A2,1: POKE A6,1: POKE A0,1:
RETURN
460  POKE A5,1: POKE A2,1: POKE A6,1: POKE A0,1:
RETURN
470  POKE A4,1: POKE A2,1: POKE A7,1: POKE A0,1:
RETURN
480  POKE A5,1: POKE A2,1: POKE A7,1: POKE A0,1:
RETURN
490  POKE A4,1: POKE A3,1: POKE A6,1: POKE A0,1:
RETURN
500  POKE A5,1: POKE A3,1: POKE A5,1: POKE A0,1:
RETURN
510  POKE A4,1: POKE A3,1: POKE A7,1: POKE A0,1:
RETURN
520  POKE A5,1: POKE A3,1: POKE A7,1: POKE A0,1:
RETURN
530  TEXT : HOME : END
==================== ======
SANDY APPLE PRESS
JULY 1982
===========================
```

YOU'LL BE AMAZED AT HOW MUCH WRITING YOU'LL DO WITH A WORD PROCESSOR

Utility Programs

What's a Utility

Utility programs are programs that help you program or access different parts of your computer. In this section we will review some of the more useful utility programs available at this time.

PLE And ACE

Two of the most useful utilities around for the Apple are PROGRAM LINE EDITOR (PLE) (Synergistic Software/Call -A.P.P.L.E.) and APPLESOFT COMMAND EDITOR (ACE) (Southwestern Data Systems). These programs allow you to easily edit program lines without having to re-write or re-trace the entire lines. For example, if you entered

```
10 TEXT HOME : D$ = CHR$(1) + CHR$(4)
```

and meant to put a colon between TEXT and HOME, and you really wanted CHR$(13) instead of CHR$(1). With PLE or ACE, changing that would be a snap. To make the changes you would simply enter CTRL-E (for edit) and after EDIT appears, enter the line number to be corrected. The line you wanted would appear. To make the changes you would enter the colon between TEXT and HOME and then using CTRL-I (for insert) add the 3 to CHR$(1) to change it to CHR$(13) and then depress RETURN to exit the editor. You would not have to retrace the entire line or put in POKE 33,33 or anything else. There is a lot more these editors do, and new versions of PLE (GLOBAL PLE) and ACE are now available that do editing and a lot more. Both programs reside at a place in memory where they will not get in the way of the program you are writing. They are the most important utility you can get.

APPLESOFT Tool Kit/DOS Tool Kit

Apple, Inc.'s APPLESOFT TOOL KIT is more than a utility. Besides APPLESOFT PROGRAMMER'S ASSISTANT (APA), it also has a hi-res character generator, an animation package and a "relocating" program. However, the APA program is the important utility. With it, you can renumber programs, have automatic line numbering, hold and merge programs, cross reference variables and perform other useful tasks. Like PLE and ACE, APA resides in a place in memory that will not get in the way of most of your APPLESOFT programs. Once it is loaded, it is possible to renumber your program for purposes of blocking or giving yourself more room between line numbers simply by entering &R. Likewise, you can load one program, and using &H, hold it in memory and load another program and then use &M to merge the programs together.

DOS Boss

Sometimes a utility is both fun and useful. Beagle Bros.' DOS BOSS is both useful and entertaining. It is useful for customizing your disks (e.g., having your name appear instead of VOL. 254 on disk headings). With DOS BOSS, it is possible to rewrite error messages, change DOS commands, and do all other kinds of things with your disks that you normally could not. Perhaps the best thing about DOS BOSS, as well as all other Beagle Bros. disks, is the extras you get with them that are both entertaining and educational. I am referring to their famous Tip Books. In these little books are hints on how to maximize the use of your Apple, programs and lots of nutty insights to help you get going in various areas of computing. Moreover, Beagle Bros. disks are listable. That means you can learn how they did something with a program by listing them.

Routine Machine

A final programming utility you may want to purchase is ROUTINE MACHINE (Southwestern Data Systems). This program allows you to imbed machine language routines into Applesoft programs. What this means is that after learning how to program in APPLESOFT, you can virtually write programs with the speed of machine language. Several routines, such as sort, search, input, and many more are on the ROUTINE MACHINE disk. When writing an APPLESOFT program, all the user has to do is to enter an ampersand before a function (e.g., & SORT) and ROUTINE MACHINE will enter a binary routine into the APPLESOFT program that will jump to the machine language routine executing the desired function. Programs can be increased in speed by a factor of 10 or more with this utility, a shortcut to machine-level programming.

Other Utilities

There are several other utilities on the market and in the public domain that will help you in programming, and there are certain to be more available as time goes on. The ones I have suggested are the most useful based on my own experiences in programming. If you join an Apple Users Group, you will learn about a lot more and other's experiences. Like all other programs that you are thinking of buying, ask other users about them and get a demonstration of their use first!

Word Processors

Your Apple computer can be turned into a first class word processor with a word processing program. Word processors turn your computer into a super typewriter. They can do everything from moving blocks of text to finding spelling mistakes. Editing and making changes is a snap, and once you get used to writing with a word processor, you'll never go back to a typewriter again. This book was written with a word processor, and it took a fraction of the time a typewriter would have taken. (Believe me, I wrote 9 books with a typewriter!)

There are some limitations with word processors. First, the Apple screen displays only 40 columns. Since the standard page size is 80 columns, this bothers some people since what appears on the written page is different from what appears on the screen. You can buy an 80 column card for the Apple or word processors with 70 columns done with software (even though a full horizontal page is 80 columns, the margins take up at least 10 columns). Also, some word processors will "scroll" horizontally, to give you a pretty good idea of what your page will look like. Since I write in everything from double column (two 40 column groups) to 132 columns (using condensed type), I was never bothered by 40 columns on the screen and 80 (more or less) on the printed page. A second difference some users find annoying is the different set of conventions used on word processors and typewriters. For example, to get upper case, word processors use the ESC key or CTRL-A instead of the SHIFT key as on typewriters. It is possible to make simple changes on your Apple to get the SHIFT key to give you upper case. However, I find it much easier to use either ESC or CTRL-A for getting upper case since you do not have to hold the SHIFT key down while hitting another key. Finally, as it comes, the Apple II does not have lower case. Again, this can easily be remedied with a lower-case adaptor (a chip installed under the keyboard). Also, some word processors have lower case in software, not requiring any special hardware. (My own preference is the chip since it allows me to use lower case with any program.)

Before we proceed with a list of suggested word processing packages, let me offer a word of caution. If you meet other Apple users who have a certain type of word processor they have worked with for a while, they will swear it is the best available. Never argue about politics, religion or word processors with Apple users! This is because word processors are fairly sophisticated programs, and it takes a while to become accustomed to all of their strengths and weaknesses, and by the time a person does, he/she has invested a good deal of time and has a become quite skilled in the program's use. Thus, users are convinced that their own word processor is the best there is, and it can be difficult to determine which one is best for you. To give you some help in making up your mind, the following are some features you might want to look for:

1. **Find/Replace.**
   Will find any string in your text and/or find and replace any one string with another string. Good for correcting spelling errors and locating sections of text to be repaired.

2. **Block Moves.**
   Will move blocks of text from one place to another (e.g., move a paragraph from the middle to end of document). Extremely valuable editing tool.
3. **Link Files.**
   Automatically links files on disks. Very important for longer documents and for linking standardized shorter documents.
4. **Line/Screen Oriented Editing.**
   Line-oriented editing requires locating beginning of line of text and then editing from that point. Screen-oriented editing allows beginning editing from anywhere on the screen. The latter form of editing is important for large documents and where a good deal of editing is normally required.
5. **Automatic Page Numbering.**
   Pages are automatically numbered without having to determine page breaks in writing text.
6. **Imbedded Code.**
   In word processors, this enables the user to send special instructions directly to the printer for changing tabs, enabling special characters on the printer and doing other things to the printed text without having to set the parameters beforehand and/or having the ability to override set parameters.

These are just a few of the things to look for in word processors. As a rule of thumb, the more a word processor can do, the more it costs. If you only want to write letters and short documents, there is little need to buy an expensive word processor. However, if you are writing longer, more complex, and a wider variety of documents, the investment in a more sophisticated word processor is well worth the added cost. If you have specialized needs (e.g., producing billing forms), you will want to look for those features in a word processor that meets those needs. Therefore, while a word processor may not do certain things, it may be just what you want for your special applications. As with other software, get a thorough demonstration of any word processor on an Apple before laying out your hard earned cash.

Inexpensive, Simple Word Processors

1. **Apple Writer (Apple,Inc.).**
   Basic word processor, 40 columns, "wrap around," ESC key upper/lower case toggle. Very simple to use with good documentation.
2. **The Correspondent (Southwestern Data Systems).**
   Uses 80 column "scroll" to format text (e.g., view half of 80 column page and scroll horizontally to view other half), imbed-

ded code, flexible. Good for letters and short documents, forms, etc.

Medium-priced, More Sophisticated Word Processors

1. **Super Text (Muse).**
(a) **Super Text 40/56/70.** Provides upper/lower case and up to 70 columns on screen without hardware attachments. Can design your own fonts and convert to and from non-Super-Text files.
(b) **Super Text 40/80.** Requires lower case adaptor or Videx 80-column card. This book was written with Super Text and is my personal favorite. It has excellent screen-oriented editing, software type-ahead buffer, relative page numbering, parameter subroutines for various printers, preview mode, automatic file linking, excellent documentation and very fast execution in addition to several other features. Excellent for a variety of documents and different printers.
2. **Screen Writer II (On-Line).**
Line-oriented editing, excellent documentation/tutorial, flexible, simple to use, limited software printer spooling, 70 columns in software. Somewhat slow, but handles different types of documents well.
3. **Apple Writer II (Apple, Inc.).**
Vastly improved version of Apple Writer. Still simple to use, but vastly improved over original Apple Writer. Can be used with certain 80 column cards and on variety of documents.
4. **Write-On (Datamost).**
Well documented, simple to use but very flexible word processor. Excellent for a wide variety of documents but one of the most simple word processors to learn to use.

Expensive Super Word Processors

Word-Star (Micropro, Inc.).
Requires 80 column card and Z-80 (CP/M) card. For those who have close to $1000 to invest in the hardware/software required for the use of Word-Star, it is a professional-level word processor that will do just about anything you want. It requires a good deal of study to use all of its functions, and in addition to the manual that comes with it, there are separate tutorials on the market. However, once mastered, there is very little by way of word processing it will not do.

The list of word processors suggested is only a partial one of what is now available. Other popular word processors include MAGIC WINDOW,

EXECUTIVE SECRETARY, EASY WRITER, LETTER PERFECT and WORD HANDLER. In addition, there are programs that will check your spelling and catch errors for you. One of the best I have seen is APPLE SPELLER (Sensible Software), which can be used with most word processors other than WORD STAR. For WORD STAR users, there is SPELLSTAR (Micropro). Also, there are programs that will merge other programs with word processors. For example, ADDRESS BOOK and FORM LETTER (both by Muse) can be used together with SUPER-TEXT to write several form letters and automatically address them. GRAFTRIX can be used with APPLE WRITER to print graphics within a word processor file. The only question is what CANNOT be done with your Apple and word processing!

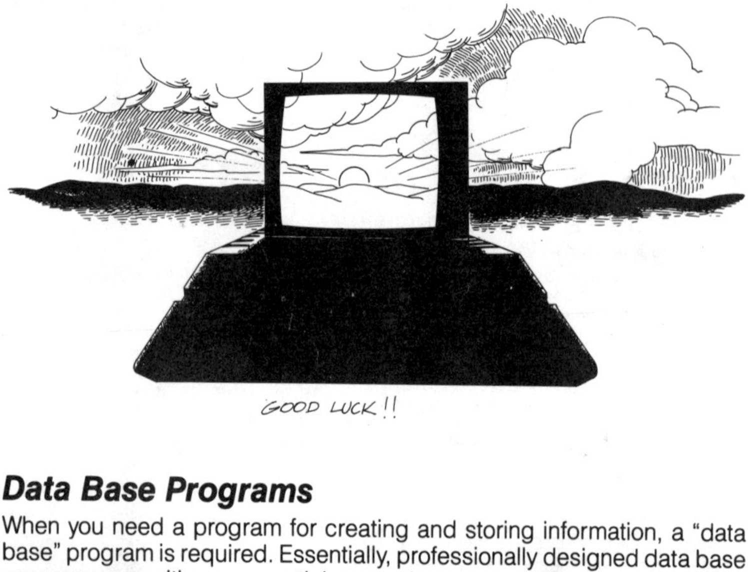

GOOD LUCK!!

Data Base Programs

When you need a program for creating and storing information, a "data base" program is required. Essentially, professionally designed data base programs are either sequential or random access files. When you use one, all you have to do is to use the pre-defined fields provided or create fields. For example, a user may want to keep a data base of customers. In addition to having fields for name and address, the user may want fields for the specific type of product the customer buys, dates of last purchase, how much money is owed, date of last payment, etc. The following are some popular data base programs.

File Cabinent — This program has been around a long time, but is still a nice little data base program. You can find it on public domain disks available through your local Apple Club or the International Apple Core. It is comparatively limited, no documentation, but it is useful for personal, non-professional applications.

Personal Filing System (Software Publishing Corp.) — Written in PASCAL, this popular data base system is very simple to use and can hold large amounts of information in a single record. Reports for PFS can be generated with PFS: REPORTS, a separate program also by Software Publishing Corp. which allows user to sort, calculate, and generate compiled information from PFS data files.

DB Master (Stoneware) — In its latest version, this is a total data base package for creating data base files, generating reports, sorting, calculating and doing just about everything a data base system can do. Written in machine language to maximize speed. Works best with multiple disk drives.

The Data Factory (Micro Lab) — Very good data base program for creating and changing data bases. Allows user to transfer records to new data base, so that once records are entered, it is unnecessary to re-enter records when new data base is developed. Gets very high marks from users.

dBase II (Ashton-Tate). — An extremely powerful relational database management system for professional applications. Handles multiple databases and can be used with only a single drive. Extensive documentation and requires CP/M to use.

Probably more than most other packages, data base programs should be examined carefully before purchasing. Some of the more expensive data bases can be used with virtually any kind of application, but if you're only going to be using your data base to keep a list of names and addresses to print out mailing labels, for example, a data base program designed to do that one thing will usually do it better and for a lot less money. On the other hand if your needs are varied and involve sophisticated report generation and changing record fields, then do not expect a simple, specialized program to do the job.

Business Programs

There are so many different business programs that do so many different things, not including data base programs or word processors, that this section will necessarily be somewhat sketchy. However, it will give you an idea of where to start and a spectrum of what is available for your Apple. Included are programs that range from general spreadsheet calculations to food/nutritional planners.

VisiCalc (VisiCorp) — The consistent best selling program for the Apple, according to *Softalk* magazine, has been VisiCalc. It is an electronic spreadsheet that can be used to calculate numerous rows and columns of numeric data. It is extremely flexible, and the user can devise worksheet formats to do anything from calculating payrolls to expense accounts. There are several supporting programs available separately to use with VisiCalc for plotting, data base files, forecasting, etc.

Financial Management System II (Jarvis/Southwestern Data Systems) — Sets up multiple accounts against a common budget for keeping track of expenses, income, taxes, etc. Has several macros for abbrievating budget categories.

Real Estate Analysis Planner (R.E.A.P.) (Datamost) — A program for the analysis of real estate costs, payments, interests, equity, etc. By entering different costs and payments, the program will analyze various other elements of real estate buying and selling, including tax advantages, annual income from property, general forecasting, etc. Prints out all facts and figures for prospective buyer.

Tax Preparer (Howardsoft) — Allows user to enter income, deductions, etc. for preparing federal income tax returns for 10 schedules and 11 forms. Printouts are in IRS forms for direct filing. After user buys original package, yearly updates are supplied at nominal cost.

B.I.S. General Ledger On Line (Broderick & Associates) — An electronic general ledger and business information system for producing selected business activity reports quickly. Written in machine language for maximizing speed.

Nutri Planner–800 (Praxis Associates, Inc.) — Presented in an electronic spread sheet fashion, Nutri Planner–800 gives instant information on 800 food items in 25 nutritional categories such as calories, vitamins, minerals, etc. It is used for nutritional assessment, recipe analysis, and food budgeting primarily for institutional uses, e.g., hospitals, schools, etc. It is easy to use and fast, written in FORTH.

Graphics Packages

In our chapter on graphics, we discussed some of the Apple's capabilities with graphics. However, certain uses require either highly advanced programming skills or a good graphics package. The following is a list of some excellent graphics programs.

Alpha Plot (Beagle Bros.) — A simple to use graphics drawing package, including, keyboard or paddle drawing, hi-res "typing" text fonts, space saving "scrunch" routine for saving hi-res files to disk at less than 34 sectors, special keyboard chart for ease of use, numerous image options for special effects plus little "extras" on disk.

The Complete Graphics System II (Penguin) — A combination two/three dimensional drawing, shape making, hi-res font, and animation package at a low cost. A bit awkward to use, but is reasonably priced.

GraFORTH (Insoft) — A combination, drawing, font editor, two/three dimensional shape editor, turtle graphics, animation and music language package. This package is actually a special version of the FORTH language for doing graphics on the Apple. It comes with a 200 page manual for both learning how to program in GraFORTH and using the several editors, fonts, etc. Allows user to produce really first class, professionally looking graphics, animation and music. Very fast and could be used to produce graphic games with sound. A personal favorite.

The Printographer (Southwestern Data Systems) — This is a simple to use but very powerful graphics dump program. Picture cropping, magnification, "cameo" and "diamond" cropping, sector compactor, single or multiple disk drive use, horizontal placement, rapid loading of graphics files, printing to printer or disk plus compatibility with virtually every printer makes this graphics dump package one of the best available.

Zoom Grafix (Phoenix Software) — A popular graphics dump routine with screen preview of graphics before printing and will print out selected portion of picture.

Apple Mechanic (Beagle Bros.) — Combination graphics/disk zap. Has excellent shape table editor and shape "driver" routines. In addition, it has a number of hi-res fonts, a font editor and a font writing routine. (The disk zap program allows you to write directly to any track and sector on your disk—not graphics, but a nice thing to have for customizing and recovering blown disks.) Comes with tip book on how to use programs and teriffic tips for your Apple.

Hardware

There is so much hardware for the Apple, that like our other lists, this one is only a sampling. In Chapter 1 we discussed 16K RAM cards, modems, and other hardware for your computer. Here, I want to point out some specialized hardware other than what has already been mentioned. There are several excellent RAM cards, from 16 to 256K, and modems on the market for your Apple; they will not be reviewed here.

Dithertizer II (Computer Station) — This is a hardware package with a video camera and plug-in adaptor along with software for taking disk "photographs." The "photos" may then be printed out to your printer.

Doubltime Printer (Southwestern Data Systems) — This is a hardware/software system (ROM chip/interrupt card/disk) for "printer spooling" that allows user to perform multi-functions with printer and computer. Unlike a printer buffer that is limited to the buffer size, spooling will print out single/multiple files of any size from disk while allowing user to write and/or run other programs while printing is carried out.

Microbuffer (Practical Peripherals, Inc.) — This is a buffer that is placed inside your printer so that when text/graphics are dumped to the printer they go into the buffer and are printed from there. This frees the computer to do other things. Comes in 8K and 16K versions.

System Saver (Kensington Microware) — This is a combination fan, socket box, and surge protect system. Slides on the side of Apple II and forces air over hot chips for cooling and reducing chances of system failure due to overheating and/or line surges. Comes with two extra sockets for monitor and printer plug-in. On/off switch on front of box saves time and Apple switch's life.

Appli-Card (Personal Computer Products, Inc.) — This is a "super-card" with a combination of Z-80, 64K RAM, real time clock, 40–255 column horizontal scroll, 70 column screen display, and other features that allow the user to take up only 1 slot where normally it would take up to 4 slots and have CP/M, more than 40 columns, and 64K of additional RAM. Available in 4 and 6 mhz versions, and can be used for CP/M applications such as WordStar.

Summary

The most important thing to understand from this last chapter is that we have only scratched the surface of what is available for the Apple II computer. There is much, much more than a single chapter could possibly cover, and as you come to know your Apple, you will find that the choice of software and peripherals is limited only by the confusion in making up your mind. There were other items for the Apple that came to mind, but this chapter and book would have never ended were I to indulge myself and keep prattling on. The software and hardware I suggested were based on personal preferences, and I would suggest that you choose on the basis of your own needs and preferences and not mine. Think of the items mentioned as a random sampling of what one user found to be useful, and then after your own sampling, examination and testing, get exactly what you need.

As you end this book, you should have a beginning level understanding of your computer's ability. Whether you use it for a single function or are a dedicated hacker, it is important that you understand the scope of its capacity to help you in your work, education and play. It is not a monstrous electronic mystery, but rather a tool to help you in various ways. You may not understand exactly how it operates, but you probably do not understand everything about how your car's engine works either, but that never prevented you from driving. Furthermore, like your car, you should think of your computer as a vehicle that will take you where you want, and never again consider it a machine that you must follow.

INDEX

APPENDIX A
Error Messages

The following are the codes for the various error messages on your Apple. Whenever you have an error handling routine using ONERR and PEEK (222) you will be given a code representing an error. For example, an error of 42 means that you are OUT OF DATA when your program contains a READ statement and a number of DATA statements.

0	=	NEXT WITHOUT FOR	22	=	RETURN WITHOUT GOSUB
1	=	LANGUAGE NOT AVAILABLE	42	=	OUT OF DATA
2,3	=	RANGE ERROR	53	=	ILLEGAL QUANTITY
4	=	WRITE PROTECTED	69	=	OVERFLOW
5	=	END OF DATA	77	=	OUT OF MEMORY
6	=	FILE NOT FOUND	90	=	UNDEFINED STATEMENT
7	=	VOLUME MISMATCH	107	=	BAD SUBSCRIPT
8	=	I/O ERROR	120	=	REDIMED AN ARRAY
9	=	DISK FULL	133	=	DIVISION BY ZERO
10	=	FILE LOCKED	163	=	TYPE MISMATCH
11	=	DOS SYNTAX ERROR	176	=	STRING TOO LONG
12	=	NO BUFFERS AVAILABLE	191	=	FORMULA TOO COMPLEX
13	=	FILE MISMATCH	224	=	UNDEFINED FUNCTION
14	=	PROGRAM TOO LARGE	254	=	BAD INPUT RESPONSE
15	=	NOT DIRECT COMMAND	255	=	CONTROL-C INTERRUPT
16	=	PROGRAM SYNTAX ERROR			

APPENDIX B

ASCII Screen Chart

INVERSE		
$00	@	0
$01	A	1
$02	B	2
$03	C	3
$04	D	4
$05	E	5
$06	F	6
$07	G	7
$08	H	8
$09	I	9
$0A	J	10
$0B	K	11
$0C	L	12
$0D	M	13
$0E	N	14
$0F	O	15
$10	P	16
$11	Q	17
$12	R	18
$13	S	19
$14	T	20
$15	U	21
$16	V	22
$17	W	23
$18	X	24
$19	Y	25
$1A	Z	26
$1B	[	27
$1C	\	28
$1D	]	29
$1E	∧	30
$1F	—	31

INVERSE		
$20		32
$21	!	33
$22	″	34
$23	#	35
$24	$	36
$25	%	37
$26	&	38
$27	′	39
$28	(	40
$29	)	41
$2A	*	42
$2B	+	43
$2C	'	44
$2D	-	45
$2E	.	46
$2F	/	47
$30	0	48
$31	1	49
$32	2	50
$33	3	51
$34	4	52
$35	5	53
$36	6	54
$37	7	55
$38	8	56
$39	9	57
$3A	:	58
$3B	;	59
$3C	<	60
$3D	=	61
$3E	>	62
$3F	?	63

FLASH

$40	@	64
$41	A	65
$42	B	66
$43	C	67
$44	D	68
$45	E	69
$46	F	70
$47	G	71
$48	H	72
$49	I	73
$4A	J	74
$4B	K	75
$4C	L	76
$4D	M	77
$4E	N	78
$4F	O	79
$50	P	80
$51	Q	81
$52	R	82
$53	S	83
$54	T	84
$55	U	85
$56	V	86
$57	W	87
$58	X	88
$59	Y	89
$5A	Z	90
$5B	[	91
$5C	\	92
$5D	]	93
$5E	∧	94
$5F	—	95

FLASH

$60		96
$61	!	97
$62	″	98
$63	#	99
$64	$	100
$65	%	101
$66	&	102
$67	′	103
$68	(	104
$69	)	105
$6A	*	106
$6B	+	107
$6C	,	108
$6D	-	109
$6E	.	110
$6F	/	111
$70	0	112
$71	1	113
$72	2	114
$73	3	115
$74	4	116
$75	5	117
$76	6	118
$77	7	119
$78	8	120
$79	9	121
$7A	:	122
$7B	;	123
$7C	<	124
$7D	=	125
$7E	>	126
$7F	?	127

CONTROL

$80	@	128	(0)
$81	A	129	(1)
$82	B	130	(2)
$83	C	131	(3)
$84	D	132	(4)
$85	E	133	(5)
$86	F	134	(6)
$87	G	135	(7)
$88	H	136	(8)
$89	I	137	(9)
$8A	J	138	(10)
$8B	K	139	(11)
$8C	L	140	(12)
$8D	M	141	(13)
$8E	N	142	(14)
$8F	O	143	(15)
$90	P	144	(16)
$91	Q	145	(17)
$92	R	146	(18)
$93	S	147	(19)
$94	T	148	(20)
$95	U	149	(21)
$96	V	150	(22)
$97	W	151	(23)
$98	X	152	(24)
$99	Y	153	(25)
$9A	Z	154	(26)
$9B	[	155	(27)
$9C	\	156	(28)
$9D	]	157	(29)
$9E	^	158	(30)
$9F	—	159	(31)

NORMAL

$A0		160	(32)
$A1	!	161	(33)
$A2	"	162	(34)
$A3	#	163	(35)
$A4	$	164	(36)
$A5	%	165	(37)
$A6	&	166	(38)
$A7	'	167	(39)
$A8	(	168	(40)
$A9	)	169	(41)
$AA	*	170	(42)
$AB	+	171	(43)
$AC	,	172	(44)
$AD	-	173	(45)
$AE	.	174	(46)
$AF	/	175	(47)
$B0	0	176	(48)
$B1	1	177	(49)
$B2	2	178	(50)
$B3	3	179	(51)
$B4	4	180	(52)
$B5	5	181	(53)
$B6	6	182	(54)
$B7	7	183	(55)
$B8	8	184	(56)
$B9	9	185	(57)
$BA	:	186	(58)
$BB	;	187	(59)
$BC	<	188	(60)
$BD	=	189	(61)
$BE	>	190	(62)
$BF	?	191	(63)

NORMAL

$C0	@	192	(64)
$C1	A	193	(65)
$C2	B	194	(66)
$C3	C	195	(67)
$C4	D	196	(68)
$C5	E	197	(69)
$C6	F	198	(70)
$C7	G	199	(71)
$C8	H	200	(72)
$C9	I	201	(73)
$CA	J	202	(74)
$CB	K	203	(75)
$CC	L	204	(76)
$CD	M	205	(77)
$CE	N	206	(78)
$CF	O	207	(79)
$D0	P	208	(80)
$D1	Q	209	(81)
$D2	R	210	(82)
$D3	S	211	(83)
$D4	T	212	(84)
$D5	U	213	(85)
$D6	V	214	(86)
$D7	W	215	(87)
$D8	X	216	(88)
$D9	Y	217	(89)
$DA	Z	218	(90)
$DB	[	219	(91)
$DC	\	220	(92)
$DD	]	221	(93)
$DE	∧	222	(94)
$DF	—	223	(95)

LOWER CASE

$E0	,	224	(96)
$E1	a	225	(97)
$E2	b	226	(98)
$E3	c	227	(99)
$E4	d	228	(100)
$E5	e	229	(101)
$E6	f	230	(102)
$E7	g	231	(103)
$E8	h	232	(104)
$E9	i	233	(105)
$EA	j	234	(106)
$EB	k	235	(107)
$EC	l	236	(108)
$ED	m	237	(109)
$EE	n	238	(110)
$EF	o	239	(111)
$F0	p	240	(112)
$F1	q	241	(113)
$F2	r	242	(114)
$F3	s	243	(115)
$F4	t	244	(116)
$F5	u	245	(117)
$F6	v	246	(118)
$F7	w	247	(119)
$F8	x	248	(120)
$F9	y	249	(121)
$FA	z	250	(122)
$FB	{	251	(123)
$FC	|	252	(124)
$FD	}	253	(125)
$FE	~	254	(126)
$FF	?	255	(127)

APPLESOFT/DOS
Example Glossary

This glossary is arranged in *alphabetical* order and contains both APPLESOFT and DOS commands. The examples are set up to show you how to use the commands and their proper syntax. In some cases when a command has different contexts of usage, more than a single example will be used. Some examples are given in the immediate mode and some in the program mode (those with line numbers) and some with both. Results are given to show what a particular configuration would create in some examples for clarification. Some of the more advanced commands were not covered in the text, but are provided here for a complete reference.

ABS( ) — Gives the absolute value of a number or variable.

```
PRINT ABS(123.45)
```

AND — Logical operator used in IF/THEN statement.

```
140 IF A$ < > "Y" AND A$ < > "N" THEN GOTO 100
```

APPEND — (DOS) Adds data to end of existing sequential text file.

```
200 PRINT CHR$(4); "APPEND NAMES"
```

ASC( ) — Returns ASCII value of first character in string.

```
PRINT ASC ("W")
```

or

```
A$ = "APPLE" : PRINT ASC(A$)
```

ATN( ) — Returns arctangent of number or variable.

```
PRINT ATN(123)
```

BLOAD — (DOS) Load binary file into memory. Does not need address to load, but can be included.

Immediate mode:

```
BLOAD GRAPHICS FILE
```

or

```
BLOAD GRAPHICS FILE, A$4000
```

Program mode:

```
100 PRINT CHR$(4); "BLOAD GRAPHICS FILE"
```

BRUN — (DOS) Runs binary file from disk.

Immediate mode:
BRUN SPACE APES

Program mode:
100 PRINT CHR$(4); "BRUN SPACE APES"

BSAVE — (DOS) Saves binary file to disk. Must include both starting address and length in either hexadecimal or decimal.

Hexadecimal:
BSAVE ZOOM BLAST, A$300, L$3DF

Decimal:
BSAVE SPACE SHIP, A801, L1234

CALL — Goes to machine subroutine at a given decimal address.

CALL −936.

CATALOG — (DOS) Prints the file names on the disk to screen or printer.

CATALOG,D1

or

CATALOGD1

CHR$( ) — Returns the character with a given decimal value.

PRINT CHR$(65)

CLEAR — All variables are reset to zero.

120 CLEAR

CLOSE — Closes text file.

210 PRINT CHR$(4); "CLOSE NAME LIST"

COLOR= — Sets color in lo-res graphics in values from 0 to 15.

30 COLOR = 9

CONT — Continue program after a STOP, END or CTRL-C

CONT

or

300 CONT (e.g., RUN 300 to continue)

COS( ) — Returns the cosine of variable or number.

PRINT COS(123)

DATA — Strings or numbers to be read.

1000 DATA 2,345,HELLO,"WALK"

DEF FN( ) — Defines a substitute function for real variable.

DEF FN A(X) = X * X
PRINT FN A(4)
(Results = 16)

DEL — Deletes range of line numbers.

DEL 120,200

DELETE — (DOS) Deletes file from disk.

DELETE ADDING MACHINE

DIM — Allocates maximun range of array.

130 DIM A$(100)

DRAW – AT — Draws a hi-res shape table on hi-res screen at X,Y coordinates.

150 DRAW 5 AT 100,40

END — Terminates running of program.

200 END

EXEC — (DOS) Executes the contets of a text file without removing program in memory.

EXEC PROGRAM SETUP

EXP( ) — Returns e=2.718289 to indicated power.

PRINT EXP(3)

FLASH — Turns on flashing mode

30 FLASH : PRINT "HELLO"

FOR — Sets up beginning of FOR/NEXT loop and top limit of loop.

40 FOR I = 1 TO 100

FP — Sets to 'floating point' or APPLESOFT language. Also clears memory.

FP

FRE( ) — Returns available memory.

PRINT FRE(0)

GET — Halts execution until single entry received from keyboard.

30 GET A$ (or GET A or GET A%)

GOSUB — Branches to subroutine at given line number.

100 GOSUB 200

GOTO — Branches to given line number.

100 GOTO 200

GR — Sets lo-res graphics mode.

120 GR

HCOLOR= — Sets hi-res color to values of 0 to 7.

40 HCOLOR = 3

HGR — Sets page 1 hi-res graphics mode and clears hi-res screen 1.

120 HGR

HGR2 — Sets page 2 hi-res graphics mode and clears hi-res screen 2.

130 HGR2

HIMEM: — Sets memory to highest available location for a program within a range of −65535 to 65535, depending on RAM memory.

10 HIMEM: 40123

HLIN – AT — Draws a horizontal line in lo-res graphics at given vertical position.

40 HLIN 10,20 AT 11

HOME — Clears screen and places cursor in upper right hand corner of text window.

HOME

HPLOT – TO — Plots single point or points on hi-res screen at given X,Y coordinate to another X,Y coordinate.

40 HPLOT 10,50 : REM SINGLE POINT
50 HPLOT 0,0 TO 279,151 : REM RANGE OF POINTS

HTAB — Horizontal tab position set.

50 HTAB 30 : PRINT "HERE"

IF/THEN — Sets up conditional logic for execution.

60 IF A$ = "Q" THEN END

IN# — (DOS) Takes input from indicated slot #.

IN#6

INIT — (DOS) Initializes diskette.

INIT HELLO

INPUT — Halts program execution until string or numbers entered and RETURN key is pressed. May enter message within INPUT statement.

90 INPUT "ENTER WORD – > "; W$(I)
100 INPUT "ENTER NUMBER-> "; A 110 INPUT "ENTER
INTEGER NUMBER – > "; N%
120 PRINT "HIT 'RETURN' TO CONTINUE ";
130 INPUT R$

INT — Sets to INTEGER BASIC language and clears memory.

INT

INT( ) — Returns the integer value of real variable or number.

PRINT INT(123.45)

INVERSE — Turns on inverse mode.

50 INVERSE : PRINT "APPLE"

LEFT$(,) — Returns specifed number of characters from a given string beginning with character at far left.

10 A$ = "GOODBYE"
20 PRINT LEFT$(A$,4)
(Results = GOOD)

LEN — Returns the length in terms of number of characters of a specified string.

PRINT LEN(A$)

LIST — Lists program currently in memory.

LIST

LOAD — (DOS) Loads APPLESOFT or INTEGER program specified.

LOAD CALENDAR PLOT

LOCK — (DOS) Prevents file from being overwritten or deleted.

LOCK CALENDAR PLOT

LOG( ) — Returns logarithm of specifed number or variable.

PRINT LOG(15)

or

PRINT LOG(G)

LOMEM: — Sets memory to lowest location available for a program within a range of –65535 to 65535, depending on RAM memory.

LOMEM: 1234

MAXFILES — (DOS) Reserves specified number of buffers for files within a range of 1–16.

MAXFILES 10

MID$(, ,) — Returns a portion of a string beginning with the nth number from the left to the length of the second number.

```
10 A$ = "WONDERFUL"
20 PRINT MID$(A$,4,3)
(Results = DER)
```

MON — (DOS) Turns on screen display of computer-disk communication.

MONCIO

or

MON C,I,O

NEW — Clears program in memory.

NEW

NEXT — Sets the top of the loop begun with FOR statement.

```
10 FOR I = 1 TO 100
20 PRINT "THIS" ,
30 NEXT I
```

NOMON — (DOS) Turns off screen display of computer-disk communication.

NOMONCIO

or

NOMON C,I,O

NORMAL — Returns screen to standard display from INVERSE or FLASH modes.

```
10 FLASH : PRINT "FLASHING MODE"
20 NORMAL: PRINT "NORMAL MODE"
```

NOT — Logical negation in IF/THEN statement.

```
60 IF A NOT B THEN GOTO 100
```

NOTRACE — Turns off TRACE mode.

NOTRACE

ON — Sets up computed GOTO and GOSUB.

```
190 ON A GOSUB 1000,2000,3000
```

ONERR — Branches to specified line when error encountered.

```
40 ONERR GOTO 1000
```

OPEN — (DOS) Creates or starts new text file.

```
500 PRINT CHR$(4); "OPEN NAME LIST"
```

OR — Logical OR in IF/THEN statement.

```
130 IF A=10 OR B=20 THEN GOTO 190
```

PDL( ) — Returns value of specified paddle number 0–3.

```
PRINT PDL(0)
```

PEEK — Returns memory contents of given decimal location.

```
170 PRINT PEEK (768)
180 IF PEEK(768) = 5 THEN GOTO 200
```

PLOT — Plots point in lo-res graphics in X,Y coordinates, visible in colors other than black.

```
PLOT 10,15
```

POKE — Inserts given value in specified memory location.

```
POKE 768,10 (Sets memory location 768 to decimal value 10)
```

POP — Used in GOSUB context, it removes top line number in the stack and makes the second to last line number the "return" point when the next RETURN is encountered.

```
10 GOSUB 100
20 END
100 GOSUB 200
200 PRINT "HELLO"
210 POP
220 RETURN
(Result = HELLO; without POP it would be HELLO HELLO)
```

POS( ) — Gives the current horizontal position of the cursor.

```
10 PRINT "THIS LINE"; : PRINT POS(0)
```

POSITION — (DOS) Used in sequential text files to begin read files at specified postion rather than first file.

```
10 D$=CHR$(13) + CHR$(4)
20 PRINT D$ "OPEN NAME FILE" : PRINT D$ "POSITION
NAME FILE,R9" : PRINT D$ "READ NAME FILE"
```

PR# — Sends output to specified slot number.

```
PR#1
```

PRINT — Outputs string, number or variable to screen or printer.

```
PRINT 1;2;3; "GO"; F$; A; N%
```

READ — Enters DATA contents into variable.

```
10 READ A : READ B$
20 DATA 5,"BATS"
```

READ — (DOS) Reads contents of text file.

```
40 PRINT CHR$(4) "READ NAME FILE"
```

RECALL — Loads array from tape that has been recorded with STORE.

```
RECALL Z
```

REM — Non-executable command. Allows remarks in program lines.

```
10 BELL$ = CHR$(7): REM RINGS BELL
```

RENAME — (DOS) Renames files on disk.

```
RENAME FAST SORT, SHELL SORT
```

RESTORE — Resets position of READ to first DATA statement.

```
10 FOR I = 1 TO 5 : READ A$(I) : NEXT
20 RESTORE
```

RESUME — Goes to statement where error occurred in error-handling routine.

```
10 ONERR GOTO 50
20 INPUT V%
30 END
50 PRINT "ENTER ONLY INTEGER NUMBERS!" : RESUME
```

RETURN — Returns program to next line after GOSUB command.

```
500 RETURN
```

RIGHT$(,) — Returns the rightmost n characters of given string.

```
10 A$ = "DATAMOST" : PRINT RIGHT$(A$,4)
(Results = MOST)
```

RND( ) — Generates a random number less than 1 and greater than or equal to 0.

```
PRINT RND(5)
```

INT(RND (1) * (N) + 1)—Generates whole random numbers from 1 to N, with N being the upper limit of desired numbers.

ROT= — Used to rotate shapes on hi-res screen. Can be set to angles between 0 to 255. Number of angular positions recognized depends on SCALE value of shape.

```
60 ROT = 64
```

RUN — Executes program in memory, or if file name included, executes program from disk.

Immediate mode:
RUN FLYING MACHINE (executes disk file)
RUN (executes program in memory)

Program mode:
150 PRINT CHR$(4); "RUN FLYING MACHINE"

SAVE — Records program on disk.

SAVE GRAPH PLOT

SCALE= — Specifies size or scale of shape on hi-res screen.

40 SCALE = 5

SCRN(,) — Returns the color code (0–15) in lo-res graphics of plot at X,Y coordinates.

30 PRINT SCRN(10,20)

SHLOAD — Command for loading shape table from tape.

SHLOAD

SIN( ) — Returns the sine of variable or number.

PRINT SIN(123)

SPC( ) — Prints specified number of spaces.

PRINT SPC(29); "HERE"

SPEED — Sets speed of execution from 0 to 255. (Default speed is 255.)

50 SPEED = 100

SQR( ) — Returns the square root of variable or number.

PRINT SQR(64)

STOP — Halts execution and prints line number where break occurs. (CONT command will re-start program at next instruction after STOP command.)

100 STOP

STORE — Records array values on tape.

STORE Z
10 STORE Z

STR$( ) — Converts number/variable into string variable.

20 T = 123 : T$ = STR$(T) : TT$ = "$" + T$ + ".00"

TAB( ) — Sets horizontal tab from within a PRINT statement.

PRINT TAB(20);"HERE"

TAN( ) — Provides the tangent of number or variable.

```
40 T = 34 : V = 55
50 R = T + V : PRINT TAN(R)
```

TRACE — Turns on TRACE function for display of program execution. (Turned off with NOTRACE.)

```
TRACE
```

UNLOCK — (DOS) Removes LOCK status from file on disk allowing it to be removed with DELETE statement or overwritten.

```
UNLOCK TAX CHART
```

VAL( ) — Used to convert string to numeric value.

```
30 H$ = "123" : PRINT VAL(H$)
```

VERIFY — (DOS) Examines disk file to check for errors. If no errors, nothing happens.

```
VERIFY TAX CHART
```

VLIN — AT – Draws vertical line in lo-res graphics AT given horizontal position.

```
50 VLIN 1,30 AT 10
```

WAIT — Stops execution until memory location values meet given conditions.

```
80 WAIT -16384,128
```

WRITE — (DOS) In making text files, specifies file name to which following PRINT statements will be written.

```
50 D$ = CHR$(13) + CHR$(4)
60 PRINT D$"OPEN NAMES": PRINT D$"WRITE NAMES"
70 PRINT "TOM" : PRINT "DICK" : PRINT "HARRY"
```

XDRAW — Used with shape tables to draw a specified shape in complimentary color on hi-res screen. Similar to DRAW.

```
70 XDRAW 3 AT 150,55
```

MONEY SAVING COUPON

MONEY SAVING COUPON

MONEY SAVING COUPON